The Rise of
FASCISM

F. L. Carsten

Second Edition

UNIVERSITY OF CALIFORNIA PRESS
Berkeley and Los Angeles

First Published, 1967
© *F.L. Carsten, 1967*
Second edition, 1980
Made and printed in Great Britain
by Billing & Son Ltd,
Guildford & Worcester

University of California Press
Berkeley and Los Angeles

ISBN 0-520-04307-3

Library of Congress Catalog Card Number 80-51592

1   2   3   4   5   6   7   8   9

Contents

Preface

This is a book on the history of the principal Fascist movements as they developed in the course of the 1920s and 1930s. For obvious reasons, the attention is focused, above all, on the countries in which Fascism originated and achieved power: Italy, Germany and Austria. The history of the Fascist movements in these countries is described in detail: but the book does not include the period when the Fascists and the National Socialists exercised power—a different topic which would require a separate volume. For an understanding of the subject, however, it has proved necessary to give brief sketches of the Fascist movements in several European countries outside the triangle Rome–Berlin–Vienna. But the book does not attempt to discuss the history of Fascism in every European country: an undertaking that would become rather tedious and repetitive. In Chapters 5 and 6 those countries have been selected in which the Fascist movements were either particularly strong in their own right, or presented special traits which differed from the pattern established in Italy and Germany.

Therefore, for example, the small and unimportant Fascist movements of Norway and the Netherlands have been omitted because they only leaped into a short-lived prominence during the period of the German occupation when they were fostered from Berlin. Equally, there is nothing on the French Fascist parties—except a sketch of the *Action Française* in the first chapter—because they all remained small and uninfluential. The most important among them, the *Parti Populaire Français* of Jacques Doriot, was mainly distinguished by its violent anti-Communism, not unnatural in a party led by a former high-ranking Communist. But violent anti-Communism alone is not the same as Fascism (as little as violent anti-Semitism is): the true Fascist parties developed an ideology of their own which was a very important element in their history, and which will be discussed on the following pages. The dictatorships of Portugal, Spain and certain East European countries (such as Poland or Lithuania) were not

8 PREFACE

established by the advance and ultimate triumph of Fascist parties; but they represent a much more old-fashioned and conservative type of dictatorship similar to those which had existed in the Iberian peninsula—and elsewhere—in earlier decades. Although these dictatorships were influenced by the rise of Fascism in Italy and Germany and show certain 'Fascist' traits, their history has been omitted here because it differs in vital points from that of the Fascist movements in other European countries. But the development of the true Fascist party of Spain, the *Falange*, is included. If the reader feels that this division is somewhat arbitrary, the author can only plead that he had to use his own judgement and that he hopes that some of his readers may be convinced by the arguments put forward in the course of the narrative. He has not aimed at including everything, but at giving a number of significant examples. Above all, he hopes to have explained how it was possible that Fascist movements not only developed, but were able to become mass movements and to seize power, in countries of ancient culture, a high level of education, and a tradition of civilized behaviour.

The author grew up in Berlin during the years of the rise of National Socialism. What is contained in Chapter 4 thus partly describes events which he has observed himself, and these personal recollections are incorporated into the narrative. They may colour his judgement: he vividly remembers the atmosphere of those years, the discussions with National Socialist students, their strong influence in the universities, the meetings he attended where Adolf Hitler, Otto Strasser and other National Socialists spoke, the clashes in the streets and meeting halls. The chapter tries to convey to the reader this political atmosphere which was a highly important element in the rise of National Socialism.

Finally, the author wishes to express his grateful thanks to those of his colleagues who read the whole or part of the manuscript or gave him their advice: Professor Gordon A. Craig, Dr Harry Hearder, Dr István Deák, and Professor Eugen Weber. The staff of the Bundesarchiv at Koblenz and of the Hoover Library at Stanford, California, have supplied him with extremely valuable documents and pamphlets without which the book would have been far less interesting: to them too the author owes a great deal. But most of all he owes to his wife with whom he has discussed the subject of the book on innumerable occasions and who has suggested to him many improvements and changes in detail.

London, October 1966 F.L.C.

I | Nationalism and Anti-Semitism before 1914

There was no 'Fascism' anywhere in Europe before the end of the first world war. Without the slightest doubt, it was this great upheaval, the destruction and the crises resulting from it, and the fear of 'red' revolution which arose in many European countries, that brought forth the movement which—after the Italian example—we call 'Fascist'. In comparison with the world after 1918—a world torn by bloody conflicts, political hatred, civil wars, revolutionary and counter-revolutionary convulsions—the world of the years before 1914 was a haven of peace. Nowhere in western and central Europe were law and order seriously threatened. Prosperity and economic progress were the order of the day. The proclamation of the *Commune* of Paris in 1871 did not inaugurate a new era of revolutions in Europe, but was the last of the revolutionary events of the nineteenth century, however this rising of the Paris proletarians may have been interpreted by Marx and his disciples. It was only in Tsarist Russia that a new violent revolution broke out in 1905 at the end of the lost Russo-Japanese war— the harbinger of things to come. It had no repercussions in other European countries. There the security of the governing orders, the economic and social system, the prosperity of the middle classes seemed established for all eternity. Colonial expansion and the partition of other continents contributed to this prosperity, in spite of the conflicts which resulted from them. The ever-growing expenditure on armaments on land and at sea—ominous in retrospect—created more employment and brought in vast profits. If there were clouds on the European horizon, they did not seem very threatening.

One of these clouds was a result of the economic development itself. The position of the lower middle classes, which in most towns formed the bulk of the population, was threatened on the one hand by the process of concentration in industry and trade, the foundation of larger and larger enterprises, and on the other hand by the rise of the working classes and their vociferous demands for equality and political rights. At least in some western countries—Italy, for example, or France—there were truly revolutionary movements of the extreme Left, and everywhere there were strong socialist parties and trade unions. Marx had prophesied that the large majority of the middle and lower middle classes would be pushed down to the level of proletarians; even if this prophecy turned out to be incorrect, many of their members feared lest they would lose their safe and privileged positions. This could also be threatened by newcomers and immigrants and, in many areas of central Europe, by the rise of new or less favoured nationalities which, until recently, had not possessed a middle class of their own. In a world which was becoming far more competitive the Jews, but recently emancipated, provided such a threat in many a country; but the advance of other minorities—Protestants, Czechs, or Poles, as the case might be—could cause similar fears among those who thought their positions undermined, or their traditional ways of life eroded. Their reaction to real or imagined threats did not bring about 'Fascism', but it created the pre-conditions for the development of 'Fascist' movements after the world of the pre-1914 years had been destroyed by an earthquake. It is for this reason that we must, in the first instance, look at these groups as they developed in several European countries. Before 1914, they had no chance of coming into power; their influence was confined to comparatively small minorities, to the disinherited and the disgruntled. Yet their ideologies were to be carried over into the post-war period when they were to thrive in a far more promising climate. And their members—and in some important cases their leaders too—remained active and provided a coherent link between the pre-war and the post-war worlds.

Although these movements differed widely from country to country, there were certain features which they had in common. They were violently nationalist—a nationalism very different from that of nineteenth-century conservative or liberal groups, so much so that the term 'the *new* Right' has been coined to describe them. They were also, in most cases, strongly anti-Semitic, using the Jews as a convenient scapegoat for the ills of capitalist society. Finally, they were appealing not only to the middle and lower middle classes, but also to the lower classes, attempting to wean them from the ideals of socialism and internationalism, and to provide a popular basis for the new movements. This was not yet the era of mass democracy, but the leaders clearly recognized that such a mass basis was essential if the ideas of liberalism and democracy, of socialism and syndicalism, were to be opposed with any chance of success.

France

France had been defeated in the Franco-Prussian war of 1870–71 and had lost Alsace and Lorraine to the victor. The result was an upsurge of nationalism—by no means confined to the political Right—and a demand for revenge. In the 1880s the movement of General Boulanger —'General Victory' who would march across the Rhine and free the lost provinces—had for the first time posed a clear threat to the Republic from the Right. Paul Déroulède and his 'League of Patriots' constituted an extreme right-wing organization preparing a *coup d'état*, fanning the embers of discontent and eager to lead the General to the Élysée; but the movement collapsed ignominiously, Boulanger fled the country, and the Republic was saved. Yet only a few years later the collapse of the Panama Company and the resulting scandal provided new food for vehement attacks upon the Republic and, more specifically, upon the Jewish financiers responsible for the scandal.

It was then that a new journal was founded to fight the influence of 'international Jewish finance', *La Libre Parole*, and that this journal and its editor leaped into prominence. This was Edouard Drumont who, in 1886, published a book that was to make him famous: *La France juive*, which soon sold many thousands of copies. It painted an idyllic picture of the old France, a France that had been destroyed and conquered by the Jews. It was an attack on modern civilization which debases and humiliates man, on the world of the *bourgeoisie*. It appealed to the economic fears and resentments of the middle classes: the Jew, detested by the small shopkeepers, businessmen and artisans, became the symbol of financial power, of the capitalist order. 'The only one who profited from the Revolution was the Jew.' Jewish immigrants, such as the Rothschilds, had amassed vast fortunes in France: their wealth caused all the evils from which France was suffering. Jews had committed many other crimes throughout history; they were the devil from whom France must be delivered. But Drumont included in his attacks leading politicians and financiers, the Pope, the bishops and the Catholic Church, great noblemen and members of the royal family, all those who in his opinion aided or courted Jews. The Panama scandal provided him with the material he required. He was the founder of organized anti-Semitism in France, and he gave it a definite anti-bourgeois tinge. In anti-Semitism he discovered an issue which had a mass-appeal.

Other forces in the France of the late nineteenth century were strongly opposed to the Republic as such and to the traditions which it incorporated, those of the French Revolution and the Enlightenment, of rationalism and liberalism. An open clash between the pro-republican and the anti-republican forces, which shook the very foundations of the established order, occurred at the very end of the century over the question whether Captain Alfred Dreyfus, accused of espionage on behalf of Germany, was innocent or guilty. It so happened that Dreyfus was a Jew—a fact not unconnected with the suspicion that fastened upon him, and with his degradation and sentence to life imprisonment by a court-martial. During the following years the agitation for a retrial slowly mounted; at the beginning of 1898 Émile Zola published his famous *J'Accuse* in defence of Dreyfus. Soon after, it was established that the principal document on which the prosecution and condemnation of Dreyfus rested was a forgery; and the officer responsible for this forgery, Colonel Henry, was arrested and committed suicide. Yet these events did not bring about the end of *L'Affaire Dreyfus*, nor did they silence his numerous enemies. Too many people in prominent positions were involved, and too many strongly established prejudices were at stake.

In the spring of 1898—a few months after Zola's *J'Accuse* and the foundation of the *Ligue des Droits de l'Homme* in response to his appeal—two young men, who were sickened by these events and by the plight of France, founded a *Comité d'Action française*. These were Maurice Pujo, the twenty-six-year-old editor of a literary review founded by him, and Henri Vaugeois, a philosophy teacher aged thirty-four. The committee's appeal presented the campaign of the *Dreyfusards* as a revival of the Panama scandal, serving only the interests of corrupt politicians and financiers. At the end of the year Pujo in an article, *L'Action française*, sharply attacked parliamentarianism and individualism; France must become as strong as she had once been, must be 'remade . . . into a state as organized at home, as powerful abroad, as she had been under the *Ancien Régime*', before the Revolution of 1789. In June 1899 Vaugeois lectured on the *Action française* to the nationalist public, deeply stirred by the *Affaire Dreyfus*;

soon after, the first issue of its bulletin appeared. The movement was launched. Its leaders were a group of intellectuals, busy with interminable discussions and determined to fight against the ideas of the French Revolution and all it stood for. The leading spirit among them was Charles Maurras, a writer who was then hardly thirty years old.

Maurras was born in the south of France, in a royalist family which had adhered to Napoleon III; to him the Republic was the last stage of French decadence. He was firmly convinced of the justice of the verdict passed on Dreyfus, but that was not the main issue: even if Dreyfus were proved innocent, it would not excuse the agitation which divided France, weakened the army and jeopardized the existence of the country. In his opinion, Colonel Henry had been murdered in prison, he was a hero, and his blood must be avenged; Germany was and remained the national foe. But Maurras' enemies were not only the Germans and the British—Frankfurt and London were the two capitals of international finance which personified the two hostile nations—but even more so the Jews, freemasons and Protestants, the protagonists of a devilish conspiracy directed against France and Catholicism. Four interconnected Estates made up what Maurras called 'anti-France': the Jews—foreigners in France; the Protestants—Frenchmen who accepted the non-French ideas of Germany, Switzerland and England; the freemasons and other anti-clericals—who agreed with the ideas of their anti-French allies; and finally the métèques—a term borrowed from ancient Athens, signifying resident foreigners. All fattened on the wealth of the country. All were equally hostile to a strong army, to French tradition and to its core, Catholicism.[1] The spirit of 'anti-France' in Maurras' opinion pervaded the teaching of history in French schools and universities which were dominated by the four hostile Estates; hence so many intellectuals were on the side of Dreyfus. The Jews were an element of disintegration; their tradition forced them to be hostile to that of France, while the Huguenots, centuries ago, had cut themselves off from the true national tradition; the loyalty of all these groups was not to France, but to foreign authorities.

To Maurras France was a Goddess, 'the miracle of miracles', the beautiful par excellence, and she demanded absolute devotion. He

---

[1] Quoted from Maurras' *La Démocratie religieuse*, p. 90, by D. W. Brogan, 'Nationalist Doctrine of M. Charles Maurras', *French Personalities and Problems*, London, 1946, p. 69; and from *L'Enquête sur la monarchie*, pp. 535-6, by E. R. Tannenbaum, *The Action Française*, New York, 1962, p. 73.

venerated the *Ancien Régime* and hated the French Revolution and the Enlightenment which had brought disorder and decline to the country. 'The fathers of revolution are in Geneva, in Wittenberg, and in earlier times in Jerusalem; they derive from the Jewish spirit and from the varieties of an independent Christendom which raged in the oriental deserts and the primeval forests of Germany, the different centres of barbarity.'[2] Democracy was equal to anarchy; it lacked the manly principles of action and initiative; it made the state the prey of rapaciousness and group interests; it was feminine, weak and evil. If France was to become as strong as she had once been, the monarchy must be reestablished; for only a hereditary monarchy could give the nation unity, stability and authority, without which it would break to pieces. Among the leaders of the *Action française* Maurras was at first the only monarchist, but he succeeded in converting the others— at a time when royalism was declining in France. The monarchy must be restored by force; against this, the government would be powerless, unable to organize its own support; it could thus be overthrown by a 'conservative revolution'.

The task of the *Action française* was the formation of this minority, 'which will make history and which the crowd will follow', of an élite which would become the ruling group of the new France.[3] This élite, in Maurras' opinion, would be formed by 'the best' from all trades and professions, the best officers, the best writers and philosophers, the best civil servants, it would be an intellectual élite. Thanks to Maurras, the *Action française* acquired a doctrine, which the other groups of the French Right lacked, and thanks to this doctrine it was able to grow and to survive. But at the same time it was too conservative and traditionalist, too exclusive and intellectual, and—with its royalism—too old-fashioned, hence unable to appeal to the masses, especially the industrial workers. The middle-class origin of its leaders and their intellectual pursuits made them unfit to become the leaders of a revolutionary movement.

At the beginning of 1906 the Institute of the *Action française* was opened. There Maurras held the chair of political science, and courses were given in politics, history, foreign relations, nationalism and social sciences, courses which were later published in book-form. A few months later the *Cour de Cassation* annulled the verdict against

---

[2] Quoted from the preface to *Romantisme et Révolution*, *Œuvres Capitales*, II, p. 33, by Ernst Nolte, *Der Faschismus in seiner Epoche*, Munich, 1963, p. 170.
[3] Quoted from *L'Enquête sur la monarchie*, pp. 469, 500, 509, ibid., p. 179.

Dreyfus and declared him innocent; but the *Action française* refused to accept his acquittal and revived its agitation against the *Dreyfusards*. Young royalists attacked and mutilated the statues of men who had supported the campaign for a revision of the sentence. In 1908 the *Action Française*—first issued as a *Revue* every other week—became a daily paper, with money provided by the writer Léon Daudet and by public subscriptions. But many more copies were printed than could be sold, and heavy losses were incurred; there were in addition frequent expensive court actions, and heavy fines to be paid by the paper. The influence of the *Action française* was growing, especially among intellectuals and in the universities. In May 1908 it fomented riots against a professor of the Sorbonne because he had taken a student group to Germany during the holidays to promote better understanding between the two countries: he was forced to suspend his lectures. Early in 1909 rioters disrupted the lectures of another professor who had expressed 'anti-national' opinions on the subject of Joan of Arc; pitched battles were fought inside and outside the Sorbonne. The young nationalists began to dominate the university district. Jewish teachers became the victims of similar campaigns.

In these street battles and disturbances a leading part was played by an organization which had been founded in 1908 to sell the new daily paper: the *Camelots du Roi*. They were the militant wing of the *Action française*, animated by a military spirit, fighting a 'holy war' against the old order, the Jews and their other enemies. The organization was hierarchical and para-military. Its composition was allegedly 'classless', but in reality few workmen became members. Within twelve months there were 600 *Camelots* in Paris alone, and sixty-five sections outside the capital; but only a minority were active members. In 1910 an élite formation was organized within the *Camelots*, the *Commissaires*, who were armed with clubs and similar weapons and had to guard the party's offices and leaders, to protect its parades, to disrupt public functions, and—like the *Camelots*—engaged in frequent riots and deeds of violence. These assumed such proportions that the Duc d'Orléans, the royalist candidate for the throne, publicly dissociated himself from the violence of the *Camelots*. The leaders of the *Action française* had to promise to give up 'the politics of the barricades' and of street violence, but their paper passionately denounced the duke's 'evil counsellors' who were sowing discord among his supporters and splitting their ranks.

At the third *Action française* congress, held in December 1910, all important reports had to be submitted in advance to Maurras, who more and more became the movement's acknowledged leader, and were approved without discussion. There was mounting enthusiasm, of which not the royalist idea, but Maurras and his closest associates were the true focus. In all 300 delegates attended the congress, representing over 200 sections, but only sixty to sixty-five were from the provinces. The party's support came above all from army officers, members of the professions, especially lawyers, teachers and priests, but there were also many white-collar workers, commercial travellers, insurance agents, etc.: the lower middle classes were strongly represented. They detested the republican régime which had brought no glory to France and did not help them to overcome their economic difficulties, while many priests and monks resented the 'monstrous Judeo-Masonic régime' that had brought about a separation of Church and state and severely curtailed the influence of the Church on education. In this struggle the *Action française* strongly supported the Church and the Catholic hierarchy from which it received much valuable help, not only in money. In response to the demands of its lower-middle-class followers the *Action française* proposed to replace the system of economic liberalism by a corporate order, in which labour was to be organized in guilds.

Yet persistent attempts to win over the industrial workers met with little success. The anti-Semitic propaganda, the shrill denunciations of 'Judeo-Masonic conspiracies', which identified bankers, rapacious employers and trade union leaders with the Jews, did not attract the workers. Nor were attempts to reach an understanding with certain syndicalist leaders, above all Georges Sorel, more successful. The militants of the extreme Left also hated the existing régime, but they had too little in common with the *Action française* leaders to make more than mere flirtations possible. In spite of all the verbal attacks on certain features of capitalism the *Action française* maintained close links with capitalist and industrialist circles, and Maurras showed a marked deference to big business; his movement depended on the support of these groups and on that of the Church, and they were anathema to the radical Left. During the war years Maurras emerged as a veritable champion of the Catholic Church, defending the Pope and the clergy and attacking their critics in many articles which were published as a book in 1917. It was these traits which marked the *Action française* clearly as a movement of the Right and decisively separated it from the revolutionaries of the Left.

ITALY 17

Long before 1914 the *Action française* showed many of the characteristics which later distinguished Fascist movements. Its hatred of
liberalism, democracy and the parliamentary system, its glorification
of power and violence, which it did not hesitate to use against its
enemies, its advocacy of strong leadership, its marked anti-Semitism
and anti-Freemasonism were features which we shall find time and
again among the Fascist groups of the post-war period. Yet for the
time being Maurras exercised little influence outside France, and even
inside the country the virulent attacks in which he and his followers
specialized made little impression on the Third Republic. Maurras was
no Mussolini, and no Hitler. The *Action française* was and remained
the movement of a small minority, and its ideology orientated towards
the past rather than the present.

Italy

Like Germany, Italy was united only in the third quarter of the nineteenth century, between 1860 and 1870, and there was little that was
'natural' or 'inevitable' about this unification. While Germany was
welded together by three victorious wars, a spectacular growth of
prosperity, and a rise to the status of a great power, Italy remained
desperately poor. Even in the military field, it was only thanks to the
good services of the French and the Prussians that she had become
united at all. After Cavour's untimely death in 1861, the Italian governments proved weak and inefficient. But it was the economic question
which bedevilled the existence of the new state, and it was in this field
that the failure of the government was most clearly marked. While
there was no knowledge of economic issues in the kingdom, a glowing
optimism about the country's resources was prevalent; it was considered the 'garden of Europe', overflowing with wealth. In reality,
the mountain and hill areas were arid, the plains often marshy and
malarious; the soil was exhausted; agricultural methods were primitive;
the rivers and streams carried the top soil down to the sea. Soil erosion
was a problem no one was able to master. While Germany had vast
coal and mineral deposits, these were absent in Italy and all essential
raw materials had to be imported. Industrialization had barely started
and no capital was available for investment.

These problems were much worse in the south. Its economic life had
been disrupted by the removal of trade barriers between the north and

the south as a result of unification; its protected industries and its system of trade had been destroyed. Many peasants were practically serfs, the victims of malaria, usury and rack-renting, and brigandage was endemic. A southern Italian bitterly described the south as 'a kingdom apart and isolated, a kingdom of discontinuity, with confused labyrinths of broken mountains, with wild torrents in place of rivers, with great expanses of desert neither irrigated nor capable of irrigation, deserts over which malaria reigns supreme. . . .'⁴ From the north, as a result of unification, the heavy northern system of taxation and a new bureaucratic and political machine had been imported into this arid area, which had no industry and no middle class, but a rate of illiteracy of over ninety per cent.

In this poor and backward country, parliamentary government and institutions rested on a very weak basis, and the masses were utterly uninterested in politics. Until 1882 only 600,000 out of a total population of more than twenty-five millions were entitled to vote, and of these the majority usually abstained, so that deputies were elected by very small numbers. Then the property qualification was replaced by a test of literacy, or the proof of the payment of a certain sum in direct taxes; in addition, officials and those who had been decorated were enfranchised, increasing the electorate to over two millions, about eight per cent of the population. It was only in 1912 that all men aged thirty years or more were enfranchised. Governments were frequently changing; widespread corruption in governing circles did not increase the respect for the new institutions, which did not rest on any traditions and were widely distrusted.

Yet the kingdom, with its weak economic and political structure, indulged in ambitious dreams of great-power politics. At home, there were the 'unredeemed' areas of the Alto Adige (South Tyrol) and of Trieste which had remained under Austria, but were considered Italian by the large majority of the Italians, although only part of their inhabitants spoke Italian. The Speaker of the Italian Chamber publicly referred to 'our Trento', and government's funds were used to assist the Italians in the Trieste municipal elections. Yet politically Italy remained linked to Germany and Austria by the Triple Alliance, which had been concluded in 1882 and was periodically renewed. In reality, there was strong enmity, if not to Germany, then at least to Austria. The dreams of conquest and expansion went much further, and were

---

⁴ Quoted by Margot Hentze, *Pre-Fascist Italy—The Rise and Fall of the Parliamentary Régime*, London, 1939, p. 225.

in particular directed towards the northern shores of Africa just across the Mediterranean. In the 1880s the Italians established themselves at Assab and Massawa on the Red Sea. In 1887 Francesco Crispi became prime minister and extended the Italian zone of influence in north-east Africa into the colony of Eritrea; but he aimed at establishing a protectorate over the whole of Ethiopia, where an Italian protégé was established as emperor. In 1896 Crispi ordered the Italian army to occupy Tigré, to the south of Eritrea, and to march into the Ethiopian highlands. There at Adowa it was disastrously defeated by the Ethiopian forces. Crispi fell from power; but one of the few who ardently defended 'the hero, the only true Italian' was the young writer and teacher Enrico Corradini (born 1865).

Seven years later, in 1903, Corradini founded a nationalist journal, *Il Regno*, which was anti-parliamentarian, anti-democratic and anti-socialist and denounced 'bourgeois' society as cautious, unheroic and pacifist. In juxtaposition to it he asserted the moral values of war and imperialist expansion. The Italian nationalists were fascinated by foreign examples, especially those of Germany and Japan; these they considered the rising nations whose example Italy must follow; they thought of Britain and France as conservative powers, merely defending their possessions. Germany and Japan with their half-autocratic régimes also furnished proof that there was a modernity entirely different from liberal democracy which evoked the ideas of 1789. To Corradini, nationalism was the antithesis of democracy; liberty and equality should be replaced by obedience and discipline. At the end of 1910 the Italian Nationalist Party, *Associazione Nazionalista Italiana*, was founded at Florence. Its foundation conference was addressed by Corradini who emphasized the poverty of Italy and its lack of natural resources: its misery could only be overcome by greater efforts.

The main theme of his speech, however, was that, exactly as there were proletarian classes which had adopted socialism, so there were proletarian nations which must adopt nationalism: 'nations, that is to say, whose living conditions are disadvantageously lower than those of other nations. . . . As socialism teaches the proletariat the value of the class struggle, so we must teach Italy the value of the international struggle. . . . But if the international struggle means war, well then, let there be war!'[5] Hence the programme of the new party advocated an increase in the strength of the army and colonial conquests; the

[5] Quoted by Hentze, op. cit., p. 286.

Italians were to be reawakened to a consciousness of the greatness of
Rome and the Roman Empire. Parliamentarianism and democracy,
freemasonry and international socialism were denounced as the
enemies of the nation. Indeed, the second party congress, held in 1912,
decided that freemasonry and all universal ideas—pacifism, internationalism, egalitarianism—were incompatible with nationalism.

At the first party conference, too, Luigi Federzoni (who in 1922
became Mussolini's minister for the colonies) called for an invasion of
Libya, at that time still under Turkish suzerainty. Corradini promised
that Libya would fall without a shot being fired, and that the African
desert would bloom. To him, the Arabs were mere beasts who should
be whipped and hanged if they dared resist. This propaganda for once
was successful. A few months later Libya was invaded by the Italian
army, but the war—far from being a walk-over—was very protracted
and costly. In the end an army of 100,000 men was required, and the
Senussi tribes continued their fierce resistance for many years. Italian
control remained limited to the coastal area, and the number of Italian
settlers who were established there was very small. Imperial conquest
did not prove rewarding to the country; but Corradini continued to
speak of the Libyan and Balkan wars as the struggles of proletarian
nations against 'European plutocracy'. The most plutocratic nation to
him was France, dominated by democrats and freemasons, who had
prevented Italy from gaining Tunisia. As with the *Action française*,
the influence of the Italian Nationalist Party remained small, mainly
confined to intellectual circles. At the elections of 1913 only three
Nationalists were elected to the chamber. The propaganda in favour of
conquest and expansion had not aroused any mass enthusiasm.

The most violent opposition to the war in Libya came from the extreme left-wing Socialists, while some moderate Socialists, Bonomi and
Bissolati, supported the war and for that reason were expelled from
the party. The most vociferous opponent of Bissolati within the party,
and of any reformist tendency as such, was the young Benito Mussolini, then the local leader in the area of Forli where he had been born
in 1883, the son of a village smith and a village school teacher. 'In case
of war,' he proclaimed, 'instead of hastening to the frontiers, we shall
foment rebellion at home.' And after the outbreak of the war: 'The
Arab and Turkish proletarians are our brothers, and the Turkish and
Italian *bourgeois* our irreconcilable enemies.'[6] Mussolini was a con-

6 Quoted from Mussolini's *Opera Omnia*, iii, p. 137, and iv, p. 130, by Nolte,
op. cit., p. 215.

vinced internationalist and revolutionary, violently opposed to parliamentary activities and to the Socialist acceptance of parliamentary procedure. For his violent agitation against the Libyan war of 1911 he was sentenced to five years' imprisonment, but actually only served five months of the sentence.

In 1912, at the congress of Reggio Emilia and on the motion of Mussolini, the right-wing leaders were expelled from the party; Mussolini himself was appointed the editor of the party paper, *Avanti!* His revolutionary fervour was in no way dampened by this promotion and he continued to despise the intellectuals who led the party. He advocated the use of force in the class struggle against the landowners and the Church, but he nourished the same hatred against the reformist leaders of his own party. Soon after Reggio Emilia, Angelica Balabanoff remembers, Mussolini stopped near some trees on his way home and declared: 'One day we shall hang Turati and other reformists on one of these trees.'[7] Filippo Turati was the man who, in the 1890s, had founded the Italian Socialist Party. Mussolini's hero was the French revolutionary leader Blanqui, 'the man of the barricades', the organizer of revolutionary violence. From another French revolutionary, Gustave Hervé, Mussolini took over the slogan: 'To us the national flag is a rag to be planted on a dunghill.' It was his love of violence in word and deed which made Mussolini conspicuous among his fellow-Socialists. He believed in a 'state of permanent war between bourgeoisie and proletariat' that 'will generate new energies, new moral values, new men who will be close to ancient heroes'.[8]

If Italian socialism, in the form it was preached by Mussolini, was more radical and violent than its French and certainly its German counterparts, Italian nationalism had much in common with that of the *Action française*. It was equally anti-liberal and anti-democratic, its aim too was power and the exercise of power, it too dreamt of 'action', action by an élite. Corradini proclaimed that with a hundred men ready to die he would give new life to Italy. But the emphasis was much more on war, the glorification of war, and the conquest of colonies than was the case in France, which possessed a large colonial empire, and in Corradini's eyes was the most 'plutocratic' country. There was a marked affinity of his thought with that of the Socialists in his

[7] Angelica Balabanoff, *Erinnerungen und Erlebnisse*, Berlin, 1927, p. 84. At that time she was a leading Italian Socialist and personally close to Mussolini.

[8] From a review of Sorel's *Réflexions sur la violence* written by Mussolini in *Il Popolo*, which he edited at Trento in 1909, and quoted by Laura Fermi, *Mussolini*, Chicago, 1961, p. 77.

definition of Italy as a proletarian nation, engaged in a struggle against the 'plutocratic' nations of Europe. It was the class struggle elevated to the international plane. All these ideas were to exercise a profound influence on the later Fascists.

One characteristic trait, however, which we have noticed in France, and shall find again in Germany, Austria and elsewhere, was absent in Italy: anti-Semitism. It was to be absent too in Italian Fascism until it was imported from Germany in the course of the second world war. This may perhaps be explained by the fact that Jews were much less wealthy and less prominent in Italian economic and intellectual life than they were in the more northern countries. In Italy the Jews were hardly more than 0·1 per cent of the population, about 45,000 in all; nor were they conspicuous. Thus 'racialist' ideas made little headway in a country where Jews and Gentiles looked hardly different. As late as 1943 Mussolini himself had to admit to Kállay, the prime minister of Hungary, that there was virtually no anti-Semitism in Italy, and that the number and the position of the Italian Jews were quite insignificant.

Germany

Compared with the poverty-stricken Italy, and even with the defeated France of the Third Republic, the German Empire founded by Bismarck was a country of great strength and energy. There was rapid economic progress, especially in heavy industry, railway building and banking. The 1870s were a time of tremendous boom, interrupted by two short depressions caused by too rapid expansion. Between 1870 and 1900 many towns more than doubled their population; Berlin grew from a city of 775,000 to one of 1,888,000 inhabitants. While in 1870 only thirty-six per cent of the Germans had lived in towns, by 1900 the percentage had increased to 54·4, with a corresponding increase of the numbers employed in industry and trade. Germany—with her great deposits of coal and metals in the Ruhr, the Saar and Upper Silesia—was becoming a country of factory chimneys, mines and large urban conglomerations. The working-class quarters of Berlin and many other towns acquired their endless dreary streets of *Mietskasernen* (literally, 'barracks for hire', likening them to military barracks). There, in spite of all prosperity, numerous working-class families lived in poverty and squalor. The industrial and other workers began to organize themselves into trade unions, and a Social Democratic Party became the opposition party on the Left. It grew quickly after 1875— when several rival factions combined into one party; but it polled less than half a million votes in the general elections of 1877, and only gained twelve seats in the German parliament.

The German Empire was neither democratic, nor particularly liberal, but rather conservative, a country in which the old authorities— the princes, the army, the bureaucracy—retained much of their power; hence there was no place in it for a party of the type of the *Action française*, with its right-wing extremism directed against the republican régime as such, and hardly any place for a party of the 'new Right'. The first attempt in this direction was made in 1878 when the court preacher Adolf Stoecker in Berlin attempted to found a 'Christian-Social Workers' Party'. This was not a radical party, for it emphasized its 'love of king and fatherland', and its main endeavour was at first directed towards winning over Social Democrats: the working class was to be induced to make its peace with the Church and the existing state. But when Stoecker tried to address the Berlin workers the meeting ended in complete failure and a triumph for the Social Democrats. In the following year, however, Stoecker discovered in anti-Semitism a new weapon which made a strong appeal—not to the workers, but to the lower middle classes of the capital which were politically entirely loyal and much closer to his own world of ideas.

The German Jews had been emancipated in the early nineteenth century and were often active in trading and in finance; but they had also entered the professions and were prominent in politics, especially in the different liberal parties and in journalism, and they were particularly prominent in the capital. In 1879 Stoecker proclaimed that their temple was the stock exchange, that they were not clothed with the mantle of the prophet but with the finery of mammon; they were an irreligious power, and through their wealth they were making Berlin a Jewish town and themselves into the new aristocracy. Small traders, craftsmen, shopkeepers and other groups which suffered under the *laissez-faire* policy of the 'liberal era' and felt threatened by the growth of capitalism provided Stoecker with a mass following. But, according to police reports, in addition many officers and educated people attended his meetings. Stoecker was determined to 'demonstrate to the people the roots of its misery, the power of finance, the spirit of mammon and the stock exchange', to make known 'the sighs of the peasants and craftsmen who are writhing under the Jews'.

There was tumultuous applause when he proclaimed at a mass meeting in 1883: 'We offer battle to the Jews until final victory has been gained, and we shall not rest here in Berlin until they have been thrown down from the elevated platform which they have occupied into the dust where they belong.'[9] He demanded administrative measures to curtail the Jewish advance in the fields of education and law, and wanted to gain protection for the workers and the middle classes by social legislation. He soon acquired tremendous popularity.

That Stoecker's propaganda was falling on fertile soil soon became evident. In April 1881 an 'Anti-Semite Petition' was submitted to Bismarck signed by 225,000 people. It demanded the prohibition of any further Jewish immigration from eastern Europe, the exclusion of Jews from the teaching profession and certain high offices, the limitation of their number in secondary schools and the legal profession; it ominously referred to the Jews as a 'race', while Stoecker desired to bring about their baptism and assimilation. In Pomerania in the same year there were anti-Jewish riots; crowds, shouting the anti-Semitic cry of 'hep, hep!', stormed Jewish shops; the police who tried to intervene were stoned, so that the military had to be brought in to reestablish order. In the opinion of the provincial governor it was Jewish money-lending and price-cutting, and Jewish competition in general, that had caused the troubles. In Neustettin the synagogue was burnt down. On New Year's Eve 1881 masses demonstrated in the centre of Berlin and shouted, 'Kick out the Jews!'. Dresden, the capital of Saxony, became another centre of anti-Semitic propaganda.

There were earlier examples of a more violent and racial anti-Semitism in some literary productions. In 1868 Hermann Gödsche, a journalist on the staff of the conservative *Kreuzzeitung*, published a novel which described a meeting of Jewish conspirators in the ancient Jewish cemetery of Prague, where they plotted to take over the world: an early version of the *Protocols of the Elders of Zion* which were to furnish 'proof' of a Jewish world conspiracy. In 1871 August Rohling, a teacher at a Prague church seminary, produced an edited version of the Talmud to prove that their doctrine commanded the Jews to commit ritual murder. This book was then edited by Edouard Drumont in a French version, and with his preface published in German. In

⁹ Quoted by Walter Frank, *Hofprediger Adolf Stoecker und die christlichsoziale Bewegung*, 2nd ed., Hamburg, 1935, p. 84. The other quotations, ibid., pp. 77–8. In 1880 about 54,000 Jews were living in Berlin, less than five per cent of the population.

1873 Wilhelm Marr, a journalist, brought out a book on 'The Victory of the Jew over the German, looked at from a non-religious point of view', which went into twelve editions within six years. In 1879 he founded the 'League of Anti-Semites'. He argued that this was 'a question of race' and that 'the difference lies in the "blood"...'; but he advocated the use of 'strictly legal methods' to prevent 'the further displacement of Germanism by Judaism'.[10]

These feelings were echoed in very respectable and academic circles. In 1879 the famous historian Heinrich von Treitschke published a series of articles in the well-known *Preussische Jahrbücher* which ended with the sentence: 'The Jews are our misfortune.' Treitschke deeply influenced a whole generation of German students; his lectures at Berlin University were attended by vast numbers. Both he and Stoecker were highly respected people, not rabble-rousers, and Stoecker was connected with the royal court. Remarks made by such men provided anti-Semitism with an aura of respectability. To Eugen Dühring, a blind lecturer in economics and philosophy at Berlin University, it was a question of 'racial honour' to drive the Jews, this 'incomparably inferior race', from all public offices and from the world of business and finance.

The man, however, who more than any other can be regarded as the prophet of things to come and whose *Deutsche Schriften* exercised a strong influence on later generations, was Paul Bötticher, who called himself de Lagarde. He too was an academic, an authority in the field of oriental studies, but he had to earn his living as a secondary school teacher and only late in life became a professor at Göttingen University. Lagarde started writing in the 1850s (he was born in 1827). Already then he decided it an impossibility to endure the Jews who formed 'a nation within a nation', and whose nationality could only be eliminated if they were deprived of their religion; either they must renounce this, or they must leave central Europe. But in his ambitious schemes for this area he went much further: German emigration must be directed, according to a carefully worked-out strategic plan, to Posnania, Bohemia, Slovakia, Hungary, Galicia and Istria; their native populations must be hardened by mixing them with a German alloy, and thus the degenerate subjects of small German states would become free men.[11]

[10] Quoted from Peter G. J. Pulzer, *The Rise of Political Anti-Semitism in Germany and Austria*, New York and London, 1964, pp. 50–1.
[11] Paul de Lagarde, 'Über die gegenwärtigen Aufgaben der deutschen Politik' (written in 1853!), *Deutsche Schriften*, 4th ed., Munich, 1940, pp. 30, 33, 42.

In his later writings de Lagarde merely expanded this programme. The countries bordering upon Germany and Austria in the east were to be Germanized. Russia was to be defeated in war and forced to cede to Germany a broad belt of territory from the Baltic to the Black Sea but *without* the inhabitants. These lands were to be settled with German peasants, and the Jews from Poland and Galicia to be expelled to Palestine. Only through a German colonization of eastern Europe and the separation of Russia from the southern Slavs could Austria, Germany's natural ally, be preserved in an efficient state; Austria must be most thoroughly Germanized; and the German Jews must either emigrate or become Germans. 'The *Alliance Israélite* is nothing but an international conspiracy—similar to Freemasonry—to promote the Jewish domination of the world, in the Semitic field the same what the Jesuit Order is in the Catholic one. . . . Any alien body within a living organism creates ill-feeling, disease, even festering sores and death. Even if the alien body were a jewel, it would have the same effect as a piece of mouldering wood. The Jews as Jews are aliens in every European state, and as aliens nothing but carriers of putrefaction. . . .'[12] And even more sharply some years later: 'One does not negotiate with trichinae and bacilli, nor can one educate them; they are destroyed as quickly and as thoroughly as possible. . . .'[13] It is not surprising that de Lagarde also fulminated against Bismarck's foreign policy, against parliament and the political parties; the Reichstag must be replaced by an advisory council; a leader must unite and command the nation. During his life-time de Lagarde mainly influenced certain student circles; but there is no doubt that, many years after his death (in 1891), his ideas were revived and taken up by the National Socialists. Almost their whole programme can be found in his writings.

Much more widely read at the time was the book of a younger man who was strongly influenced by de Lagarde, Julius Langbehn. In 1890, when he was almost forty years old, he published his 'Rembrandt as an Educator', which immediately had a great popular success. But while Stoecker, and largely de Lagarde too, aimed at the assimilation of the German Jews, Langbehn did not object to orthodox Jews, but believed that 'the modern, plebeian Jews are a poison for us and

---

[12] The quotation is from 'Die Stellung der Religionsgesellschaften im Staate' (written in 1881), ibid., pp. 295–6. The other ideas are taken from de Lagarde's writings in the 1880s, ibid., pp. 98, 332, 354–5, 413–15, 422, 476.

[13] de Lagarde, *Juden und Indogermanen*, Göttingen, 1887, p. 347. In general cp. Fritz Stern, *The Politics of Cultural Despair*, Berkeley and Los Angeles, 1961, pp. 60 ff.

must be treated as such. . . . They are democratically inclined; they have an affinity with the mob. . . .' And in a later edition: 'Germany for the Germans. A Jew can no more become a German than a plum can turn into an apple. . . .'[14] Anticipating the Nuremberg Laws by almost half a century Langbehn also advocated an investigation into people's ancestry as a condition of granting German citizenship to them. To him the Jews were particularly obnoxious because they represented political and economic progress, democracy, liberalism and capitalism.

All this, for the time being, had only a limited influence in the realm of practical politics. About 1885 anti-Semitism declined as a political movement in Berlin and Dresden, but it gained new strength in west Germany, in the area of Hesse where many peasants were indebted to Jewish money-lenders. There a librarian of Marburg University, Otto Böckel, became the highly popular leader of an anti-Semitic movement which aimed at excluding Jews from the cattle markets and providing credit facilities for the peasants. On the basis of a radical social pro-gramme Böckel was elected a deputy for Marburg in 1887—in a constituency which had been considered a safe conservative seat. In the same year he declared: 'Through anti-Semitism the German people shall learn to feel itself again as a Germanic race opposed to the Jewish race.' In 1890 he and four other anti-Semites were elected Reichstag deputies, all in Hesse. By 1893 their number had increased to sixteen, and the votes polled by the party to 264,000, nearly three per cent of the electorate. In 1898 its votes further grew to 284,000, but then the movement began to decline. Hesse and Saxony remained its strongholds. But strong differences arose between the conservative anti-Semites and the radicals, men such as Böckel or Hermann Ahl-wardt, who in Pomerania campaigned 'against Junkers and Jews!' and attacked high society as sharply as he did the Jews. These internal conflicts were one of the causes of the movement's decline; another was the sharp rise of general prosperity at the end of the nineteenth cen-tury which continued into the twentieth, with only a minor depression during its first two years.

This decline also affected Stoecker's party which had always re-mained closely linked with the Conservatives. The draft programme submitted to the Conservative conference in Berlin in 1892 proposed: 'We fight the often aggressive and disintegrating Jewish influence on

[14] Quoted from *Rembrandt als Erzieher*, 33rd ed., 1891, p. 284, 38th ed., 1891, p. 292, 49th ed., p. 348, by Stern, op. cit., p. 141, and Pulzer, op. cit., p. 242.

our national life', with the additional clause: 'We reject the excesses of anti-Semitism.' But this addition met with heated opposition from the delegates; when Stoecker moved its rejection they gave him an ovation, and only seven votes were cast in its favour. But four years later Stoecker was forced to resign from the party executive; the agrarian interest which now dominated the party feared that his tendency towards social reform might invade the estates of the Junkers. The combination of radicalism and anti-Semitism in Ahlwardt's agitation was certainly ominous. In Germany, in contrast with Austria, there was no future for a Christian-Social Party.

Yet anti-Semitism survived as a small political force, and there was even personal continuity with the later National Socialist Party. From the later 1880s Theodor Fritsch, a Leipzig engineer, published an 'Anti-Semitic Correspondence'; he wrote that true Germans must reject the Old Testament, a 'story glorifying the Jews', that Christ was an Aryan and anti-Semite, hated and rejected by the Jews, and that Judaism was the enemy of German life. There followed a *Handbook of the Jewish Question* and an *Anti-Semitic Catechism*, both of which had numerous editions. Fritsch eagerly corresponded with Langbehn who exercised a strong influence on this group. From 1902 onwards Fritsch published a journal, *Der Hammer*, in which he extolled racial purity. Its readers soon formed local groups, the 'Hammer Communities', but their number remained very small. In 1912 a 'Reich Hammer League' and a 'Germanic Order' were formed at a meeting in Leipzig, the members of which had to guarantee that they were of pure 'Aryan' descent. It was in these circles that the Swastika was soon used as a symbol of the Sun-Wheel that had been taken to the south by the Aryans, and that was to announce the Sun-Rise 'brilliantly on a Germanic field'. A post-card of the year 1903, from which this theme has been taken, showed a black Swastika on a white field surrounded by a red circle: the later emblem of the Hitler Party.[15] These circles too propagated the revival of Germanic customs, names and months in place of the Christian ones.

Fritsch's Hammer League was a corporate member of another and much larger association that was devoted to the preservation of Germanism, to the promotion of a 'sense of racial and cultural kinship among all sections of the German people'. This was the *Alldeutscher Verband* (Pan-German League) which was formed in the 1890s and

[15] Interestingly enough, this swastika post-card is among the papers of no less a person than Julius Streicher, Hitler's chief Jew-baiter.

soon attracted thousands, especially teachers and white-collar workers. In 1901 it had 22,000 active members. Another corporate member was the *Deutschnationaler Handlungsgehilfenverband*, a nationalist trade union of clerical workers. The Pan-German League engaged in a vigorous propaganda for a more militant foreign policy, for German expansion abroad, be that in eastern Europe or by the acquisition of new colonies. In the last decades of the nineteenth century Germany had indeed gained a colonial empire; but the colonies were small and scattered from West Africa to groups of islands in the Pacific, and little benefit was derived from them. Officially the League was not anti-Semitic, but many of its members were, and its deputies in the Reichstag cooperated with the anti-Semites. The leader of the League, Heinrich Claß, later acknowledged that his teacher Heinrich von Treitschke had implanted in him the conviction that the Jews were noxious to Germany. In 1907 he launched a campaign against the Jews as carriers of modern materialism: they should be treated as foreigners and heavily taxed, excluded from teaching, banking and the civil service, forbidden to own land, and their immigration and their activities should be curtailed. Claß considered that the universal franchise which Bismarck had introduced was bad for Germany and ought to be replaced by a class and plural franchise: if the Reichstag refused to accept this, a new constitution should be imposed from above. He favoured an Imperial dictatorship to save Germany from liberalism. Claß and his League maintained close relations with powerful organizations, such as the *Bund der Landwirte* (Agrarian League), and with important politicians in the conservative and national liberal camps.

It was from organizations such as the Hammer League, the Pan-German League and the *Deutschnationaler Handlungsgehilfenverband* that the National Socialist Party was to draw many of its early members. The nationalist, anti-liberal, racist and anti-Semitic propaganda spread by these organizations prepared the soil on which National Socialism was to grow. Its ideology was already familiar to many thousands of Germans. Theodor Fritsch, during his later years, became a National Socialist deputy in parliament. His *Handbook of the Jewish Question* and other publications were well known to Hitler. The 'Hammer' publishing house later also published a popular edition of the *Protocols of the Elders of Zion*, a work which strongly influenced Hitler and many of his followers.

This applies equally to a curious, semi-philosophical work written by an Englishman who made his home in Germany, the son of a British admiral, Houston Stewart Chamberlain. At the very end of the nineteenth century he published in German his *Foundations of the Nineteenth Century*: it contained a purely racialist interpretation of history. 'It is clear that, in a certain sense, we may regard the intellectual and moral history of Europe from the moment of the entry of the Teuton to the present day as a struggle between Teuton and non-Teuton, between Germanic sentiment and anti-Germanic disposition. . . .' In the creation of a new civilization 'it was Teutonic blood and Teutonic blood alone (in the wide sense in which I take the word, that is to say, embracing the Celtic, Teutonic and Slavonic, or North European races) that formed the impelling force and the informing power. . . .' But to Chamberlain only northern Europe was 'pure Teutonic in the narrowest sense of the word', while in Germany 'the fusion of the three branches—Celts, Teutons and Slavs—took place, a fact which explains the distinct national colour and the richness of the gifts of this people', and France too, before the French Revolution, had a 'predominantly Teutonic character'. In this respect Chamberlain differed from later National Socialist ideologists who were strongly anti-Slav and convinced of the purity of the German race.

Chamberlain was strongly anti-Semitic, but to him—again in contrast with Nazi racialism—'the term Jew rather denotes a special way of thinking and feeling. A man can very soon become a Jew without being an Israelite. . . . On the other hand, it is senseless to call an Israelite a "Jew", though his descent is beyond question, if he has succeeded in throwing off the fetters of Ezra and Nehemiah, and if the law of Moses has no place in his brain, and contempt of others no place in his heart. . . . A purely humanized Jew is no longer a Jew because, by renouncing the idea of Judaism, he *ipso facto* has left that nationality. . . .' Chamberlain even spoke of 'the perfectly ridiculous and revolting tendency to make the Jew the general scapegoat for all the vices of our time' and wrote that 'the Jew is no enemy of Teutonic civilization and culture'. He expressed his admiration for the Sephardic Jews in eastern Europe [*sic*] with their 'genuine nobility of race! Beautiful figures, noble heads, dignity in speech and bearing.' But in Germany 'our government, our law, our science, our commerce, our literature, our art . . . have become more or less willing slaves of the Jews', and the Indo-Europeans had been infected with Jewish blood; if this process continued unchecked, 'there would be only one people of pure race left in Europe, that of the Jews, all the rest would be a herd of pseudo-

Hebraic mestizos, a people beyond all doubt degenerate physically, mentally and morally. . . .'[16] Thousands of 'racially-minded' Germans believed in pronouncements of this kind, in pseudo-learned and high-faluting phrases. More than any other book *The Foundations of the Nineteenth Century* became a kind of bible of the German racialists, which, even before 1914, sold 100,000 copies. Before he died in 1927 Chamberlain was firmly convinced that he had found in Hitler the German saviour; in an article published in 1924 he hailed Hitler as destined by God to become the leader of Germany.

It was this racialism, the firm belief in the natural superiority of an allegedly Germanic race and in the great destiny of their *Volk* (people), that distinguished German right-wing extremism from that of the Latin countries. It often went hand in hand with a veneration of 'blood and soil', with an Aryan mysticism, neo-paganism and rejection of Christianity, which the more rationally-minded French or Italians would have found rather ridiculous. So, of course, did many Germans—until these hare-brained schemes were translated into a frightening reality in the years after 1933. In the opinion of the racialists, the German *Volk* was not identical with the nation, but it included all those of German blood, wherever they lived, from Brazil in the west to the Volga in the east, from Scandinavia in the north to the Tyrol in the south; it had no geographical limits. The belief in a German *Volk* superior to all other peoples was particularly strong in certain academic circles. As early as 1861 the poet Geibel had expressed it in the verse:

> *Und es mag am deutschen Wesen*
> *Einmal noch die Welt genesen.*

(Roughly, 'Germanhood one day may heal the whole world.') Not included in the *Volk* were the Jews and other 'inferior' peoples. In 1896 a conference attended by representatives of all the *Burschenschaften* (students' corporations) proclaimed: 'The *Burschenschaft* rests on the basis of German *Volkstum*. . . . Jewish citizens of the *Reich* are not to be regarded as Germans.' This *völkisch* concept was to remain a distinguishing mark of the new German Right. It was not shaken, but on the contrary strongly reinforced by Germany's defeat in the first world war.

---

[16] The quotations are from the English translation of *The Foundations of the Nineteenth Century*, 2 vols, London, 1911, I, pp. lxxviii, 273, 330–1, 491–2, 563, II, pp. 187, 231. It is difficult to say what influence Chamberlain had upon Hitler: it seems unlikely that he ever read these bulky semi-philosophical volumes.

Austria and Bohemia

The Dual Monarchy of Austria-Hungary was a much weaker state than the German Empire. It possessed no military laurels on which it could rest, its economic progress was much slower and uneven, and large parts of it were very poor and backward. Above all, only the political aspirations of the Hungarians were satisfied by the *Ausgleich* of 1867, while those of the many Slav nationalities remained unfulfilled. In the course of the nineteenth century the Czechs, the Poles, the Slovenes acquired their own middle and educated classes, hence their demands for political concessions became louder. But such concessions would have threatened the position of the Germans who were the leading nationality in the Austrian half of the dual monarchy, especially in areas with a mixed population, such as Bohemia. The population of Vienna, Prague and other towns was growing apace—by 1910 Vienna had more than 2,000,000 inhabitants—but the middle and lower middle classes felt far from secure. Apart from the political demands of the rising non-German nationalities, there was the growing economic concentration which deprived many a small man of his livelihood. In the thirty years following upon the abolition of guild privileges in 1859 in Vienna alone the enterprises of 35,000 artisans were seized for default.

There was another threat, much more real than in Germany. Until the middle of the nineteenth century the Jewish population of Vienna had been very small, but in 1910 175,000 inhabitants of the capital were classified as Jews, more than eight per cent of the population. Jews were not only extremely prominent in banking, but also in other branches of economic life; 'it is safe to say that by 1914 the industry and trade of Vienna were to an overwhelming extent in Jewish hands'.[17] Many Jews entered the professions, journalism or the civil service. In the University of Vienna in 1880 38·6 per cent of the medical students were Jewish, and 22·3 per cent of the students reading law—at a time when the Jewish percentage of the population in general was perhaps five per cent. In 1890 the figure for the whole university was 33·6 per cent. In literature, the theatre, and in intellectual affairs in general, Jews soon occupied the leading positions. If Jews were politically active they were Liberals, hence any anti-liberal tendency might easily turn into anti-Semitism. Moreover, in addition, many of the Jews

17 Arthur J. May, *The Hapsburg Monarchy 1867–1914*, Cambridge, Mass., 1960, p. 177.

living in Vienna and other towns had but recently come from Galicia or another eastern province of the monarchy. They differed strongly from the other inhabitants in their language, their clothing, their whole way of life, and aroused wide-spread anti-Semitic feeling. Growing competition by Jewish traders and craftsmen had the same result. Anti-Semitism equally appealed to the students and the members of the professions in which many Jews were to be found. Open and organized anti-Semitic propaganda resulted from the financial crash of 1873 which affected large numbers of the Viennese. Popular passions were aroused by it and remained strong thereafter. Large numbers held the Jews responsible for the crash which was caused by the failure of a leading bank and the collapse of many companies in its wake.

Anti-Semitism became particularly strong among the students. The Viennese *Burschenschaft* 'Libertas' expelled its Jewish members in 1878, and soon after forbade its members to accept Jews as partners in a duel. The Prague 'Teutonia' excluded Jews in 1879; ten years later all the Austrian *Burschenschaften* decided to accept only Aryans as members. The tendency spread to gymnastics associations; eight branches of the *Turnerschaft* in Lower Austria barred Jewish members. In the *Burschenschaften* this went parallel with Pan-German (*großdeutsch*) sentiments, which—in Austria—meant a desire to join the new German Reich, preferring the Hohenzollern to the Habsburg Empire. At Graz University a students' meeting had to be closed officially in 1875 because many students interrupted the singing of the Austrian national anthem by whistling and sang demonstratively the German anthem *Deutschland über Alles* ('Germany above Everything'). In the same year the Austrian flag and national anthem were insulted openly in the same city at a congress of scientists. When the deputy Schönerer in parliament during the debate on the budget in 1878 exclaimed that 'throughout Austria's German provinces the cry could be heard "if only we belonged to the German *Reich*"', hundreds of students and other academics the same evening sent him their visiting cards as a sign of approval. In the same year several *Burschenschaften* elected him an honorary member and invited him to their drinking parties. Henceforth they provided him with an enthusiastic following.

Georg Ritter von Schönerer was born in 1842, the son of a well-known and wealthy railway builder and official, who had been ennobled for his services to the monarchy. From his father he inherited the title and the estate of Rosenau in Lower Austria where he lived the life of a landed gentleman. In 1873 he was elected to the Austrian parliament, the Reichsrat, for his rural constituency and in parliament first joined the progressive club. During his early years he stood out for a markedly radical programme, demanding for example the nationalization of the railways and the introduction of a universal and direct franchise, but also a political and economic union with Germany. Nor was he particularly anti-Semitic: well-known Jews—the later Socialist leader Victor Adler and the famous historian Heinrich Friedjung—were at first his close associates. It was his fervent nationalism, his *großdeutsch* (Pan-German) attitude, that made Schönerer follow a more and more extremist course; and it was his intimate connexion with the nationalist *Burschenschaften* of Vienna University that brought this about.

It seems that Schönerer's anti-Semitism also derived from these circles. At first it was fired by economic motives, dislike of the effects of Jewish capitalism, the Jewish press and the Jewish liberal propaganda. At an artisans' meeting in 1882 he exclaimed against 'the ubiquitous and dumbfounding rise to prosperity of the Jews', who had 'risen to almost a hegemony in the economic sphere, . . . a symptom of the general economic disease. . . .'[18] But it soon developed into racial anti-Semitism. In 1883 he wrote in his journal *Unverfälschte Deutsche Worte* ('Undiluted German Words'): 'We shall never be willing to recognize a Jew as a German because he speaks German or even behaves in a German national way, or to aim at a mixture of Germans and Jews, or to consent to it. Adopting the "brutal racial point of view" we must on the contrary declare that we consider much more feasible a mixture, or in certain circumstances an alliance, with the Slavs and Latins than any intimate connexion with the Jews. For the former are Aryans and related to us, while the latter are completely alien to us by descent. . . . If one or the other Jew voluntarily joins our German ranks, he may work with us in God's name, but only as a common soldier and not in a leading position. . . .'[19]

In the Reichsrat in 1883 Schönerer demanded the dismissal of all Jewish teachers; all true Germans must oppose 'the international speculators without a fatherland, whose goal is the corruption of the Germanic race already at the primary school stage'. Four years later he demanded special legislation against the immigration of foreign Jews, for 'the customs and ways of life of these alien parasites are hostile to the Aryan descent and to the Christian culture of the Ger-

[18] Quoted by Pulzer, op. cit., p. 146.
[19] *Unverfälschte Deutsche Worte*, 1 July 1883.

man nation'.[20] But less than half the members of the 'German Club', which had meanwhile been formed in parliament by the nationalists, voted in favour of his motion, and the Club split up. Among the small traders, craftsmen and shopkeepers of Vienna, on the other hand, Schönerer became highly popular, for to them Jewish competition was a real problem. Yet his journal, the *Unverfälschte Deutsche Worte*, in 1885 sold only 1,700 copies, and the 'German-National Association' which he founded in 1882 never acquired a large membership; when it was dissolved in 1889 it had only about 1,200 members. It was much more the students who followed Schönerer than the Viennese population, although he did his best to rouse the rabble in great mass meetings.

Schönerer's popularity in Vienna was soon overshadowed by that of another man, a much more astute politician, a very gifted orator and organizer: Dr Karl Lueger, who was only two years his junior. Lueger who had a lower-class social background knew far better how to appeal to the little man and his unspoken aims and desires. Like Schönerer he started his politics as a Liberal. First elected to the city council in 1875 on a radical platform, ten years later he entered parliament where he supported Schönerer's anti-Semitic motions and cooperated with him. From the beginning he also maintained close relations with the Catholic reform movement which was then being organized by Austrian clergymen and noblemen. It was, above all, as a Christian-Social leader that Lueger made his mark and mobilized a mass support far greater than Schönerer ever enjoyed, and became one of the most popular mayors Vienna has ever had.

When Lueger noticed how strongly the masses were attracted by anti-Semitic slogans he too adopted them. In 1887 he was to address a meeting after the Hungarian anti-Semitic leader Komlossy, who received an ovation and was frequently interrupted by cries of assent. Lueger then turned to the chairman and enquired what he should say to compete successfully with Komlossy, and the chairman advised him to outdo the first speaker's anti-Semitism. This Lueger proceeded to do and earned storms of applause. Yet Lueger never mustered the hatred of the Jews which was shown by the fanatics of his party, and his anti-Semitism always remained a qualified one. In this respect too he resembled Stoecker in Berlin. He informed one of the Viennese

Jewish leaders: 'I dislike the Hungarian Jews even more than I do the Hungarians, but I am no enemy of our Viennese Jews; they are not so bad and we cannot do without them. . . .'[21] He also coined the famous phrase: 'I decide who is a Jew'.

To Lueger, anti-Semitism was a handy weapon, useful above all to wrest Vienna from the bourgeois Liberal Party in which Jews were very prominent. In this he was completely successful. In 1895 his party gained control of the Vienna city council: it won all the seats in the popular, third curia, and in general twice as many seats as the Liberals. By 1900 the Christian-Social Party had virtually a monopoly of seats, 131 out of 154. In 1895 Lueger was for the first time elected mayor, but not confirmed in office by the Emperor Francis Joseph. The resulting re-election of the city council only increased Lueger's majority. In 1897 he was elected for the fourth time and then confirmed in office. Until his death in 1910 he remained the master of the capital for which he achieved much. The Socialist *Arbeiter-Zeitung* in its obituary notice admitted that Lueger was 'the first bourgeois politician who reckoned with the masses, moved the masses, and sank the roots of his power deeply into the soil'. That Lueger was no racialist was also shown in his attitude towards the Slav nationalities of the monarchy. In parliament he declared in 1891: 'In Austria I only know nations with equal rights; I see in every Czech, in every Slovene my Austrian co-citizen.'[22] In a strongly Catholic country, Lueger never opposed the Church and the established monarchy, and received much valuable support from the Catholic side. In both respects he strongly differed from the more extreme Schönerer.

It was, above all, Schönerer's Germanism which became extreme during these years, his veneration for things Germanic or Prussian, his hatred of the Habsburg monarchy and Catholicism, feelings that were echoed by the German racialists. He signed his letters '*mit deutschem Gruß*' ('with German greetings'), as the National Socialists were to do later. His paper recommended parents to give to their children truly Germanic names—another fashion which was later adopted by many thousands. He tried to revive the Midsummer and Yuletide festivals, Germanic cults, and the Germanic names of the months—practices also followed by *völkisch* circles in Germany. Celebrations were held to commemorate the battles of Noreia, where the Cimbri had defeated the Roman legions in 113 BC, and of the

21 Quoted by Pulzer, op. cit., p. 204.
22 Quoted by Kurt Skalnik, *Dr Karl Lueger*, Vienna and Munich, 1954, p. 73.

Teutoburg forest, where Varus' legions had been slain by the Cherusci in AD 9. In the place of the Christian calendar a Germanic calendar starting in 113 BC was to be introduced; a festival was organized in 1888 to inaugurate the year 2001 starting from Noreia. There was constant praise of Prussia and the Hohenzollerns. Some years later Schönerer launched the 'Break with Rome' movement 'against the anti-German power of Rome' to achieve 'the final victory of Germandom over the un-German, quarrelsome Roman Church', which had allied with 'Slav insolence . . . in order to annihilate Germandom in this Empire which has been built on German foundations'.[23] His followers were enjoined to leave the Catholic Church and to become Protestants, but few did so. Others—to prove their anti-Semitic convictions—were wearing on their watch-chain a pendant showing hanged Jews.

In the Reichsrat Schönerer and his followers time and again staged tumultuous scenes and obstruction tactics which brought parliamentary work to a standstill: particularly so in 1897 when the Badeni government tried to satisfy the legitimate wishes of the Czechs and other Slavs by the introduction of new language ordinances. The deputy Karl Hermann Wolf referred to Czech and Slovene as 'mere Slav dialects' and called the Reichsrat chairman a 'Polish scoundrel'. The Pan-German deputies incessantly blew trumpets and whistles, banged the lids of their desks, and free fights ensued. Finally Wolf and Schönerer were forcibly removed by the police. Outside there were monster demonstrations, and in Prague martial law had to be proclaimed. The Badeni government was forced to resign and parliament was prorogued. The last chance of solving the problem of the nationalities within the monarchy had passed. In the elections of 1901 twenty-one Pan-German deputies were elected to the Reichsrat, nineteen of them in the German districts of Bohemia where the party had its main strength. But in the following year the party split. Wolf increasingly resented Schönerer's autocratic methods in controlling the party and founded his own more moderate 'Free Pan-Germans' which, being more opportunist, soon became considerably stronger than the parent body. In the elections of 1907, the first held under universal male franchise, the 'Free Pan-Germans' won fifteen seats, the Schönerer group only three. Schönerer himself was heavily defeated in the Bohemian district of Eger (Cheb) by a Social Democrat who gained more than five times his opponent's votes. In Lower

[23] *Unverfälschte Deutsche Worte*, 16 November 1898.

Austria and Vienna Schönerer's adherents went over to Lueger's Christian-Socials. Gradually he was deserted by all. Neo-Paganism had no attraction for the masses; the 'Break with Rome' slogan and the propaganda for the Hohenzollern House did not make Schönerer precisely popular. The Christian-Social Party was the chief gainer.

In the German districts of northern Bohemia, however, the seed sown by Schönerer continued to germinate because here the position of the Germans was truly threatened. In the course of the industrialization of the area many Czech workers migrated into the towns where they formed strong non-German pockets. They were accustomed to lower living standards and accepted lower wages than the German workers, in the lignite fields as well as in the factories. At a meeting of German workers' associations held at Reichenberg (Liberec) in 1888 a textile worker complained that the Czech workers were undercutting the legitimate demands of German craftsmen and accepting living conditions which no German would tolerate. Ten years later a bookbinder from Brüx (Most) and a typesetter from Hohenstadt brought together the representatives of several thousand German workers; they founded the 'Federation of the German Assistants and Workers' Associations of Austria' to protect the interests of the German workers; the new Federation accepted Schönerer as its patron. The Badeni crisis—the proposed ordinances applied in particular to Bohemia—and Schönerer's campaign against the government caused tremendous excitement among the German Bohemians. In May 1899 several hundred delegates representing more than 4,000 workers met at Eger (Cheb); the majority came from the industrial districts of northern Bohemia, others from Vienna, Graz, Munich and Berlin. A textile worker proposed to send greetings to Schönerer, 'the leader of the German people of the Ostmark' (Eastern March); the proposal was carried unanimously.

From these modest beginnings developed the Deutsche Arbeiterpartei (German Workers' Party) which was founded at Trautenau (Trutnov) in 1904 by German workers from Bohemia and Moravia and from Austrian towns, such as Linz, where a strong Czech immigration had recently occurred. The programme of the new party was radical rather than right-wing,[24] demanding the introduction of the universal and equal franchise, freedom of speech and the press, of association and meetings, and an extension of political self-government.

[24] The programme of 15 August 1904 is printed in A. Ciller, Vorläufer des Nationalsozialismus, Vienna, 1932, pp. 135-6.

The party proclaimed itself a '*freiheitliche nationale Partei*' ('liberal national party'), 'which is fighting with all its strength against the reactionary tendencies, feudal, clerical and capitalist privileges as well as all foreign national influences', so as to overcome the 'untenable conditions of the society of to-day' and to secure 'the social rise of the workers'. It was a mixture of political, social and national demands, born out of the fierce struggle in a frontier area which had strong social and national implications.

In 1913 a new party programme was adopted which was much more outspoken, especially against 'the teachings of the Social Democratic Party Saint Marx'. His doctrine of internationalism was pronounced 'wrong and of immeasurable damage to the Germandom of central Europe'. The poor German-speaking workers, 'who with their contributions had made Social Democracy powerful, were in many areas pushed out of their jobs by the Slav comrades whom they had heartily welcomed. The German employer took the cheaper Slav worker; but the red organization refused to give the German party veterans the protection to which they were entitled. . . .' Hence the Germans began to recognize 'the perniciousness of the international doctrines' and 'the insincerity of Social Democracy which is led by Jews and closely allied with the mobile big capitalists'.[25] What is interesting in this programme is not so much the description of the dangers threatening the German workers—which was based on reality—but the close connexion seen between Jews, Social Democrats and big capitalists, which was to figure so prominently in *Mein Kampf* and in National Socialist propaganda. Meanwhile the first three deputies of the party had been elected to the Reichsrat, all for industrial districts in northern Bohemia. When the first world war broke out the *völkische* German trade unions had 611 local branches and 45,000 members. Among their leaders several later became prominent National Socialists. They refused to acknowledge that the existence of the Germans in Bohemia depended upon reaching an agreement with the Czechs, on a compromise between the two nationalities. They were on the contrary convinced that the areas of German influence must be extended and the Czech competition eliminated from them.

These political influences shaped the mind of the young Adolf Hitler, who was born at Braunau on the Inn in 1889 as the son of an

[25] The programme of September is printed by Andrew G. Whiteside, 'Nationaler Sozialismus in Österreich vor 1918', *Vierteljahrshefte für Zeitgeschichte*, ix, 1961, pp. 344–5.

Austrian customs official. When he came to Vienna as a young man of eighteen his political sympathies were with Schönerer and the Pan-Germans. He was impressed by Schönerer's enthusiasm for the House of Hohenzollern and his advocacy of joining the German *Reich*. But he was critical of Schönerer's lack of understanding of social issues and of the importance of the lower classes: his appeal was directed too exclusively to *bourgeois* groups. In Dr Lueger, on the other hand, the young Hitler found the man who understood the importance of the social question, recognized the value of large-scale propaganda and was a virtuoso in playing on the instincts of the masses, while he avoided any attack on the Church and thus gained its support. Many years later Hitler still expressed his admiration for him. Last, but not least Hitler encountered in Vienna the fierce anti-Semitism preached there by leaders of both parties. But he reacted equally negatively to the other nationalities of the Habsburg monarchy which he encountered in Vienna for the first time: 'Disgusting to me was the conglomerate of races which characterized the capital of the Empire, disgusting this whole mixture of peoples, of Czechs, Poles, Hungarians, Ruthenians, Serbs and Croats, etc., but between them all as the eternal morbid growth (*Spaltpilz*) of humanity —Jews and more Jews. . . .'[26] In later years, there was to be found framed above Hitler's bed Schönerer's slogan: 'Without Juda, without Rome, let us build Germania's dome.'

There is no doubt that the young man received his decisive political impressions in the Vienna of the early twentieth century, from the newspapers which he read avidly, and from the heated discussions in which he engaged with his room-mates and casual acquaintances.[27] It was a mixture of social and national ideas which he absorbed eagerly, but above all it was the world of the Pan-Germans and anti-Semites of the most extremist hues which he entered. Yet this world was doomed. Even if war had not broken out in 1914, the Germans—a minority of about thirty-five per cent in the Austrian half of the monarchy— could not have held their own against the rising tide of Slav nationalism. Indeed, since 1880 this percentage had not increased but slightly decreased. Any attempt at the Germanization of the non-Germans, at

---

[26] *Mein Kampf*, 97th ed., Munich, 1934, pp. 59, 106, 108, 110, 133–5.

[27] Ibid., p. 137. August Kubizek, *Adolf Hitler, mein Jugendfreund*, Graz, 1953, has tried to prove that Hitler was already a convinced Pan-German and follower of Schönerer before he came to Vienna; but this view has been disproved by Franz Jetzinger, *Hitlers Jugend—Phantasien, Lügen—und die Wahrheit*, Vienna, 1956, especially pp. 212–13, 236. In general, there is little reason to doubt Hitler's own version in this respect.

reducing their influence or rights, at making the Germans the sole ruling group was bound to end in failure. Somewhat more realistic, was the expectation of the break-up of the Habsburg monarchy which might allow its German parts to join the German *Reich*—a goal which Schönerer proclaimed so loudly. But this would have meant that this *Reich* would lose its only reliable ally—a severe setback to the dreams of expansion and world power cherished in Pan-German circles. There was no way out, and the sharp decline of Schönerer's political influence in the decade before 1914 seemed to prove this.

Russia

In Russia too, the dawning of a more liberal age and the outbreak of revolution in 1905 led to the formation of a party of the 'new Right', opposed alike to liberalism, parliamentarianism, socialism and the Jews. The defeat of the Russian army and navy by the Japanese caused the outbreak of mass strikes and revolutionary disorders all over Russia, and the government was forced to make concessions. In June 1905 Nicholas II promised that a national assembly would be called, that the Tsarist autocracy would give way to a new régime. In August an imperial decree was promulgated which instituted a State Duma, to be elected on the basis of a very restricted class franchise. In October, however, an imperial manifesto promised a wide extension of the franchise for the Duma which was to have wide legislative powers; inviolability of the person, freedom of conscience, speech, and assembly were to be established. It seemed as if the autocracy would soon be transformed into a constitutional monarchy, although the word 'constitution' was not mentioned in the manifesto.

Significantly, it was during the same month, on 22 October 1905, that a new party was founded which called itself the 'Union of the Russian People' (*Soiuz Russkogo Naroda*). It did not consider itself to be a party, but a spontaneous popular movement for the defence of the Tsar, the Church and the fatherland, of the autocracy against any attacks, representing the Russian people (*narod*) itself. But it conceded that the voice of the people should be heard in the councils of the government and that the grievances of the peasants and workers were to some extent justified. It was thus able to attract genuine support from the lower classes and above all from the lower middle classes, from tradesmen and clerical workers, as well as from the lowest sections of the community, those below the proletariat. Its leaders, however, came from much higher sections: landowners, lawyers, merchants, engineers, former officers, etc. Its first leader, Dr A. I. Dubrovin, was a physician who gave up a large and profitable practice in St Petersburg to devote himself to politics. He was elected the party's leader at the foundation meeting, and he remained in that position until 1909.

The new party in its policy and tactics was more flexible than the traditional Right; it soon became the strongest and best-organized force on the Right, with over 200 branches and more than 20,000 members. Although its deputies sat in the Duma, it remained hostile to it and dedicated to the maintenance of the Tsarist autocracy. Its deputies in the second Duma, which met in March 1907, made every effort to discredit it by creating scandals and tried to prevent it from doing any useful work. In the third Duma—elected in November 1907 on the basis of a much more restricted franchise—there were about fifty deputies of the extreme Right, more than ten per cent of the total. They shrilly denounced the actions of 'liberal' or 'constitutional' ministers, the Jewish infiltration of the press and schools, the detractors of the monarchy and the army, the national minorities and their aspirations, and all those who aimed at converting the Duma into a genuine parliament. Dr Dubrovin claimed that only Jews and free-masons wanted to see the Russian village community, the *mir*, destroyed, while he considered it an embodiment of social justice. In the party's opinion the country's worst enemies were the Liberals and their party, the Constitutional Democrats, while the Socialists were merely acting at the bidding of the secret forces which stood behind them, the Jews and the Liberals, who were more or less identified with each other. The Jews were to be eliminated from economic life through legislation, boycott and expulsion from the country; business and financial enterprises only benefited Jews and foreigners and were classified as essentially un-Russian.

In its fight against these hostile forces the party frequently resorted to violence, strike-breaking and boycotts. To promote this more violent side of its activities secret fighting groups were organized in Moscow, St Petersburg and other towns, as well as para-military units, for example in Odessa the 'Yellow Shirts', to beat up political ad-versaries and Jews—the forerunners of the Black, Blue and Brown Shirts of later years. Some sections of the Union of the Russian People took the political radicalism of the leaders seriously; if as a result government subsidies were withdrawn from them, this would only increase their extremism. The fourth party congress, held in April 1907, demanded that the Duma be converted into a purely consultative assembly, and its members be drawn from all estates of the orthodox Russian people. In spite of all its extremism, however, the party never broke entirely with the government; it remained loyal to the monarchy, on whose support it depended. Its violent methods frightened many Conservatives, but the connexions with the administration were maintained. It was not a really revolutionary party, nor did it possess a clearly defined programme.

In 1909 the party split. Its leader in the third Duma, Markov, retained the name, the apparatus and the majority of the party members and then moved closer to the Conservatives. Dr Dubrovin became the leader of a more radical group which remained very small. Further splits followed, and the movement gradually lost much of its support. But, thanks to the continued help of the authorities, the party was able to make certain gains in the elections to the fourth Duma of 1912. In areas of mixed national population it retained some importance because there national and religious differences and conflicts played into its hands. Its last 'triumph' occurred in 1911. In a cave near Kiev there was found the body of a schoolboy, thirteen years of age, who seemed to have been murdered by a gang of thieves who feared that he would betray them. The Union of the Russian People immediately launched a campaign against a Jewish clerk, Beilis, whom they accused of ritual murder, and succeeded in having him arrested and charged with the crime. For several years, the party leaders and deputies proclaimed his guilt and tried to make its acknowledgement the touchstone of political reliability. They even achieved that the case came up for trial in 1913, but Beilis was acquitted by the jury. A similar case had occurred in Bohemia in 1899, when a Jewish vagabond, Hilsner, had been tried for the ritual murder of a girl and had been stoutly defended by Thomas Masaryk; thereupon anti-Semitic students of Prague University violently disturbed his lectures and forced him to interrupt them. This kind of propaganda transcended the frontiers, and anti-Semitism was always a popular war-cry.

Thus extreme right-wing movements from the later nineteenth century onwards affected all major countries on the European continent. These groups and parties had much in common. They were not only nationalist and expansionist, but at the same time anti-liberal, anti-parliamentarian, anti-democratic and anti-freemason, as well as—outside Italy—anti-Semitic. They used violent methods and several of them formed their own para-military shock troops. They desired strong, authoritarian or autocratic government. They appealed to the masses, especially of the industrial workers, attempting to wean them from socialism. But this appeal to the masses was on the whole not successful; it was only locally in exceptional circumstances and for short periods that the masses could be mobilized, for example during the Badeni crisis of 1897 in Vienna. Moreover, not only in Austria, but also in France, Germany and Russia these movements began to decline in the early twentieth century, and internecine conflicts further weakened them. On the other hand, it is surprising how strongly they attracted educated people, especially university students, in several countries. It is easy to say that youth always tends to extremes; it is also easy to underestimate the magnetism which emanated from the hotch-potch of racialism, imperialism, nationalism and hankering after the glorious past that was preached by these parties.

The leaders of these parties, moreover, were usually respectable academics, writers, professional people or intellectuals, often men of means, and not the type of rabble-rouser and popular demagogue of low social origin we shall meet during the post-war period. Perhaps these older leaders were not primitive and unscrupulous enough to play the part of a Mussolini or a Hitler, hence their success was limited. But they did recognize and exploit the real grievances of the lower middle classes, the small people who were the victims of economic change and capitalist concentration; and they deeply impressed a part of the academic youth which was destined to lead their countries during the post-war years. It was the war itself that uprooted the masses, that organized and sanctioned violence on a scale far greater than any of the nationalist and anti-Semitic leaders had ever dreamt of. The crises which followed upon the war did not only affect certain social groups, they affected society as a whole. The great empires which had ruled over so much of Europe for so long toppled to the ground; the stability and security which they had furnished disappeared. Upon war there followed revolution and open or disguised civil war. In large parts of Europe the old order collapsed and the Era of Violence began.

2 | The Italian Example

The War and its Aftermath

The months preceding the outbreak of the first world war saw strikes and rioting in many Italian towns. In June 1914, during demonstrations by anarchists and republicans, violence broke out at Ancona, a port on the coast of the Adriatic. A general strike was then proclaimed by the Socialists and the General Confederation of Labour, and rioting became general. In the Romagna and the Marches of central Italy there were violent revolutionary outbreaks. Local republics were set up in many smaller towns, and the red flag was hoisted on the town hall of Bologna. Officers were disarmed; the military barracks were besieged in many places. Reservists had to be called out to prevent a railway strike, and the prestige of the civil authorities declined. While parliament remained inactive, there was in Rome a reaction of a different kind. Tens of thousands, mobilized by the Nationalists, marched through the streets, ready to meet force by force. In Bologna the Nationalists organized patrols of volunteers to preserve law and order; they demanded the shops to reopen and the houses to show the national flag. Thus, while the authorities remained passive, the Nationalists were the only group which dared to do something to stem the red tide. The crowds often did not know what they were marching for, but seemed ready to accept a leadership of any kind, and demanded 'action' as a sign of their protest.

When the war broke out a few weeks later the Socialist and Social Democratic parties of all the belligerent countries—Britain, France, Germany, Austria, and even Russia—decided to support the war efforts of their governments and to 'defend' their countries which had been 'attacked' by the others. The wave of patriotic enthusiasm which swept over Europe engulfed all countries and buried the Socialist International which had preached international solidarity and the calling of a general strike if war should be declared. Only small minority groups of the extreme Left—notably Lenin's Bolsheviks, Rosa Luxemburg's circle in Germany, and similar groups elsewhere— remained loyal to the ideas of proletarian internationalism and revolutionary action against the war. Their cry was a cry in the wilderness. Their leaders were either in exile, or were soon imprisoned; nationalism triumphed everywhere.

Italy, however, remained neutral although she was a partner of Germany and Austria in the Triple Alliance of 1882; while the Italian Socialist Party at the outbreak of the war reaffirmed its opposition to war and any imperialist adventure. Mussolini at first, in some articles and in a meeting held at Milan, went so far as to declare that a German victory would bring greater advantages to the proletariat than a victory of the Entente powers. But a war on the side of Germany and Austria would have been very unpopular in the country. On 22 September 1914 he published an article in the party organ *Avanti!* which proclaimed: 'The Socialist Party reaffirms its eternal faith in the future of the Workers' International, destined to bloom again, greater and stronger, from the blood and conflagration of peoples. It is in the name of the International and of Socialism that we invite you, proletarians of Italy, to uphold your unshakeable opposition to war.'[1] This attitude he maintained until the end of the month; but by the beginning of October rumours began to circulate that Mussolini was wavering, that he favoured the side of the Entente, that his old hatred of Austria—shared by so many Italians—was gaining the upper hand.

Meanwhile a strong nationalist agitation had started in Italy demanding that the country should renounce its policy of neutrality and enter the war on the side of the Entente, to conquer the 'unredeemed' territory of the Alto Adige, to come to the aid of France and Belgium who had been invaded. Gradually many Italians changed their attitude from one of 'absolute neutrality' to that of 'watchful neutrality' which favoured the western powers. To Mussolini inaction was repugnant; an alliance with the Nationalists did not seem unnatural in a country in which they hotly opposed the neutralist and passive attitude of the government and demanded intervention. On 18 October—without informing any of his colleagues—Mussolini published an article in *Avanti!* with the title 'From absolute to active and working neutrality',

[1] Quoted by Laura Fermi, *Mussolini*, Chicago, 1961, p. 104.

in which he claimed that, from the beginning of the war, the Socialists' neutrality had had an anti-German and anti-Austrian flavour; 'absolute neutrality' was a dangerous and immobilizing slogan; a war against Germany and Austria could free Italy from the possibility of suffering any reprisals in the future; did the Socialists want to remain mere spectators of the drama that was being enacted before their eyes? The Socialist Party executive which met on the same day replied by depriving Mussolini of his editorship of *Avanti!*

Only four weeks later Mussolini announced that he would publish his own paper, in favour of Italian intervention in the war on the side of the Entente. On 15 November his editorial in the first issue of *Il Popolo d'Italia* attacked the anti-war propaganda as cowardice: 'My cry is a word that I would never have pronounced in normal times, and that today I raise loudly, with my full voice, with no attempt at simulation, with a firm faith, a fearful and fascinating word: *war!*'[2] Soon after Mussolini was expelled from the Socialist Party as a traitor—the party to which he had devoted his life and his revolutionary energies for so many years, and which he was henceforth to persecute with his undying hatred. At that time it was rumoured that right-wing circles had produced the funds which enabled him to publish his new paper; but probably the money came from French Socialist circles. During the previous month the first *fasci* (literally 'bundles', from the Latin *fasces*, bundles of rods from which an axe protruded, a symbol of Roman justice) were formed to promote the intervention of Italy in the war. In December Mussolini and his followers formed a *fascio d'azione rivoluzionaria* (group of revolutionary action) with the aim of 'destroying the Germany of the Hohenzollerns and of Scheidemann', one of the moderate Social Democratic leaders who had come out strongly in support of the German war effort. It was a revealing equation.

It is difficult to explain this complete volte-face which propelled Mussolini at one stroke from the extreme Left to the extreme nationalist side. But most likely he sensed the nationalist mood prevailing in the country and was carried away by his thirst for action and his hatred of Austria, by a belief in war as a means to obtain revolutionary ends. At first he may not have realized the consequences and did not have the courage to tell his comrades of his change of mind. But outside the Socialist camp there were many who agreed with him. In May 1915

[2] Quoted ibid., p. 107. The scenes leading to Mussolini's expulsion from the Socialist Party are best described by Balabanoff, op. cit., pp. 89–95.

the poet Gabriele d'Annunzio hailed 'an Italy that shall be greater by conquest, purchasing territory not in shame, but at the price of blood and glory. . . . After long years of national humiliation, God has been pleased to grant us proof of our privileged blood. . . .'[3] During the same month Italy declared war on Austria. The poet immediately volunteered and performed legendary deeds of valour, among them daring flights over the unredeemed cities of Trieste and Trent on which he dropped messages of encouragement—the first leaflet raids of propaganda warfare. Mussolini, on the other hand, waited until he was called up and served in the front lines for only a few months; then he was wounded in the leg and had to stay in hospital for a considerable time. This enabled him to resume his journalistic activities: he did not return to the front. In October 1917 the Italian army suffered a severe defeat by the Austrians and Germans at Caporetto, a defeat which led to an outbreak of panic and an almost unchecked advance of the enemy to the Piave river, to the north of Venice. Mussolini now advocated in his paper the suppression of the Socialist press, the persecution of any-one who was not doing the utmost for the war or undermined the spirit of resistance, and the establishment of a non-parliamentary government to lead the nation—the first time that he voiced such demands. Some months later, in May 1918, he exclaimed: 'We, the survivors, we who have returned, demand the right of governing Italy. . . .'

In the autumn of 1918 first Austria, and then Germany collapsed: victory was gained at last. In the Peace Settlement of 1919 Italy obtained the Alto Adige—including a large German-speaking minority, thus creating a new *Irredenta*—and Istria with Trieste, but her larger territorial aspirations remained unsatisfied. In particular, there was no extension of the Italian colonial empire in Africa, and the eastern shore of the Adriatic from Fiume southwards was assigned to the new king-dom of Yugoslavia. It was in vain that the Italians, under the terms of the secret Treaty of London—concluded in April 1915 to induce them to enter the war—laid claim to northern Dalmatia, which had once belonged to the Republic of Venice. The Adriatic Sea was not to be-come *mare nostrum*. To Yugoslavia too was assigned the port of Fiume, to the east of Istria, which was mainly Italian-speaking.

This treatment by the victorious powers aroused intense indignation in Italy and led to a temporary withdrawal of the Italian delegation from the peace conference. Soon it was said all over Italy that the war

[3] Quoted by Dennis Mack Smith, *Italy—A Modern History*, London, 1959, p. 300.

had been won, but the peace lost; the Italians felt cheated of the fruits of victory. The Italian government, when it finally accepted the peace terms, aroused the fury of the nationalists, among whom Mussolini figured prominently. In January 1919 he combined forces in Milan with the *arditi*—shocktroops with a distinctive uniform and armed with daggers, formed during the war for raids on the enemy positions— to break up a meeting of Bissolati who favoured an exchange of the Alto Adige and Dalmatia for Fiume. D'Annunzio in his turn proclaimed: 'Dalmatia belongs to Italy by divine right as well as human law, by the Grace of God who has designed the earth in such a way that every race can recognize its destiny therein carved out. . . . It was ours and shall be ours again. . . .'[4] The nationalist passions which had been aroused by the war were reaching fever heat.

Radicalism in the Ascendant

Only a few weeks after the break-up of the Bissolati meeting Mussolini founded in Milan the *Fasci di Combattimento*, similar to the *fasci* formed during the war to promote the intervention of Italy or the defence of the country. The meeting of 23 March 1919 was attended by about a hundred people, half of them from Milan, the others from other north Italian towns. The chairman was a captain of the *arditi*; other *arditi* were present and served to protect the meeting against any interference from outside. The alliance with this military élite formation was firmly cemented. Mussolini proclaimed: 'As the succession to the régime is open we must not vacillate. We must hurry. If the régime is to be overthrown, it must be we who occupy its place. Therefore we create *fasci*: organs of creation and agitation, capable of descending into the streets and crying: "We, we alone have the right to the succession, because we, we were the men who forced the country into the war and into victory." '[5] It was the first time that he so openly and clearly stipulated his aim, to take over the succession, to overthrow the existing régime, to achieve power.

The programme adopted unanimously at the meeting reflected the nationalist and social demands arising from the war and a determined opposition to all who had not supported it. It supported the claims of the organizations of ex-servicemen and demanded an Italy 'on the

[4] Quoted ibid., p. 318.
[5] Quoted by Hermann Finer, *Mussolini's Italy*, 2nd ed., London, 1964, p. 116.

Alps and the Adriatic Sea with . . . the annexation of Fiume and Dalmatia'; the imperialism of other nations to the detriment of Italy and any Italian imperialism to the detriment of other nations were condemned; in electoral contests any candidates who had been neutralists in the war were to be opposed strenuously. The political battles which Mussolini had fought during the war were to be continued. A few months later, in June, a more detailed programme was published. It contained several demands which were decidedly radical: a progressive tax on capital and a tax of eighty-five per cent on war profits, universal franchise for men and women, a national militia, a minimum wage, nationalization of the munition industries, workers' participation in the management of industrial enterprises, the confiscation of all ecclesiastical property—in a country in which much ecclesiastical property had already been secularized in the course of the nineteenth century.

Most of these demands were left-wing, rather than right-wing. Only the demand for workers' participation in industrial management coincided with a demand of the Nationalists, put forward in March 1919, for a corporative organization of industry based on workers' and employers' syndicates, but it could equally be understood in a more radical sense. There was much truth in the comment of a Rome newspaper that the new *fasci* did not aim at the defence of the ruling class or the existing state, but wanted to lead the revolutionary forces into the nationalist camp so as to prevent a victory of Bolshevism. The *fasci* soon reported a membership of 15,000 organized in eighty-two sections. On 15 April they gained their first 'victory' in Milan. They attacked a Socialist mass meeting, and then proceeded to set fire to the building of *Avanti!* and to wreck the paper's offices and printing machines. Mussolini was avenged on the paper whose editor he had once been: it was the first of many similar acts of revenge. Mussolini, however, declared that he was fighting the Socialists, not because of their socialism, but because they were anti-national and reactionary. This action too had been organized in close cooperation with the *arditi* whose military experiences proved invaluable. The police did not intervene, as was to happen time and again during the years to come. It was this weakness of the state and its organs, their willingness to condone illegality, which greatly facilitated the rise of Fascism.

This weakness was also proved in the case of Fiume. After riots had broken out in the town the Allied command insisted that the Italian garrison must be withdrawn; but one of its officers made his soldiers swear that they would return and take Fiume, and he asked the poet D'Annunzio to lead the expedition. On 12 September 1919 he marched into Fiume at the head of a column of some thousand men, demobilized soldiers, *arditi* and others, but also military units which had deserted and furnished him with the necessary weapons and supplies. Every day more volunteers arrived and brought with them guns, aeroplanes, motorboats, etc. Ships were boarded and taken to Fiume with their supplies and weapons. D'Annunzio declared that Fiume was annexed to Italy and granted the town a constitution based on corporations—a model of the later corporative state. His legionaries wore black shirts decorated with a skull and crossbones and saluted by raising their arms in 'Roman fashion'. They swore loyalty to the *commandante* who frequently addressed vast and enthusiastic audiences. They responded with chants and rhythmic cries which were later adopted by the Fascists, and shouted '*Italia o morte !*' ('Italy or death!'). Time and again D'Annunzio emphasized the historical importance of his action, the purity of his motives and the baseness of his enemies: 'Today Fiume is the example for Italy: it is the honour of our conscience, the honour of the great Latin conscience, which alone through the centuries has created and today still creates truly free men. . . . We are standing alone against a threatening and insatiable monster. We are standing alone "against the foolish and vile world". . . . We are standing alone against the immense power established and supported by thieves, by usurers, and by forgers. . . .'[6] D'Annunzio was convinced that he was defending Italy against a 'flood of Slav barbarians', tribes without any history or civilization. He preached a 'new crusade of the poor and exploited nations, the new crusade of all poor and free men against the nations that have usurped all the wealth',[7] an echo of the ideas of Corradini at the time of the Libyan war. But his ardent followers hoped that Fiume would be the beginning of a general attack on the government, that D'Annunzio would lead them to seize Rome. A legionary leader wrote to the *fascio* of Trieste: 'the exploit of Fiume must be consummated in Rome'.

A private army had come into being; high-ranking army officers encouraged and helped D'Annunzio. Without the connivance of these circles the whole enterprise could never have been successful. The state abandoned its authority. The Nationalists too organized their

[6] Eugenio Coselschi, 'La Marcia di Ronchi', in *Il Decennale*, ed. by Oddone Fantini, Florence, 1929, p. 226.
[7] D'Annunzio, *Italia e Vita*, Rome, 1920, pp. 32, 42.

own shocktroops wearing blue shirts, the *squadre azzurre*, to fight
socialists, democrats and freemasons. Socialist deputies were attacked
in the streets of Rome. D'Annunzio was planning to march on the
capital. On 30 October Mussolini wrote to him from Milan: 'We are
organizing bands of twenty men each with some kind of uniforms and
weapons' which 'are awaiting your orders'.[8] The king was to be
deposed, and a republic to be proclaimed. D'Annunzio remained in
Fiume for fifteen months, but then the venture collapsed. In November 1920 Italy and Yugoslavia signed a treaty which assigned
Dalmatia to Yugoslavia and made Fiume a free city. The government
of Giolitti who had become prime minister in June ordered D'Annunzio to evacuate Fiume, which he refused to do. Giolitti then instituted
a blockade of the town, whereupon D'Annunzio issued a declaration of
war. But one shell from a battleship which slightly wounded him
made him change his mind; he quietly left Fiume and retired into
private life. The first energetic action by the government was sufficient to terminate a movement which had done great harm to Italy and
to the authority of the state. Above all, the whole affair served as a
dress-rehearsal for the march on Rome.

Meanwhile the economic situation worsened and the value of the
lira declined rapidly. Political and social unrest broke out in many
parts of Italy. In the summer of 1919 crowds, indignant about recent
price increases, invaded the shops, looted goods, and insisted on price
reductions. Mussolini and his *fasci* proclaimed their solidarity with the
rioters. The *Popolo d'Italia* suggested that it would set a good example
if some profiteers were strung up on lamp-posts and some hoarders
smothered under the potatoes and the sides of bacon they were hiding.
'Squeeze the rich!' was the Fascist slogan. From the towns the unrest
spread to the countryside, where much of the fertile land belonged to
a few great landowners. Recently demobilized peasants, wearing their
war decorations, occupied large estates and settled on them. They
belonged to no party or trade union, and sometimes took the field under
the Italian tricolour, with bands playing and church bells ringing.
The movement spread in the area of Rome, in the Po valley and in
southern Italy, but the Socialists took no notice of the peasants' land-
hunger. In the north their hold over many towns had been strengthened
during the war. In the Romagna and Emilia 'Red Leagues' were
formed between Socialist municipalities.

The ideas of the Russian Revolution, brought back by embittered

[8] Quoted by Fermi, op. cit., p. 177.

soldiers from the front, were spreading. In August a Socialist manifesto proclaimed: 'The proletariat must be incited to the violent seizure of political and economic power, and this must be handed over entirely and exclusively to the Workers' and Peasants' Councils.' In October a Socialist congress met at Bologna. It decided in favour of adherence to the newly formed Communist International, which was dominated by the Bolsheviks, and of the formation of Workers' Councils, which should one day develop into Soviets. Turati, the leader of the party's right wing, was heavily outvoted; but he was not expelled from the party, as the left wing had demanded.

In November 1919 general elections were held. The Socialists campaigned under the slogan 'all power to the proletariat united in its Councils!'. They polled about one-third of the total vote and obtained 156 seats out of 508 in parliament (compared with fifty-two in 1913). By contrast, Mussolini, who stood in Milan as an independent, received less than 5,000 votes out of 268,000, while his Socialist adversary polled more than fifty per cent of the total. The danger from the Left seemed far greater than that from the Right.

This was apparently confirmed by the events of the following year. Peasant unrest was getting stronger and many more estates were occupied. The Nitti government was forced to sanction many of the seizures of land after they had been carried out. The seizures spread into the field of industry. Already in the autumn of 1919 the workers had occupied the Mazzoni factory at Pinerolo when the owner refused to grant their wage demands, and the government had then appointed an official as the provisional director of the factory. In August 1920 new wage demands were raised on account of rising prices, but the employers refused and decided on a lock-out. The workers resorted to obstruction tactics and at the end of August occupied the factories. In Milan alone 280 factories were occupied day and night, and Red Guards were formed to protect them. The movement spread all over Italy. Two hundred factories were occupied in Turin. Workers' committees controlled the occupied factories and maintained output. But soon there were no raw materials to carry on production and no money to pay the wages. Many workers got tired of staying in the factories, and the Red Guards now had to prevent large numbers from deserting. The government wisely did not intervene. Giolitti assumed that the movement was not the beginning, but the end of a wave of revolutionary unrest; if it failed on its own account, this would not be due to government intervention, and the prestige of the leaders would suffer. After

twenty-two days the factories were evacuated and solemnly returned
to their owners. The action had ended in a fiasco.

Yet in the local elections held in November 1920 the Socialists
achieved further gains. They now controlled 2,162 out of 8,059 communes, and twenty-five out of sixty-nine provinces, and were particularly strong in the industrial north. In Emilia they predominated in
223 out of 280 communes. At the end of the year the party had more
than 200,000 members, perhaps ten times the number it had had at
the end of the war, and the socialist General Confederation of Labour
over 2,000,000. There was great economic distress owing to rising
prices and mounting inflation. At the end of 1920 the lira was worth
only three-and-a-half American cents as against nineteen before the
war; the public debt had soared to 95,017 million lire, seven times
the pre-war figure.

These developments aroused the fears and the hatred of the middle
and lower middle classes. They thought that Italy was at the brink of
a red revolution. They hated the workers who had occupied the
factories, the trade unions, the strong organizations of the agricultural
labourers, and the peasants who had seized the land. They did not realize
that the danger had past its peak, that the workers felt tricked and beaten
after the fiasco of September 1920. The middle classes also deeply
resented the competition of the workers' cooperatives, the control
exercised by powerful Chambers of Labour over the economic life of
whole districts, developments which threatened the position of shopkeepers, contractors and middlemen. To its enemies the working-class
movement seemed far stronger than it actually was. At the beginning of
1921 it was further weakened by the secession of the Communists who
formed their own party when the Socialist congress held at Leghorn
refused to accept wholesale the conditions imposed by the Communist
International[9]: a split that was never healed and crippled the Left during
the fatal years of the struggle against the Fascists. The weakness and
passivity of the changing governments did nothing to allay the middle-
class fears; the middle classes considered the state impotent, unable
to cope with the disorders; and from this it was only one step to the
cry for a strong government which would protect them and put down
all the unrest.

The Italian Socialist Party—during the war, when it adopted a

[9] At the Leghorn congress only 59,000 votes were cast for unconditional acceptance of the Comintern conditions, against 98,000 for conditional acceptance, and
15,000 against, indicating the distribution of strength within the party.

neutralist and anti-war attitude, and in the years after the war, when it strongly sympathized with the Russian Revolution and almost joined the Communist International—was considerably further to the Left than the Social Democratic and Labour parties of western Europe. It also seemed strong and powerful, with its affiliated trade unions, cooperatives, Chambers of Labour, and many other organizations. The occupation of the factories in which half a million workers participated showed the force and the spirit which animated the working-class movement. Some provinces of northern Italy were virtually under 'red' domination. It is thus somewhat superficial to consider the fears of the middle classes unjustified and exaggerated. In retrospect they certainly were, but at the time the middle classes' existence seemed at stake, and the Bolshevist danger appeared very real.

The Fascists Gain the Upper Hand

In the years 1919–20 the Fascists were still a tiny minority, unable to influence the turn of events, but after 1920 the initiative more and more passed into their hands, while the working-class movement was engaged in internecine conflicts and smarting under the defeat which it had suffered, the failure of the occupation of the factories. Initially the *fasci* were purely urban and had been concentrated in some towns of northern Italy, such as Milan, Bologna and Florence. In the autumn of 1920—after the occupation of the factories—they began to spread to the countryside and the small towns, especially in Tuscany, Emilia and the valley of the Po, often quite independently of Mussolini and his central committee in Milan. The *fasci* were supported by the big landowners and industrialists who feared the seizure of their estates and factories. They also received aid from the army—a factor which was to be of vital importance in bringing about their victory. In the streets of some Italian towns officers had been publicly insulted, spat upon or beaten up by the mob. These incidents caused deep resentment among their fellow-officers and a thirst for revenge which the Fascists promised to satisfy. In many cases they obtained weapons and ammunition from army depots.

On 20 October 1920 Bonomi, the minister of war, drafted a circular: officers who were being demobilized and joined the *Fasci di Combattimento*, to control and lead them, were to receive four-fifths of their former pay. Many ex-servicemen, especially from the ranks of the *arditi*, joined the Fascist squads. They were proud of the military victory they had won, but felt humiliated by not receiving what they considered their 'due' from the government. They thought themselves entitled to substantial rewards for their war services, but none were forthcoming. They were uprooted and no longer fitted into bourgeois society. Large numbers of students and youths, eager for adventure and action, embittered about the rising wages of the workers, and their own misery, detesting the boring routine of their daily lives, also joined the *squadre d'azione* of the Fascists. Finally, there were the toughs, never-do-wells and semi-criminal elements of Milan and other towns.

These squads soon engaged in countless deeds of violence all over northern Italy. Workers' clubs were burnt and plundered; chambers of labour and the institutions of 'red' municipalities were destroyed. The police hardly ever intervened, the landowners often provided the lorries on which the squads were transported across the country, and the authorities closed their eyes. Interestingly enough, the first actions of this kind were carried out in the spring of 1920 in Trieste and Venezia Giulia in the north-east, not against Italian, but against Slovene Socialists, and they were undertaken in cooperation with the police. In November—after a Socialist victory in the local elections— the Fascists descended upon Bologna and the Emilia; there and else- where they provoked violence, to which they could react with more violence, often using force for its own sake, and gaining widespread approval from the non-Socialists. Socialist resistance remained un- organized and sporadic. The number of local *fasci* multiplied. In July 1920 there were only 108 which were 'formed or in the process of being formed'; in October there were 190, at the end of the year as many as 800, and by February 1921 a thousand. The *fascio* of Milan remained by far the most important one.

There Mussolini was still following a distinctly radical line. He asserted that his programme was similar to that of the Socialists, that Fascism was helping their cause, that it would carry through the agrarian revolution, the only one that was possible in Italy. He even welcomed the occupation of the factories and declared: 'No social transformation which is necessary is repugnant to me. Hence I accept the famous workers' supervision of the factories and equally their cooperative social management; I only ask that there should be a clear conscience and technical capacity, and that production be increased. If this is guaranteed by the trade unions, instead of by the employers,

I have no hesitation in saying that the former have the right to take the latter's place.'[10] In spite of all the anti-Socialist violence Mussolini at that time and later still thought in terms of a possible cooperation with the Socialists, and also with another party founded in 1919, the *Popolari*, a Catholic-Social party strongly influenced by the Church. In May 1921 Mussolini termed the Socialists, the *Popolari* and the Fascists the leading forces of the nation.

This verdict, however, was not precisely confirmed by the general elections held in the same month. The Liberal prime minister, Giolitti, for this purpose formed a 'National Block' with the Fascists and the Nationalists; he thus hoped to make them more respectable, to assimilate them, and to weaken his main enemies, the Socialists and the *Popolari*. Government aid enabled the Fascists to win thirty-five seats, and the Nationalists eleven. But in spite of the Communist secession and their defeat in the preceding autumn the Socialists' strength only slightly declined; together with the right-wing Socialists they still polled more than 2,000,000 votes and with 147 deputies remained the strongest party; the *Popolari* came second, with 1,400,000 votes and 106 seats, while the National Block polled about 2,250,000.[11] Parliament refused to grant Giolitti the full powers which he demanded, and the government had to resign. The Liberals and the 'national block' were hopelessly split into several rival parties so that no stable majority could be found. The succeeding governments, first under Bonomi, then under Facta, were weaker even than that of Giolitti had been.

Fascist violence continued unchecked. The Giolitti government had aided the Fascists with money and arms and had warned the police not to intervene. The following are some extracts from an official history of the 'Fascist Revolution' for the early months of 1921. 'On the evening of 20 January, by arrangement with the troops of the garrison, an attack was made on the chamber of labour at Dignano' in Istria. When a Fascist squad from that town arrested a Slovene innkeeper, the tocsin was sounded in the neighbouring villages, and the Fascists were forced to retreat towards Carnizza where they were besieged, but they fought back: 'The rebel populations were driven from their villages which were destroyed by fire, and the districts of

[10] Quoted by Finer, op. cit., p. 128.
[11] The voting strength of the main parties was:

National Block	2,246,723	right-wing Socialists	382,458
Socialists	1,644,443	Communists	308,142
Popolari	1,407,723	Republicans	118,853
Democrats	703,132	national minorities	90,649.

Segotti, Vareschi, Zuechi and Mormorano were devastated.' On 10 April about 400 Fascists from Vicenza, Montegaldella, Poiana and Noventa assembled at Mossano in Venezia: 'They invaded the district from various points at once, dealing out fire and blood. Seven houses were attacked and their entire contents destroyed or burnt; some houses were set on fire. Many bastinados were administered.' At Poiana two weeks later 'the Fascists arrived in six lorries, invaded the place, occupied the red cooperative and the theatre, abducted the Socialist councillors and assessors from their houses and punished them severely.' Five days later the Fascists returned to beat up the Communist mayor. At Pordenone, also in Venezia, on 10 May the Fascists 'received substantial reinforcements from neighbouring districts and forced the revolutionaries to retreat to the Torre area near-by where they were besieged. A battle developed, machine-guns and even a field-gun were brought into action. Troops from the garrison of Udine intervened to aid the Fascists and the Bolshevist stronghold was stormed.' After this victory, they 'destroyed red and black headquarters, made arrests and carried out searches' in the countryside of Venezia.[12]

During the first six months of 1921 alone, the Fascists destroyed eighty-five agrarian cooperatives, fifty-nine chambers of labour, forty-three unions of agricultural workers, twenty-five people's centres, and many left-wing printing presses and newspapers. But they also took action on behalf of the local population and championed its interests. At Trieste they boarded boats laden with fruit and vegetables which had arrived there and forced the peasants to sell their produce at very low prices; at Naples they imposed a reduction of fifty per cent on prices in cafés and restaurants. In many cases the local *ras* of the Fascists—a term taken from Ethiopia where it denoted the tribal leaders—acted entirely independently: it would be quite mistaken to think of the Fascist Party of that time as a strictly hierarchical structure in which all the orders emanated from the centre. Thus Italo Balbo established his rule at Ferrara, and Roberto Farinacci at Cremona: both were to become Fascist ministers. These local leaders forced left-wing mayors or councillors to resign under the threat of dire penalties which would befall them. Thus Farinacci boasted that, within a few days, he had made sixty-four local councils dissolve them-

---

[12] The quotations are from the third volume of Giorgio Alberto Chiurco's *Storia della Rivoluzione Fascista*, Florence, 1929, pp. 272, 413-15. Chiurco himself was the secretary of the *fascio* at Siena.

selves. Or the provincial prefect would obligingly step in and dissolve such councils after the Fascists had created disturbances and interrupted their proceedings.

In the village of Roccastrada near Siena the mayor refused to resign, whereupon the Fascists descended in lorries upon the village and set some of the houses on fire, while the peasants fled into the fields. They came back when the Fascists had departed; but shortly after the Fascists returned because one of them had been shot by an unknown hand. Their revenge consisted in more houses being burnt down and in several random executions. The Socialists were incapable of countering these tactics of military concentration and assault. Their leaders were driven from the 'liberated' localities, left-wing deputies expelled from their constituencies and all opponents of Fascism humiliated in every conceivable way. Many were forced to drink large doses of castor oil and then tied to a tree or lamp post; many more were simply beaten up. A well-known local Fascist leader, Sandro Carosi, entered a working-class café and at pistol point forced one of those present to stand against a wall with a cup on his head: the Fascist would prove his marksmanship by shooting the cup down. But the shot instead killed the man, and Carosi ruefully pointed to the decline in his marksmanship. The papers reported the incident under the heading 'an unfortunate William Tell', and nothing happened to the murderer.

When Mussolini, after the elections of May 1921, became the leader of a parliamentary group he attempted to steer a more moderate course. Together with the National Liberals of Salandra the Fascists formed the 'National Right', and Mussolini in his first parliamentary speech spoke out strongly against Socialists and Democrats. Bolshevism had been defeated, force had achieved its object; now Fascism would prove in peaceful competition that it contained a vital element for the future of the country. It seems certain that Mussolini at that time did not envisage a one-party state and a seizure of power. In the summer of 1921 he on the contrary aimed at bringing about a rapprochement with the Socialists, a termination of anti-Socialist violence, and an agreement to that effect was signed on 2 August. What Mussolini had not reckoned with was the reaction among the Fascist rank and file and the local leaders. Emilia revolted first; thereupon Mussolini declared that, if they wanted to separate from him, it left him indifferent as the aims of Fascism had largely been achieved. But the revolt was joined by most of the old centres of Fascist influence: Bologna, Cremona, Ferrara, Forli, Modena, Piacenza and Venice. Mussolini had to resign his party offices: 'who has been defeated must go'.[13] In November 1921 a party congress was summoned to Rome, while he wanted it to meet at Milan where his own position was stronger.

In Rome, Mussolini had to give way to the demands of the extremists led by Balbo and Dino Grandi. The pacification agreement with the Socialists was buried, for the extremists wanted to destroy the trade unions root and branch and to continue the punitive expeditions. The movement was transformed into a political party, which at that time had 320,000 members and 2,300 local sections. Mussolini and Grandi embraced each other; the breach was healed. This, however, also meant a departure from the radicalism of the early days of the movement. Up to that time Mussolini, although no longer a Socialist, had remained faithful to some of the ideals of his youth, as was shown in the early slogans and programmes of the *fasci*. Now he moved closer to the Nationalists—an alliance that was to be consummated after the march on Rome. The main currents in the party now were: a strong nationalism, mainly among the intellectuals, a strong anti-socialism and anti-trade unionism, especially among the middle-class members, the landowners, etc., and a vivid dislike of the parliamentary system which was considered unable to achieve anything and merely promoted sectional interests.

During 1922 Fascist violence continued unhindered, and spread to parts of Italy hitherto relatively peaceful. Early in the year Balbo noted in his diary about Ferrara: 'We are masters of the situation. We have not only broken the resistance of our enemies, but we also control the organs of the state. The prefect has to submit to the orders given by me in the name of the Fascists.'[14] In April Balbo ordered the town to be occupied by his forces, and 45,000 unemployed camped in it for two days, until the prefect promised that their distress would be relieved by public works, and that a friend of Balbo, arrested after endless deeds of violence, would be released. In February there was a large Fascist demonstration at Prato in Tuscany the progress of which was impeded by royal guards. On the following day the Fascists ordered all enterprises to remain closed until the 'guilty' commissioner of police had been dismissed. This demand was granted by the prefect who also promised that the royal guards would be punished. When the demands had been obtained the enterprises were instructed to re-open. In the *Popolo d'Italia* Mussolini threatened the newspapers

[13] Quoted from Mussolini's *Opera Omnia*, xvii, p. 105, by Nolte, op. cit., p. 266.
[14] Italo Balbo, *Diario 1922*, Milan, 1932, p. 20 (1 January 1922).

who dared to attack his movement: 'You are printing useless insults, gentlemen. Our retort . . . is to break your bones: surgery, ruthlessly applied.'[15]

At the end of July the Fascists, under Balbo's leadership, descended upon Ravenna where a Fascist had been killed in a street fight: 'We undertook this task in the same spirit as when we demolished the enemy's stores in war-time. The flames from the great burning building rose ominously into the night. The whole town was illuminated by the glare. We had to strike terror into the heart of our enemies. . . . I announced to him [the chief of police] that I would burn down and destroy the houses of all Socialists in Ravenna, if he did not give me within half an hour the means required for sending the Fascists elsewhere. It was a dramatic moment. I demanded a whole fleet of lorries. The police officers completely lost their heads; but after half an hour they told me where I could find lorries already supplied with petrol. Some of them actually belonged to the office of the chief of police. My pretended reason was that I wanted to get the exasperated Fascists out of the town; in reality, I was organizing a "column of fire" . . . to extend our reprisals throughout the province. . . . This journey began yesterday morning, the 29th, at 11 a.m., and finished on the morning of the 30th. . . . We went through Rimini, Sant' Arcangelo, Savignano, Cesena, Bertinoro, all the towns and centres in the provinces of Forli and Ravenna, and destroyed and burnt all the red buildings, the seats of the Socialist and Communist organizations. It was a terrible night. Our passage was marked by huge columns of fire and smoke. The whole plain of the Romagna was given up to the reprisals of the outraged Fascists determined to break for ever the red terror. . . .'[16] Thus the description in Balbo's own diary. No wonder that the Fascist trade unions at about the same time had already half a million members, most of them among the agricultural workers. In the south the 'red' town of Ancona was conquered 'in perfect military fashion'. The last strongholds of the working-class movement succumbed to the Fascist terror.

A few days later, at the beginning of August, the Socialists made a last feeble attempt to defend the political liberties against 'reactionary factions' by calling a general strike. The Fascists replied with a declaration that, unless the strike was terminated, they would break it. They took over some of the public services whose workers had obeyed

[15] *Popolo d'Italia*, 15 July 1922.
[16] Balbo, op. cit., pp. 103, 109 (28–30 July 1922).

the call to strike, distributed mail, ran trams and trains, and proved that
the strike-weapon which the Socialists had wielded for so long was no
longer dangerous. The police nearly everywhere cooperated with the
Fascists. The strike collapsed. The Fascists had emerged as the defenders of law and order.

Mussolini meanwhile negotiated with the former prime ministers
Giolitti, Nitti and Salandra, and tried to assure everybody by declara-
tions of loyalty, in particular the king and the army, but also the
Vatican. He declared that the Fascists must have the courage to be
monarchists, and he made no attempt to conceal his objective: 'our
programme is simple: we want to rule Italy'.[17] It was indeed very
simple. Mussolini was determined to prevent Giolitti or anyone else
who might display some energy in the defence of the state from
becoming prime minister. But Giolitti was then eighty years old, and
Salandra nearly seventy, and no younger defender of the parliamentary régime emerged in Italy.

The March on Rome

On 3 October 1922 the *Popolo d'Italia* published the military regulations
and the oath of the new Fascist Militia; the country was divided into
military zones; a private army came into being wholly at the disposal
of the Fascist leaders. The government did not intervene. The prime
minister, Luigi Facta, was an honest and well-meaning, kindly old man,
helpless and utterly unfit to take any energetic action. The last was also
true of the army which might have opposed this infringement of its
military monopoly. But among the officers there were many sympathizers with the Black Shirts. Later that month six generals on the
active list took part in the march on Rome: Ceccherini, De Bono, Fara,
Novelli, Tilby, and Zamboni.

On 24 October a monster rally of the Fascists took place at Naples.
There Mussolini declared that his party wanted 'to become the state';
he also made it clear that he did not want to abolish the monarchy nor
to replace the king by another member of the royal family. In the
afternoon he inspected 6,000 Fascists who were uniformed and paraded
in military formations; 'either the government will be given to us or
we shall descend upon Rome and take it. It is now a question of days,

---

[17] Quoted from Mussolini's *Opera Omnia*, xviii, pp. 416, 419, by Nolte, op. cit.,
p. 271.

perhaps of hours', he proclaimed. His units roared in reply: 'To Rome! To Rome!' In a hotel room at Naples a secret meeting was held on the same day attended by Mussolini and the Fascist 'Quadrumvirs': General Emilio de Bono, Cesare Maria de Vecchi, Italo Balbo, and Michele Bianchi. Mussolini pronounced that the movement's aim must be the seizure of power and the establishment of a new government with a minimum of six Fascist members in the most important posts. On 27 October the Fascist militia should be mobilized; the prefectures, police stations, post offices, radio stations, anti-Fascist newspapers, and chambers of labour were to be occupied. As soon as the towns were secured the units were to be concentrated at three places within marching distance from Rome and to start their march on the capital on the following morning. On the same day the Quadrumvirs, assembled at Perugia, were to issue their manifesto proclaiming that the Fascists did neither march against the army, nor against the police, 'but against a political class of half-wits and idiots which in four long years has been unable to give a true government to our nation. . .'.[18]

Mussolini returned to Milan on the morning of 26 October and resumed his negotiations for the formation of a coalition government, which he continued until the 29th. Apparently, he was still uncertain what course he should adopt, whether the march on Rome should be carried out or not. The heads of the General Confederation of Industry, the Confederation of Agriculture and the Bankers' Association telegraphed to Rome asking that Mussolini should be appointed prime minister. Two Senators, the electrical magnate Conti, and the editor of the influential newspaper *Corriere della Sera*, Albertini, sent a telegram to the prime minister, Facta, with the same request. From Rome the Liberal Camillo Corradini wrote to Giolitti who was staying in Piedmont that the *fasci* 'intend to exert strong pressure to obtain the formation of a Fascist government. The truth, it seems, is that Mussolini shows signs of giving in to his extremists.'[19] The prefect of Milan, Lusignoli, acted as a go-between with whom Mussolini discussed his plans and who then passed them on to Giolitti.

Meanwhile the Quadrumvirs had installed themselves in a hotel at Perugia opposite the prefecture under the protection of a heavily armed guard; from there they directed the mobilization of the Black

[18] The full text quoted by Fermi, op. cit., p. 190; the previous quotation, ibid., p. 189.
[19] Ibid., p. 198.

Shirts. About midnight on 27 October they called on the prefect to give up his powers, and he duly did so. The Fascists then occupied the post office, the police station and the building of the provincial administration without encountering any resistance. The same happened all over northern Italy; in some places the military barracks too were occupied. There was hardly any opposition. In Siena and elsewhere the soldiers fraternized with the Fascists, who were usually commanded by former officers. The Blue Shirts of the Nationalists made common cause with the Black Shirts. The whole action was undertaken under the slogans: 'Long live Italy! Long live the King! Long live the Army!'

The king, Victor Emmanuel III, returned to Rome on the evening of 27 October, where Facta submitted to him the resignation of the government: another sign of his utter helplessness in a situation which required firm guidance from the top. But a few hours later, on the morning of the 28th, the government—which was continuing in office pending the formation of a new one—decided to proclaim a state of siege; and a proclamation to that effect was posted on the walls of Rome. But Victor Emmanuel refused to give his assent when Facta presented the decree for his signature. Perhaps he feared for his throne, perhaps he wanted to avoid civil war, perhaps he was afraid of a left-wing revolution which might result from a breach with the Fascists. The decree proclaiming the state of siege had to be revoked. There was to be no resistance.

The king had been assured by the generals of his army that 100,000 Fascists were marching on Rome and that the garrison could not stop them, but he had been misinformed. In reality there were only about 20,000 Black Shirts, and these were split up into four separate columns which approached Rome from the north-west, north, and east. They were poorly armed, with rifles, muskets and revolvers; they had hardly any machine-guns, and no artillery. They suffered from lack of food and other necessities. This and the steadily falling rain soon induced some of them to return home. The columns waited at a distance of twenty to thirty miles from Rome for orders to attack which never came. If they had attempted to take the capital by force they could have been repulsed with ease by the well-armed garrison of Rome.

No force was required. On the evening of 28 October the king asked the former prime minister Salandra to form a government in which the Fascists were to be represented. When De Vecchi telephoned Mussolini from Rome and advised him to accept this proposal, he refused. When the king's adjutant informed Mussolini that the king wished to see him he declined to come to Rome unless he was appointed prime minister. On the morning of the 29th De Vecchi telephoned once more that Salandra had given up the attempt to form a government and that Mussolini's demand would be met. Mussolini asked for a telegram confirming the invitation. When he had received it he took the night train to Rome and arrived there on the morning of the 30th, wearing a black shirt, black trousers and a bowler hat. Before he left Milan he ordered his followers to destroy the new offices of *Avanti!*, the fourth time that this was done since April 1919. His old hatreds were as strong as ever. Henceforth the paper had to be published in Turin.

The new prime minister was then thirty-nine years old. The government formed at the end of October 1922 was a coalition, not a one-party government, exactly as the government formed by Hitler ten years later. It is true that Mussolini himself was not only the prime minister but also responsible for the two key ministries of home and of foreign affairs. But there were only three other Fascist ministers, for justice, for finance, and for the liberated provinces. Two ministries, labour and the treasury, went to the *Popolari*; two others, education and agriculture, to right-wing Liberals, the former to the well-known philosopher Giovanni Gentile. The Democrats—another moderate right-wing party—received three ministerial posts, trade and industry, public works, and posts and telegraphs. A Nationalist, Luigi Federzoni, became minister for the colonies. High-ranking officers were appointed to the ministry of war and to the admiralty. There were more Fascists, nine in all, among the undersecretaries of state; but they too were balanced by four *Popolari*, two Democrats, one right-wing Liberal, and two Nationalists. At the appointment of the new government all constitutional forms were preserved; Mussolini took the oath to the constitution, the formula being read to him by the former prime minister Facta in the presence of the king. Was all this to indicate a return to constitutional practices?

On 16 November the new government presented itself to parliament. The declaration read by Mussolini received an overwhelming vote of confidence, 306 in favour and only 116 against. Only Mussolini's old enemy Turati, the spokesman of the Socialists, rejected the government and its methods, but not even all the Socialist deputies voted against the new government. Nor did Mussolini request from parliament plenary powers as Hitler was to do in March 1933. The enabling law put before the Italian parliament only asked for powers to issue decrees in strictly circumscribed fields: the system of taxation, the budget, reorganization and economies to be adopted in the state machinery. The powers were expressly limited to the end of 1923, and in March 1924 the government was to account to parliament for the use which it had made of them. But they were not dictatorial powers. Parliamentary institutions and the non-Fascist parties and newspapers continued to exist for several more years.

The march on Rome succeeded largely because there was no one to oppose it. All the forces of the state—the army, the police, the civil service, the judiciary—supported it in one form or the other, exactly as they had condoned Fascist violence and lawlessness during the previous years. Without this collusion the enterprise could never have succeeded. It was not that the Fascists had successfully infiltrated the state machinery before October 1922, although no doubt many officials sympathized with Fascism, but rather that the defenders of the law were completely passive. The old régime was too discredited and too weak to find any spirited defenders. Many no doubt hoped that the Fascists were just another political party, that once in power their violence and radicalism would abate, that they would become respectable; but these were illusions. Hardly anyone recognized that the Fascists represented an entirely new political and revolutionary force which could not be 'tamed' or brought under control, but would continue to develop its own dynamism, and would finally sweep away the old order. No other party could match the Fascists' ruthlessness; none was willing to employ similar methods. If the Socialists had replied to Fascist violence by organizing their own, there would have been civil war. In that case, there is no doubt who would have emerged victorious, for the army and the police were clearly on the side of the Fascists. It might have been preferable for political reasons to go down fighting rather than accept defeat without resisting; but as the example of the Austrian Socialists was to show in 1934, it made little difference in practice. The only effective answer to Fascist violence could have come from the army—and too many of the army leaders sympathized with the Fascists.

Towards Full Power

The march on Rome had given Mussolini power but by no means full power: the question was whether he would be able to convert his share of political power into complete control of the state and its machinery. It seems that Mussolini from the outset was determined to retain power in his hands; but he was uncertain of the methods to be employed towards the other political parties and their leaders, towards the press, and towards parliament. Hence it took him four to five years to achieve complete control, years that were interrupted by one very severe crisis which threatened to destroy everything—while Hitler ten years later only needed as many months as Mussolini needed years to eliminate his rivals and to establish the one-party state.

A first step in the direction of linking the Fascists with the state was made at the beginning of 1923. On 12 January the Fascist Grand Council dissolved all para-military associations and units and established in their place a 'Voluntary Militia for National Security'. The Black Shirts and armed squads of the Fascists were incorporated into this new force and thus acquired legal status. But they remained a party army, under the command of their own leaders, and subject to Mussolini's orders, 'at the service of God and the country and under the orders of the Chief of the Government', as it was put. Their oath of allegiance was to him, not to the king; but the country had to bear the cost of the Militia, and it was considered an organ of the state. It was only two years later, during the Matteotti crisis, that the Militia took an oath of loyalty to the king.

A few weeks later the Fascists succeeded in absorbing at least one other party which was represented in the government: the Nationalists. They had for some time been close to the Fascists, and their Blue Shirts had taken part in the march on Rome. But they were much more *bourgeois* than the Fascists, more traditional and less ruthless, hence unable to compete with them. At the end of February an agreement was reached according to which the Nationalists transferred to the Fascist Party; the two parliamentary groups united under Fascist leadership. Two Nationalists, Federzoni and Maraviglia, became members of the Fascist Grand Council, and the Fascists inherited the far-reaching nationalist aspirations in the field of foreign policy. During the same month the Nationalist leader Enrico Corradini proclaimed that Fascism was not the 'dictatorship of one man, or of a few, or of many', but that of 'supreme necessity, that of the nation'.[20] Yet at that stage not even Mussolini was convinced that his régime was going to last. At the first anniversary of the march on Rome he made

[20] Quoted by Salvatore Saladino, 'Italy', in *The European Right*, ed. by H. Rogger and E. Weber, Berkeley and Los Angeles, 1965, p. 254.

an impromptu speech to a large crowd in Milan; in this, he began to
discuss the probable duration of the régime and mentioned 'five years'
as a likely figure. But then he suddenly paused—apparently it had struck
him that the figure was too low—and quickly corrected himself: the
new figure he gave was sixty years,[21] far longer than Mussolini would
be able to remain at the helm.

The most important step towards a consolidation of power in Fascist
hands was taken at the end of the year, by a new electoral law adopted
on 18 November 1923. According to this, the party list leading the poll
in an election would obtain two-thirds of the seats in parliament if it
polled more than twenty-five per cent of the votes cast. Giolitti, as the
chairman of the committee discussing the bill, approved of it in principle; so did other well-known Liberal leaders, such as Salandra and
Orlando. Already in 1921 Giolitti had formed an electoral block with
the Fascists and the Nationalists and supported them with government
funds; he considered it right to continue his tactics of cooperation in
the hope of taming the Fascist flood. Salandra actually argued that the
new law, by providing Mussolini with a safe majority, would prevent
him from dispensing with parliament and breaking the constitution!
They also hoped that a safe majority would strengthen Mussolini's
position against the radicals within his own party. These were thirsting
for more violence and muttering about a Second Revolution; they
wanted 'to liberate Mussolini from the dirt of Rome, this brothel', for
as the prime minister he had in their opinion become the prisoner of
the monarchy and of the reactionaries.

The opposition to the bill was badly divided. The *Popolari* actually
suggested forty per cent instead of twenty-five as the minimum vote
required for obtaining a two-thirds majority. The Democrats and right-
wing Socialists were equally uncertain, and in the end they and the
Popolari abstained. But that was only after the sudden resignation of
Don Sturzo, an opponent of the bill, from the chairmanship of the
Popolari Party; this was probably brought about by an intervention
from the Vatican. The Socialists strenuously opposed the bill. In the
end the motion to enter a more detailed discussion was passed by 235
against 139 votes; while the *Popolari* and others abstained, most of the
Liberals voted in favour. A vote of confidence in the government was
carried by 303 against 140 votes, and the Senate voted 165 to 41 in
favour of the new law. The Liberals had signed their own death warrant.

[21] The story is related by Giuseppe Bottai, *Vent'anni e un giorno*, Garzanti, 1949,
p. 33, who was an eye-witness.

The result of the elections held in April 1924 was a foregone conclusion. Mussolini's position was strengthened by his alliance with the
Liberals in a National Block (as in 1921), by the end of the post-war
crisis and of the strikes which had disrupted the economy; the middle
classes felt reassured. In spite of this, there was much intimidation and
interference with the secrecy of the ballot and the propaganda of the
opposition parties. The National Block polled far more than the
twenty-five per cent required to give it control of parliament: almost
sixty-five per cent of the votes cast. Surprisingly high was its percentage in the south where the Fascists had hitherto been weak: 85·9 in the
Abruzzi, 83·7 in Apulia, 76·5 in Calabria and Lucania, 76·3 in Cam-
pania. That almost the entire south showed percentages far above the
national average was due to the prestige and influence of the Liberal
leaders, as well as to the hopes of a better future aroused in these
poverty-stricken areas. The opposition parties were decimated. The
Popolari were reduced to thirty-nine, the right-wing Socialists to
twenty-five, the Socialists to twenty-two, and the Communists to nineteen seats, while the government block gained 403. Even taken together the opposition parties only polled 1,745,000 votes compared
with 4,500,000 who voted for the government. It was a victory that
could not only be explained by bribery and intimidation. If large
sections of the working class remained hostile to Fascism, the other
social classes had made their peace with it.

When parliament met the Socialist deputy Giacomo Matteotti on
30 May sharply attacked the government, and in particular the malpractices which had occurred during the elections. He was constantly
interrupted by the Fascist majority, and got involved in a sharp dispute
with Mussolini himself. Matteotti demanded that the elections be
declared null and void and that freedom be restored in Italy. After his
speech Mussolini remarked: 'That man, after that speech, should not
be allowed to go around.' Two days later he wrote in the *Popolo d'Italia*
that the majority had been too lenient towards Matteotti who 'would
have deserved something more tangible'.[22] On 10 June Matteotti
disappeared. He was kidnapped in the streets of Rome and abducted
in a car which was found by the police some days later, with bloodstained upholstery and a window broken. On the same day the police
arrested a man who was well known for his participation in punitive
expeditions and acts of Fascist *squadrismo*; in his case Matteotti's
bloodstained trousers were found. His naked body was not found until

[22] Quoted by Fermi, op. cit., pp. 229–30.

16 August, in a desolated area north of Rome. The five men suspected
of the abduction and the murder were former *arditi*, said to be members
of a gang, which in Fascist circles was called the 'Cheka' (Soviet
political police) and operated from the Ministry of the Interior. During
the past years it had specialized in attacks on enemies of the régime
who had been beaten up or given large doses of castor oil. It took its
orders either from Mussolini, or from General de Bono, the head of the
police, or from another of Mussolini's close associates. A warrant was
issued for the arrest of one of them, Cesare Rossi, who was suspected
of having organized the murder.

The news of Matteotti's murder caused a political explosion. On 13
June the opposition deputies withdrew from parliament and decided
not to return there until law and order and the constitution had been
restored. Their leader was a Liberal deputy, Giovanni Amendola,
who himself had been the victim of an attack by the 'Cheka'. But the
majority of the Liberals and Democrats, under the former prime ministers Giolitti, Salandra and Orlando, did not join the opposition. They
advised the king to retain Mussolini as prime minister and continued
to attend parliament. Meanwhile the secessionists themselves were
deeply divided, the Liberals fearing the Socialists and *Popolari*, and
the latter each other. After an earlier Roman secession they became
known as the 'Aventine', but the Aventine took no action. Mussolini,
not unnaturally, claimed that he was completely innocent, but under
his windows the crowds were shouting: 'Give us back Matteotti's body!'
'We want Matteotti's body!' It seems possible that the opposition, if
it had been united and energetically led, might have been successful.
As it was, Mussolini could limit his concessions to some changes in the
government. He himself gave up the Ministry of the Interior; its
undersecretary of state, Aldo Finzi,[23] and General de Bono were induced to resign. Mussolini promised a 'normalization' of the political
and constitutional life and the elimination of all illegal methods. A
well-known professor of law, Alfredo Rocco, was made the minister of
justice, and the former Nationalist Federzoni was transferred to the
Ministry of the Interior. The Church and the king, the industrialists
and the Senate continued to support Mussolini as they feared, above
all, a revival of Socialism.

The Matteotti crisis also caused a crisis within the Fascist party itself.
With the revival of the opposition and increasing defections from the

[23] Interestingly enough, Finzi was a Jew who was shot in 1944 by the Germans
as the leader of an Italian partisan unit.

Fascist ranks the local leaders felt isolated and no longer confident that Mussolini would be able to surmount the crisis. They disliked his apparent willingness to make concessions. Their suspicions grew when a circular of 30 November recommended a more conciliatory attitude towards possible allies and condemned all illegal actions and continued violence: the party, it proclaimed, must be liberated from 'those who make violence a profession'. Some army generals were demanding a purge in the higher ranks of the Militia, and one of them declared that the army must always remain the strongest of all the forces existing within the nation. Thus there developed a movement of those dissatisfied with Mussolini's 'soft' leadership, the 'movement of the Consuls'. On 31 December thirty or more Consuls of the Militia called on Mussolini under the pretext of wishing him a happy New Year, but in reality to protest against any more changes in the command of the Militia (from which Italo Balbo had recently been forced to resign) and to inform the *Duce* that a 'second wave' of violence would start if the opposition was not suppressed more firmly. On the same day several thousand Fascists collected from all over Tuscany paraded through the streets of Florence, and a motion was carried: 'The Florentine Fascists . . . declare their loyalty to the *Duce* . . . but make their obedience and their discipline conditional on the decisive action of the government which must be demonstrated, if necessary, by dictatorial action.'[24] After the parade the printing presses of two opposition papers were destroyed, and the masonic lodge and the offices of oppositional lawyers wrecked. Similar violent demonstrations took place at Pisa, Bologna and elsewhere. They were meant as a clear warning not only to the king and the conservative forces, but also to Mussolini himself.

During the Matteotti crisis Mussolini's policy had wavered between making concessions and tightening the reins. The Militia was made to take an oath to the king and Mussolini continued to woo the right-wing Liberals whose support he needed. But as early as July the press was subjected to the authority of the prefects who were empowered to confiscate newspapers at their discretion. When the opposition press continued to denounce deeds of Fascist violence much more severe restrictions were imposed. At the end of 1925 the freedom of the press was abolished by decree; the owners were made responsible for all damages caused by their papers, and the exercise of the journalistic

[24] Quoted by Adrian Lyttelton, 'Fascism in Italy: The Second Wave', *Journal of Contemporary History*, vol. i, no. i, January 1966, pp. 87, 93.

profession was made dependent upon membership of a journalists' guild. These measures caused even Giolitti to go into opposition, and he was soon followed by Orlando and Salandra.

After the demonstrations and the renewed violence that had broken out in Florence and elsewhere Mussolini bowed to the extremists in his party and declared on 3 January 1925 in parliament: 'If two irreconcilable elements are struggling with each other, the solution lies in force. There has never been any other solution in history, and there never will be.' In the same speech, which was loudly applauded by the deputies, he accepted the personal responsibility for the conditions which had caused the deeds of violence, 'for I have created this political, historical and moral climate by a propaganda which extends from the intervention in the world war to the present day'.[25] Mussolini thus accepted Fascist totalitarian rule. A few days later the government was reorganized: the last two right-wing Liberal ministers left—the ministers belonging to the *Popolari* had resigned in April 1923. The government which originally had been a coalition government became the government of the ruling party. In March a radical Fascist, Roberto Farinacci, the party boss of Cremona, was appointed secretary of the Fascist party.

In his speech of 3 January Mussolini had promised that the situation would be clarified within the next forty-eight hours; this also was done. The Militia was mobilized. Numerous arrests were made, many houses and offices searched, hostile groups and organizations dissolved, and politically suspect places were closed. The local authorities were authorized to suppress all anti-Fascist activities and parties. Opposition newspapers were confiscated everywhere. The Aventine parties protested in vain. Their opportunity had passed. The Matteotti crisis, which had shaken the very foundations of Fascist power, had ended by strengthening them. It was the real turning point in the history of Italian Fascism. The only force left in the country which was politically still independent was the Church. Mussolini was at last securely in power. During the crisis his tactics had been rather hesitating and cautious, making concessions when he thought it necessary. One does not get the impression that he had a plan how to cope with the crisis—certainly not in the sense that he saw in it an opportunity to gain complete control—but that he was merely biding his time and waiting

<hr />

[25] Quoted by Erwin von Beckerath, *Wesen und Werden des fascistischen Staates*, Berlin, 1927, p. 83, from Mussolini's *Discorsi del 1925*, pp. 14, 16.

for the storm to blow over. From 1925 onwards caution was no longer required: the enemy was defeated.

The One-Party State

By the beginning of 1925 all opposition parties were in practice suppressed and the press virtually controlled by the government. By these measures, as Mussolini wrote nearly twenty years later, the 'foundations of the totalitarian state were laid'. During the following months and years further legislative measures completed the edifice. A law of December 1925 defined the powers of the Chief of the Government: he was to be responsible solely to the king who alone could dismiss him; he had to approve anything that was to be debated in parliament; the other ministers were responsible to him as well as to the king. Parliamentary government had come to an end. Soon after all opposition in parliament was also eliminated. In January 1926 some opposition deputies who had seceded to the Aventine attended a parliamentary ceremony in honour of the Queen Mother who had just died. This provided Mussolini with an opportunity to dictate his conditions for the return of the opposition: they had to recognize the Fascist revolution and repudiate the Aventine opposition; but all except three refused to do so. Their secession and protest were then declared unconstitutional and their seats forfeited, measures which were passed without any opposition.

Before the end of 1926 further drastic measures were taken against the opposition. In November—after several unsuccessful attempts on the life of Mussolini—all parties and organizations opposed to the government were dissolved. An 'Act for the defence of the State' prohibited the re-forming of any association or organization that had been dissolved by the police, as well as the dissemination of their doctrines and programmes. All oppositional newspapers were finally suppressed. A 'Special Tribunal' was established to deal with crimes committed against the state and any offence against the new law. Its presidents and vice-presidents were appointed by the prime minister from the ranks of the officers of the armed forces and the Militia; the judges too were officers who needed no legal qualifications and had to take an oath of obedience to Mussolini. There were no witnesses for the defence; there was no jury, and no right of appeal. Political offenders could be deported or assigned a compulsory place of residence. A sentence of deportation could be imposed by a commission consisting of the prefect of the province in question, the local chief of the *Carabinieri*, a high officer of the Militia, and the public prosecutor. A secret police was organized to track down the opposition and to arrest its members. Its powers and those of the 'Special Tribunal' were to sow fear in the hearts of all enemies of the régime.

Leaders of the opposition and men unwilling to make their peace with Fascism were forced to emigrate or were banished to far-away small islands. About 3,000 people were sent there without any trial between 1927 and 1934. Between 1927 and 1932 the 'Special Tribunal' passed nine death sentences, one condemning to penal servitude for life, and 1,902 sentences imposing a total of 10,157 years of imprisonment. Thus Mussolini attempted to transform the nation into a 'block of granite', into a 'monolith'. Those Italians who, outside Italy, spread rumours directed against the state or were active against 'the national interests' could be sentenced to terms of imprisonment of up to fifteen years if apprehended. If not, they could be deprived of their nationality and their property could be confiscated. But opposition activities continued at home and abroad, in spite of savage punishments, the employment of countless secret agents, the abduction of well-known anti-Fascists, etc. But it must be recognized that, inside Italy, the opposition was severely reduced and its activities curtailed: it only revived during the later years of the second world war.

Parallel with these measures in the political sphere went an attempt to remodel the economic structure, to organize all those engaged in production in Syndicates or Corporations as the Nationalists had demanded since 1919. Fascist trade unions or syndicates had been organized as early as 1921 and had slowly grown in numbers. At their national congress held at the beginning of 1922 it was proclaimed: 'The nation, understood as the supreme synthesis of all the material and spiritual values of the race, stands above individuals, categories and classes, which . . . are not legitimate unless they are contained within the framework of the superior national interest. . . . '[26] From the employers' point of view these Fascist syndicates had the enormous advantage that they were opposed to strikes and any other militant working-class action. In October 1925 the General Confederation of Industry recognized the Fascist syndicates as the only representatives of the workers and promised not to conclude any collective agreements

---

[26] Quoted by Finer, op. cit., pp. 495–6.

except through the syndicates, ignoring the elected committees of shop stewards.

A few months earlier the minister of justice, Alfredo Rocco, in a speech justified the intervention of the state in economic disputes and the abolition of strikes and lock-outs by this argument: 'Unlimited and unrestrained class self-defence . . . inevitably leads to anarchy. The Fascist doctrine . . . does away with the class self-defence which—like individual self-defence in the days of barbarism—is a source of disorder and civil war. Having reduced the problem to these terms, only one solution is possible: the realization of justice among the classes by and through the state. . . .' In the spring of 1926 a bill was laid before parliament which made all strikes and lock-outs illegal and punishable. On this occasion Rocco reiterated: 'The state is no longer the state, it is no longer sovereign, if it is unable to mete out justice in conflicts between social classes and categories, unable to forbid them to exercise private justice, just as this is forbidden to individuals and to families. . . .'[27] Separate syndicates for employers and employees, one for each trade or branch of industry, were established. Their task was to mediate between the interests of the employers and of the employees, according to the needs of production which were declared to be dominant. They alone were entitled to conclude any agreements which were then binding on all employed in that branch. Disputes were to be decided by labour courts. Membership dues were deducted from wages, also those of non-members. The government was to control the appointment of all higher officials of the syndicates. Mussolini himself became minister of corporations, a new office established in July 1926. In this way the political influence and the power of the economic groups was to be limited and controlled. In fact, however, not the employers' organizations, but the trade unions were eliminated.

In June 1926 the employers were granted authority to increase the working day to nine hours in industries which suffered from foreign competition, without increasing wages, while in the more prosperous branches payment for the additional hour was to be agreed on by the syndicates in question. When three peasants in the province of Lecce distributed a leaflet protesting against the additional hour they were sentenced to terms of imprisonment ranging from four-and-a-half to five years and seven months. When women went on strike at Carrosia near Genoa to oppose severe cuts in their wages, their leaders were

[27] Quoted by Gaetano Salvemini, *Under the Axe of Fascism*, London, 1936, pp. 85–6.

sentenced to six months' imprisonment in July 1926. In January 1927
the General Confederation of Labour—the Socialist trade unions—
decided to dissolve themselves. The resolution adopted by the national
committee pointed out that 'an uninterrupted series of illegal acts of
vandalism, the dissolution of trade unions for political and not for legal
reasons, . . . the continuous pressure used by the Fascist trade unions
to force the workers to join the official unions . . . prove that there is no
room in Italy for unrecognized trade unionism'. Therefore it was
announced that 'the work of the Confederation was at an end and its
affairs had been wound up'.[28]

In April of the same year a Charter of Labour was promulgated by
the Fascist Grand Council. This clearly recognized the rights and
position of the employers and reduced state intervention in industry
to a minimum: 'The intervention of the state in economic production
occurs only when private initiative is lacking, or is insufficient, or
when the political interests of the state are concerned.' Private initiative in the field of production was 'in the interest of the nation' and
the private organization of production 'a function of national concern';
the direction of an economic enterprise 'belongs to the employer' who
was responsible for it to the government.[29] The employers, freed from
interference by trade unions, factory committees and shop stewards,
were again the masters in their own house. The workers' most valuable
weapon, collective action and strike, had been made illegal. The
Corporative State, the establishment of which was hailed as a social
achievement, curtailed severely the rights of the workers, but emphasized and protected those of the employers.

The institution which became the most powerful organ of the state
was the *Gran Consiglio Nazionale Fascista*, the Fascist Grand Council.
The highest organ of the ruling party was vested with far-reaching public authority. It chose the party secretary who was also its own secretary
and had the right to appoint the provincial secretaries; the latter in their
turn nominated the lesser party officials. By a law of December 1928
the Grand Council was made part of the constitution, 'the supreme
organ coordinating and integrating all the activities of the régime
which issued from the revolution of October 1922'. Its president was
the chief of the government who alone was entitled to summon it and
to determine its agenda. It had about twenty to twenty-eight members,
the highest party officials, its secretary and deputy secretaries, the

[28] Quoted ibid., pp. 43–4 and n. 1.
[29] Quoted by Finer, op. cit., pp. 503–4.

more important ministers and former ministers, the comma
Militia, the presidents of the Senate and of the Special Tri
It thus symbolized 'the unity of party and state' at the high
It even had the right to determine the composition of what w
parliament. It chose from lists prepared by authorized organizations
400 candidates whose names were then submitted to the electors in
the form of a single list for their approval. It could also draw up a list
of names from among whom Mussolini's successor was to be chosen.
Finally the party secretary was given ministerial rank and entitled to
attend meetings of the government.

In all these provisions the predominance of the Fascist party over
the state was clearly expressed; equally in the provision that in all
questions of a 'constitutional' character the Grand Council had to be
consulted. Curiously enough, in the end—in July 1943—it was the
Grand Council that turned against its chief and by a majority of nineteen to seven passed a motion which in effect deprived him of his
powers and expressed its lack of confidence in his policy. In a completely
authoritarian state it preserved the possibility of having certain discussions and rendering advice—a possibility that was non-existent in
Hitler's Germany. In the elections held in 1929 under the new system
of a single list eight million votes were cast in favour, according to the
official figures, and only 136,000 against. Even if these figures were not
the correct ones it is fairly certain that at that time the large majority
of the Italians favoured the new régime, while the opposition was prevented from stating its case. The party and the state were increasingly
interlinked: the party symbol, the *fasci*, became a state emblem, the
party anthem the national anthem, the Militia a state force.

There was, however, one powerful force left in the country which
was not controlled by the party and its apparatus: the Church. Indeed,
ever since Italian troops had occupied Rome in 1870 and made it the
capital of the new kingdom, the Pope had refused to recognize its
existence and considered himself a prisoner in the Vatican which he
never left. Because of the existence of the Papal States the whole
national movement, the movement for the unification of Italy, had
been profoundly anti-clerical, opposed to the temporal power of the
Pope which he was unwilling to renounce. The first Fascist programme
of 1919 had called for the secularization of all Church property, and
in his earlier days Mussolini himself had made violent pronouncements against the power of the Church. But this attitude changed after
he had become prime minister, and in the end he succeeded where

every previous Italian government had failed. In February 1929 the Lateran treaties were signed between the Holy See and the kingdom of Italy by which they agreed to establish diplomatic relations and to recognize each other. A minute Papal State within Rome was established where the kingdom had no jurisdiction. There the Pope was entitled to maintain his own army, police, law courts and prison. The Church was to receive compensation for the territories which it had lost; ecclesiastical corporations were exempted from taxation, and ecclesiastical schools given preferential treatment; religious teaching was extended to the secondary schools, and the influence of the Church on education strengthened. The reconciliation between State and Church won Mussolini the hearts of the Catholics and the support of the Church and was one of his greatest successes. There was no longer any rival power to his own. He combined in his hands the two most important functions in the country: those of prime minister and *Duce* of the Fascist party, apart from several ministerial posts and the High Command of the Fascist Militia. He now stood at the height of his popularity and his power.

His success had been facilitated by several factors: the post-war crisis and economic difficulties, the widespread fear of red revolution, the ardent nationalism which permeated Italy on account of the war and its disappointing results, the weakness and ineffectiveness of parliamentary government, the help rendered by the government, the army, the police and the administrative authorities. What nevertheless seems surprising in retrospect is the ease with which Mussolini managed to seize the reins of power, in spite of all his fumblings and hesitations. It was not the case that he was swept into power by an irresistible movement, by a flood against which no dykes could be erected, but rather that his enemies were struck with blindness, unable to see the danger that threatened to engulf them—and not only them, but their whole country too. In April 1922 Mussolini had written: 'The new state, which already exists as a germ in the power of our party, must—gradually or by force—replace the liberal state.'[30] Five years later it had replaced the liberal state: this had been done gradually, but force had also been used on a considerable scale to speed up the transformation. The Fascist movement, at first weak and existing only in certain areas, had soon developed a dynamism which none of its enemies was able to rival, a ruthlessness which no other party could or would muster. Without this dynamism and ruthlessness it could never have succeeded,

[30] *Il Popolo d'Italia*, 30 April 1922, i.e. six months before the march on Rome.

however favourable the objective conditions of the post-war years were
to its quick development.

International Echoes

The march on Rome and the easy victory of the Italian Fascists evoked
immediate echoes in several European countries, especially in those
in close proximity to Italy which—in the post-war period—experienced
economic and social upheavals very similar to those which occurred in
Italy. Above all, this was the case in France, Germany and Austria,
the three countries in which violent nationalist and anti-Semitic
movements had developed already before 1914.

In France, leaders of the *Action française* went on record in praise of
Fascism even before the march on Rome. In March 1921 the well-
known historian Jacques Bainville hailed the first reports about
Fascist violence as a welcome symptom of Italy recovering her strength.
In August 1922 the writer Léon Daudet declared that Fascism was a
national reaction to the bestiality, stupidity and evil of Communism:
now the true Italian spirit was fighting back against those who were
preaching expropriation and internationalism. After the march on
Rome, Daudet was enthusiastically applauded by a student audience
when he exclaimed that the *Action française* would soon seize power
by force and that then the purges carried out by the Fascists would
pale in comparison with those in France. Hopes were running high
that Daudet would soon emulate Mussolini's example.

The first book in French on *Le Fascisme* was published by the publishing house of the *Action française*. In June 1923 its newspaper
quoted, with evident approval, the remark of an opponent that the
Action française was in reality the French brand of Italian Fascism.
The *Camelots* took another leaf out of the Fascists' book by beating up
and spattering with tar three left-wing politicians who were on their
way to address a mass meeting, called to protest against the German
policy of prime minister Poincaré which had led France into the Ruhr.
In 1924 another leader of the *Action française*, Georges Valois, fascinated by Mussolini's movement and its activism, sought to emulate it
in France by founding a movement of ex-servicemen which was to be
equally dynamic. At first its relations with the *Action française* remained friendly, even when Valois began to publish his own paper,
which was financed by the perfume manufacturer François Coty. In
October 1925 he founded an openly Fascist party, the *Faisceau*, which

even in its name copied the Italian example. The two groups soon began to quarrel, and Maurras announced that it was not permitted to belong to both.

In Germany, the movement which stood closest to the Fascists, Hitler's National Socialists in Munich, received a similar impetus from the march on Rome. Not only the National Socialists, but all the extreme right-wing forces in Bavaria were busy in 1923 to plan the 'march on Berlin' which was to overthrow the hated 'Marxist' government and to lead nationalism to victory. As the Fascists had marched south, so they would march north and overthrow *en route* the Red governments which ruled in Saxony and Thuringia, the two important states of central Germany. The great military leader of Germany in the first world war, General Ludendorff, was to lead the march; ex-soldiers and nationalists from all over Germany flocked to Munich to participate in it.

Only a few days after the march on Rome, a close associate of Hitler, Hermann Esser, proclaimed in Munich among tumultuous applause: 'What has been done in Italy by a handful of courageous men is not impossible. *In Bavaria too we have Italy's Mussolini* [*sic*]. *His name is Adolf Hitler*. . . .'[31] According to a police report of December 1922 the National Socialists in Munich had received 'a special force of gravity' through Mussolini's success. According to the local papers, National Socialist propaganda recommended to take action similar to that of Mussolini in Italy. They were to make the attempt in November 1923, but were to fail.[32]

Ten years later still Joseph Goebbels, by that time the minister of propaganda, wrote: 'The march on Rome was a signal, a sign of storm for liberal democracy. It is the first attempt to destroy the world of the liberal-democratic spirit . . .', that 'world which started in 1789 with the storm on the Bastille and conquered one country after the other in violent revolutionary upheavals, to let . . . the nations go under in Marxism, democracy, anarchy and class warfare. . . .' And he apostrophized Mussolini in this eulogy: 'Mussolini is a Prussian Roman! A Roman with Prussian discipline, Prussian love of work and Prussian heroism, a type which in this singularity could only grow in Roman soil. . . .'[33]

---

[31] *Völkischer Beobachter*, 8 November 1922, quoted by W. W. Pese, 'Hitler und Italien 1920–1926', *Vierteljahrshefte für Zeitgeschichte*, iii, 1955, p. 120.
[32] See below, pp. 112 ff.
[33] Joseph Goebbels, *Der Faschismus*, Berlin, 1934, pp. 8, 10, 18.

In *Mein Kampf*, too, Hitler expressed his 'deepest admiration for the great man to the south of the Alps, who . . . did not conclude a pact with the internal enemies of Italy, but worked for their destruction by all ways and through all means. . . .'[34] Mussolini, however, did not return this fulsome praise. Even before Hitler's Munich *Putsch* of 1923 had failed Mussolini declared—in a conversation with the Italian Consul General in Munich, Count Durini di Monza—that the National Socialists were 'buffoons'. He did not care for imitators. The buffoons, however, not only were to gain power in Germany but were to exercise a far greater influence on the Fascist movements outside Germany than Mussolini was ever able to achieve. In the 1930s it was Hitler and National Socialist Germany who were admired and imitated by Fascist circles all over Europe, and not Mussolini's Italy.

[34] Adolf Hitler, *Mein Kampf*, 97th ed., Munich, 1934, p. 774.

3 | National Socialism: the Formative Years

The First National Socialist Party

The German Workers' Party founded in 1904 had its main strength in northern Bohemia, where the position of the German workers was most directly threatened; during the first world war its political activities were reduced because many of its members and leaders were called up for military service. But a discussion was started about a change in the party's name, so as to underline its socialist character. At a party conference held at Aussig (Ústi) in April 1918 it was suggested to change the name to 'German National Socialist Party' or to 'German Nationalist Socialist Workers' Party'; yet the delegates by a large majority voted in favour of retaining the old name. During the following month, however, the party leaders reversed this decision and opted for the new name which, they hoped, would attract larger numbers. At a conference held in Vienna in August 1918 the change was approved by the party delegates, and a new programme was adopted:

> The German National Socialist Workers' Party aims at the elevation and liberation of the German working population from economic, political and intellectual suppression and at complete equality of rights for it in all fields of *völkisch* and political life . . . It rejects, therefore, as unnatural a combination on the basis of supranationalism. An improvement of the economic and social conditions can, on the contrary, only be achieved by bringing together all those engaged in work on the basis of the individual nationality. . . .
> The German National Socialist Workers' Party is not a narrow class party, but defends the interests of all those engaged in honest

productive work. The party is libertarian and strictly *völkisch*, and it opposes all reactionary tendencies, the privileges of Church, nobility and capitalists, and all alien influences, but above all the overwhelming power of the Jewish trading spirit in all spheres of public life. . . .[1]

The programme was more pronouncedly socialist than the party programme of 1904. All large capitalist enterprises which worked to the detriment of the common weal were to be taken over by the state, the province or the commune; this applied in particular to the transport enterprises, the mines, water power, insurance and advertising; the employees of public enterprises should share in the profits; the stranglehold of the Jewish banks on economic life must be eliminated and people's national banks be founded. These demands were repeated in a book on 'National Socialism' which one of the party leaders, Rudolf Jung, wrote in the same year; he was a railwayman who was convinced that Czech immigration was only part of a general conspiracy to expel the Germans from their Bohemian homelands. His book contained many of the slogans which, two years later, were to be incorporated in the programme of the Munich National Socialists, such as *'Gemeinnutz geht vor Eigennutz'* ('The common weal comes before private interest'); it also distinguished between 'disintegrating finance capital' and 'productive national capital'. Incomes should be distributed justly; monopolies, department stores and large estates must be nationalized, but not property acquired by 'honest productive work'. Czechs, Jews and other foreigners were held responsible for the difficulties experienced by the German workers. Therefore, the programme of May 1918 stipulated, the whole area of German settlement in Europe should be incorporated in one 'democratic and social German Empire'.

All these ideas were to reappear in the Munich programme of 1920, in particular the explosive mixture of radical social with extreme nationalist and anti-Semitic demands. They were the product of the sharp clash of the nationalities in the Habsburg monarchy, and they were formulated before its collapse in 1918. Yet there was one important difference: the German nationalist trade unions in Bohemia and the National Socialist Party which developed from their ranks were

[1] Quoted by Rudolf Jung, *Der Nationale Sozialismus*, 2nd ed., Munich, 1922, p. 65; Andrew G. Whiteside, 'Nationaler Sozialismus in Österreich vor 1918', *Vierteljahrshefte für Zeitgeschichte*, ix, 1961, p. 349; and Alois Ciller, *Vorläufer des Nationalsozialismus*, Vienna, 1932, pp. 140–1.

democratically organized: they elected their leaders and the delegates
to the party conferences, and their decisions were taken by voting.
Even the Greater German Empire envisaged by the party programme
was envisaged as 'democratic'. The party had no acknowledged
'leader', and it was not authoritarian.

The collapse of the Habsburg monarchy seemed to justify all the
fears of the German groups outside the frontiers of Germany. The
Germans of Austria and Bohemia were forbidden to join the new
German Republic. The German minorities in Czechoslovakia, Yugoslavia, Poland and elsewhere were endangered by the aggressive
national policy of the new Slav states. The privileged and protected
position which they had enjoyed under the monarchy disappeared
overnight. They were now minorities with lesser rights than the leading
nationality. To this threat most of them reacted, not by seeking a
compromise with the Slavs amongst whom they lived, but by an
ever sharper nationalism, which was reciprocated in kind by the
Slavs.

As far as the National Socialist Party was concerned its members,
after 1918, found themselves distributed among several states. Their
leader in Austria was Dr Walter Riehl; but the party was at first very
small and did not participate in any elections. In Czechoslovakia Hans
Knirsch and Rudolf Jung emerged as the leaders. In the Sudeten area,
its old stronghold, the party polled 168,000 votes in 1925 and 204,000
in 1929, considerably more than before the war. There was also a small
offshoot in Upper Silesia, which was now Polish, with its headquarters
at Bielsko. In 1920 the National Socialist Party recently founded at
Munich federated with the Austrian, Czech and Polish groups.
Speakers from Austria and Bohemia often supported the cause in
Germany, and Hitler addressed National Socialist meetings in his
native Austria. But the Austrian and Bohemian parties were not subordinate to Munich, and they did not acknowledge the leadership of
Hitler, but desired a federation of all these groups. Much more important in Austria were the numerous *völkisch* sports and other clubs,
the para-military associations which subscribed to a *völkisch* and pan-
German ideology, the students' corporations which upheld their old
racial anti-Semitism, and many similar right-wing organizations. In
Bohemia too, these ideas flourished in the German sports and gymnastic clubs which maintained close links with their counterparts in
Germany. It was particularly important that many of the young were
strongly attracted by this virulent nationalism and racialism; and many

came from families where these ideas were handed down from father to son.[2]

Germany after the World War

In November 1918 the German Empire collapsed, William II abdicated and fled to Holland. Beginning with naval mutinies at Kiel and Wilhelmshaven, revolutionary unrest broke out all over Germany. Workers' and Soldiers' Councils were formed in the towns and military units—their programme clearly inspired by the example of the Russian Soviets of 1917. The red flag was hoisted in place of the imperial black, white and red. The old authorities abdicated, and the Workers' and Soldiers' Councils found themselves in power. Germany seemed on the verge of following the Russian example. At the end of 1918 a number of small revolutionary groups combined to form the German Communist Party; yet the new party was much weaker than its Russian counterpart and rent by internal differences. Above all, in Russia the Bolshevists came into power because the provisional government continued the war against Germany and thus allowed the Bolshevists to pose as the champions of peace, and because the peasants were clamouring for the large estates to be shared out, a demand which the provisional government hesitated to fulfil. Neither condition existed in Germany. The war was over when the new government was formed, and there was no revolutionary movement among the peasants. Even the Council movement affected the peasantry only in some areas, for example in Bavaria, but there were few large estates in the south of Germany. Otherwise the movement did not spread to the countryside. At their first national congress, in December 1918, the Workers' and Soldiers' Councils decided with an overwhelming majority that elections to the National Assembly, which was to decide on the political future of Germany, were to be held in January 1919. There was to be no Soviet Germany. When the elections were held the two Socialist parties together only polled forty-five per cent of the votes cast; the majority voted for bourgeois parties, while the Communists did not put up any candidates.

Yet there was a Communist danger, although it was probably much

[2] See, for example, the reminiscences of Walther Klingohr who as a boy joined the *Deutschvölkischer Turnverein* at Krems and later the Austrian NSDAP, in the Hauptarchiv der NSDAP, NS. 26, no. 530, Bundesarchiv Koblenz.

exaggerated at the time. There was the danger of Russian propaganda and Russian agents who were active in the country. There were certain Workers' and Soldiers' Councils which refused to give up the powers which they were wielding. There were radical left-wing revolts, for example the 'Spartacus rising' in Berlin in January 1919. There were Red guards and units which refused to disband and to evacuate the buildings which they occupied. A veritable Soviet Republic was proclaimed in Munich after the murder of the left-wing prime minister of Bavaria in February 1919. Vast strikes occurred all over Germany endangering vital production.

An entirely different danger threatened the eastern provinces of Germany. The frontiers with the newly formed Polish Republic were undefined, and there were many districts in which Germans and Poles lived intermixed. Soon local warfare developed between German and Polish volunteer units which tried to occupy disputed areas and places. The new German government, composed of moderate Social Democrats, was weak and felt its whole position threatened by the continuous upheavals and revolts. To guard against them it called into being volunteer units, so-called free corps, to defend the government against left-wing uprisings and the eastern frontiers against the Poles. The volunteer units also marched into the former Baltic provinces of Russia where civil wars were raging between Whites and Reds, and where Baltic German volunteers were actively fighting on the White side. Soon the German units were not only fighting against the Reds, but also against the new Latvian and Estonian governments which declined to give in to their far-reaching demands.

The political complexion of most of the free corps was extremely one-sided. They were composed of professional officers and NCOs of the imperial army for whom there was no possibility of a return to civilian life, of adventurers, students and youngsters eager to prove their military valour. The officers' world had been destroyed by the revolution which they ascribed to the political machinations of the Left. Their epaulettes and shoulder straps were torn down by revolutionary mobs; their flag was insulted and dishonoured. The new republican order did not attract them, and a parliamentary régime meant nothing to them. They deeply resented the new leaders and their motives, the 'men of November', the 'profiteers' of the revolution. That these new leaders had called the free corps into being, that the new president, Friedrich Ebert, was—even in the opinion of Field-Marshal von Hindenburg—'a loyal German who loved his fatherland above everything', did not impress the officers and men of the free corps. They remained loyal to the black, white and red colours—even when these were officially abolished and replaced by black, red and gold. Their personal loyalty was to the leader of the free corps in question, and not to any government or constitution—many were known under the name of the leader, Aulock, Ehrhardt, Loewenfeld, Lützow, Roßbach, etc. The men were uprooted by the war and felt surrounded by a hostile world which they could not understand, isolated and betrayed. They were thirsting for action, action at any price, be that against Bolshevists, Poles, Reds, war profiteers, Jews, or the government which had called them into being. The song of the Ehrhardt Brigade proudly proclaimed:

> *Stolz tragen wir die Sterne*
> *Und unsern Totenkopf,*
> *Wikingerschiff am Ärmel,*
> *Kaiserkron im Knopf.*
>
> *Hakenkreuz am Stahlhelm,*
> *Schwarzweißrot das Band,*
> *Die Brigade Ehrhardt*
> *Werden wir genannt.*[3]

The free corps only too often took the law into their own hands. When they marched into Berlin to suppress the Spartacus rising they used the opportunity to kill the Communist leaders Rosa Luxemburg and Karl Liebknecht. When they conquered Munich and suppressed the 'Soviet Republic', under whose short-lived rule 'hostages' had been killed, they shot among many others the commander of the 'Red Army' and the anarchist writer Gustav Landauer; they also killed twenty-one members of a Catholic association whom they mistook for Bolshevists. Many others were beaten up or executed; many were 'shot while trying to escape'—which became a synonym for political murder. Many soldiers glorified in the deeds they accomplished for the fatherland. When the government ordered the free corps to be disbanded some replied by an open mutiny. In March 1920 the Ehrhardt Brigade —the swastika painted on its steel helmets—marched into Berlin and

[3] *Proudly we wear the stars*
And our death's-heads too,
Viking ship on the sleeves,
Emperor's crown on the buttons.

Swastika on our steel helmets,
Black, white and red our ribbon,
The Brigade of Ehrhardt,
That is our name.

declared the government deposed; a new government under Dr Wolfgang Kapp—hence 'Kapp *Putsch*'—was proclaimed; but it had to resign after a few days because the trade unions proclaimed a general strike against the Kapp 'government' which paralysed it.

Yet the free corps officers and men were not really interested in politics; they were a disruptive and destructive element, without any programme. Even during the Kapp *Putsch* Ehrhardt and his men showed little interest in the demands of the political Right. Attempts were made to indoctrinate them politically, for example by anti-Semitic lectures—taking the line that the German workers were deliberately deceived by Jewish leaders, as a former member of the Lützow free corps reported. Or, as another free corps soldier proudly related: 'when I left my unit at the end of 1919, even the last man of our battery had been confronted with the Jewish question'. When the same man was transferred to Warnemünde on the Baltic coast, a resort then much frequented by Jews, he continued his efforts there, with the result that 'the swastika was soon much in evidence on the promenade. Every day there were clashes and fights with Jews and their mates (*Judengenossen*).'[4] It was political violence on which the free corps thrived—directed not exclusively against Jews. After its dissolution the Ehrhardt Brigade continued in the form of an underground organization, the *O.C.* (Organization Consul; 'Consul' was a name adopted by Ehrhardt when the police sought to apprehend him). The *O.C.* had a strong following among the students of Munich and other universities; it soon engaged in deeds of violence. In August 1921 its members murdered the former minister Erzberger, a Catholic, and in June 1922 the German foreign minister Rathenau, a Jew; an attempt on the life of the Socialist leader Scheidemann was unsuccessful. The *O.C.*men selected for these deeds had to swear to carry out any orders given by their superior officers without asking questions; any traitor would forfeit his life; and the order was to be burnt as soon as it had been read. Their targets were: 'Judaism, Freemasonism and Jesuitism'.[5]

In the Germany of 1919–20 anti-Semitic slogans found a much

[4] Thus the autobiographical account of Otto Schroeder of 15 February 1937: Hauptarchiv der NSDAP, NS. 26, no. 528, Bundesarchiv Koblenz.
[5] Thus Heinrich Tillessen, one of the Erzberger murderers, to his brother Werner, an active naval officer, on 12 March 1921: *Vierteljahrshefte für Zeitgeschichte*, x, 1962, no. 6, p. 447, adding: 'Today one can only be for or against the Jews.' The best picture of the Ehrhardt Brigade and its ideology is drawn in Ernst von Salomon's autobiographical book *Die Geächteten*, Berlin, 1930.

readier echo than in the stable and secure country of the years before 1914. Then only certain social groups felt threatened or exploited by Jewish entrepreneurs or moneylenders. But after the revolution the very foundations of middle-class society were threatened. The lost war deprived many thousands of their livelihood; refugees from the ceded territories flocked into Germany, among them many Jews; the conditions of the Treaty of Versailles hit Germany severely. Above all, it was the inflation of the mark which ruined the German middle classes and destroyed their last feeling of security and stability: the inflation took away their savings, their pensions, and in many cases their property too. What was easier than to blame the Jews for all the ills of Germany? Were not some of them waxing rich while the masses were suffering? Could not foreigners eventually buy up whole streets for a few pounds or dollars? That by no means all the foreigners were Jews could be overlooked. Already in the election campaign of January 1919 nationalist leaflets called the Jews 'the vampires of Germany', and posters proclaimed: 'Germanism—Not Judaism! Not Religion But Race!'.

This new wind was soon noticed by the conservative leaders, men who were not inclined to excesses of anti-Semitic propaganda. One of them, Count Westarp, related more than ten years later: 'A sleepy meeting would wake up and the house applaud as soon as I started on the subject of the Jews. Not infrequently I personally felt a more important and more timely topic for discussion would have been the liberation of Germany or the fight against the republican system. But to achieve the success of the meeting the Jewish question could not be omitted. It had to be hashed over again at the expense of valuable speaking time.'[6] As early as September 1919 a conference of the German Nationalists held at Breslau in Silesia expressed its opposition to 'every un-German influence, particularly the disrupting influence of Jewry. . . . The party objects to the fact that foreign elements are grabbing the leadership and are leading the state to its downfall. . . .' During the Kapp *Putsch*, six months later, terrible anti-Semitic excesses were perpetrated by the free corps in Breslau. From there too, Professor von Freytagh-Loringhoven wrote to Count Westarp in July 1920 that the appeal of anti-Semitism was particularly strong and even

[6] From a manuscript by Count Westarp on 'Conservative Policy under the Republic', quoted by Lewis Hertzman, *DNVP–Right-Wing Opposition in the Weimar Republic, 1918-1924*, Lincoln, Nebraska, 1963, p. 129. The election leaflets of January 1919 are quoted, ibid., p. 126.

penetrated to the working classes: the racist idea had a great political potential and was a weapon which their party might use.[7] In Munich the fact that so many of the leaders of the short-lived Soviet Republic were Jews aroused popular anti-Semitism on a scale hitherto unknown. Exactly the same was true of Hungary where the Soviet Republic collapsed soon after, in the summer of 1919.

It would, however, be incorrect to assume that it was only anti-Semitism on which right-wing propaganda flourished during these years. In the defeated and deeply disturbed Germany there were many other weapons ready to hand. The Treaty of Versailles and the humiliation of its acceptance by the National Assembly, the new demands put forward by Germany's former enemies, the weak and ever-changing governments, the new republic which inspired little love and little respect, the ineptitude and inexperience of its representatives, the decline of German power and prestige, and above all the ever-worsening economic situation supplied many useful whips with which 'the system' could be scourged, and they were continuously used. All this did not create a Fascist movement, but it created the atmosphere in which it could develop. To this also belonged an ever-present Communist danger. The German Communist Party, although weak at first and defeated in 1919, steadily grew, and the working classes became more radical. A year after the Kapp *Putsch*, in March 1921, the Communists attempted a *Putsch* of their own in central Germany. While this venture ended in complete failure, the following years saw a further increase in Communist strength which caused growing fear among the middle and lower middle classes.

The situation was in many ways very similar to that which existed in Italy at the same time. In both countries, too, there was the problem of the soldiers who had returned from the front and felt cold-shouldered and betrayed by society. In the trenches they had pictured themselves as the heroes of the post-war world; many of them were unable to adapt themselves to a very different reality and were deeply disgusted by what they saw around them. They thirsted for action and for vengeance. They were the soldiers of the counter-revolution, but they also represented a new and much more radical element in society. They longed for something new, without any clear idea what they were aiming at, they were marching—but in what direction?

[7] Ibid., pp. 120, 127.

The German Workers' Party at Munich

During the last year of the world war a political circle was formed in Munich, consisting of factory workers, most of them employed at the railway repair shops. Its aims were to enlighten the workers about the war aims of Germany's enemies and thus to counter socialist peace propaganda, and to fight the war profiteers. The guiding spirit of this small circle was Anton Drexler, a locksmith employed at the railway shops, who was then thirty-four years old. After the German collapse, in December 1918, the group was addressed by the journalist Karl Harrer on the topic: 'The Jew, Germany's greatest enemy!'—a significant subject at a time when the new Bavarian prime minister, Kurt Eisner, as well as several members of the central government were Jews. During these months Drexler used every opportunity at his place of work, when workmen came to get or exchange tools, to start political discussions, to tell them who was in truth responsible for the military collapse and the outbreak of revolution: the Jews and the freemasons. Those who responded he invited to his flat where the circle met once or twice a week. It then had only a handful of members.

At the end of December Drexler suggested to his friends that a German-Socialist Workers' Party should be founded. All agreed, but Harrer objected to the word 'socialist'. On 5 January 1919 about twenty workers from the Munich railway shops and a few others met in a public house and founded the 'German Workers' Party' (*Deutsche Arbeiterpartei*), with Drexler as its chairman. While Drexler remained the chairman of the Munich group, Harrer became the president of a 'national' organization which was founded some days later, and Drexler his deputy. The attention of the members was still focused on the lost war. The meetings held during January were devoted to the topics: 'Why we had to win the war?', 'Could we have won the war?', and 'Why was the war lost?' The speaker was usually Harrer, the only intellectual present. He emphasized that Germany could never have lost the war if the people had been united to gain victory, that there were no military reasons for losing it, that only Jewish capital had an interest in making Germany lose: its numerous agents who were leaders of the parties, especially the Socialists, had worked all-out to foment revolution, a poison equally spread by Trotsky's propaganda. At the end of the meeting of 30 January a resolution was adopted: 'The Jews and their helpers are responsible for the loss of the war.'[8] No other activities of the new party are recorded from this period. On the contrary, Harrer warned the members not to divulge the internal programme to outsiders who did not sympathize with it. The new party was a semi-secret, esoteric group, like the 'Germanic Order' with which it was connected.

On 21 February 1919 the Bavarian prime minister Eisner was murdered while on his way to open the session of the Diet to which he intended to submit the resignation of his government. The result of the murder was the outbreak of a second revolution which culminated in the proclamation of a Soviet Republic in April. It only lasted a few weeks. At the end of April the free corps, assembled from many parts of Germany, succeeded in conquering Munich after severe fighting during which all prisoners of war and many civilians were shot. It was these events which gave a new impetus to the small German Workers' Party and to several similar groups. Exactly as in Italy after the occupation of the factories, the danger which had just been eliminated continued to arouse the fears of many respectable people. The Munich Soviet Republic left deep wounds; it created a trauma. Clearly it had been the dark design not of true Bavarians, but of foreigners, especially the Jews, who had stabbed the victorious German army in the back, who must be eliminated from the body politic. The party now established contacts with intellectuals of *völkisch* views, especially with some members of the 'Germanic Order': Dietrich Eckart, a writer, and Gottfried Feder, an engineer who agitated against the evils of Jewish finance capital and wrote a 'Manifesto on the *Brechung der Zinsknechtschaft*' ('Breaking the Shackles of Interest'). Drexler won them as members and speakers for his party meetings, which for the first time provided them with an audience.

Above all, the party found an influential patron in the person of Captain Ernst Röhm who, after the occupation of Munich, was appointed chief of staff to the town commandant. According to his own testimony, he soon attended every party meeting and always brought along a friend, usually a brother-officer or soldier.[9] Röhm was a political officer who was to play a very important part in Bavarian politics until 1923, and later as chief of staff of Hitler's S.A. (Storm-

[8] All details are taken from notes on the meetings of 16, 22 and 30 January 1919, in the Hauptarchiv der NSDAP, NS. 26, no. 76, Bundesarchiv Koblenz. Ibid., no. 78, reports by Michael Lotter, a founder member and the party secretary, on this period.
[9] Ernst Röhm, *Die Geschichte eines Hochverräters*, Munich, 1928, p. 108.

troopers). He early recognized the importance of political education, in the army as well as among the civilians. But he always insisted on the primacy of the soldiers over the politicians; his interest was focused on the many para-military associations which began to sprout in Bavaria and to train their members with the aim of enforcing a shift towards the Right. But military effort could be combined with political activity, hence Röhm's interest in the small party founded by Drexler.

Political interests were also shown by the new Bavarian *Reichswehr* itself, where a new propaganda department was responsible for the political indoctrination of officers and other ranks. In June–July 1919 courses were organized for specially selected soldiers, which were addressed by Munich professors, and also by Gottfried Feder. The soldiers thus trained were then to 'enlighten' their comrades and to counteract any left-wing tendency among them. It was in this way that the army 'discovered' Adolf Hitler, who throughout the war had served in a Bavarian infantry regiment, had been decorated and promoted lance-corporal, and was in hospital when the revolution broke out. As the member of a group employed to enlighten returned prisoners of war he soon attracted the attention of his superiors by a fiery oratory which fascinated his audiences. Other members of his group reported that he was 'a born orator who, by his fanaticism and his popular ways . . . holds the attention of his hearers', that his 'vigorous addresses (with examples from life) . . . inspired all present', and that he 'emerged as a first-class and very lively speaker'.[10] Hitler's political views were strongly anti-Semitic; he considered the Jews not a religious community but a race, a race preserved by in-breeding during a thousand years, neither willing nor able to give up its racial traits; anti-Semites must work for the abolition of all Jewish privileges; the Jews should be treated like other aliens and ultimately be removed. All this could only be achieved by 'a government of national strength and never by a government of national impotence', by 'a rebirth of the moral and spiritual strength of the nation'.[11]

After his successful speeches to the returned prisoners of war Hitler continued to be employed in a similar capacity by the Bavarian *Reichswehr*. Acting on its orders he attended meetings of the German Workers' Party which he soon joined. There too he drew attention by

[10] Printed by Ernst Deuerlein, 'Hitlers Eintritt in die Politik und die Reichswehr'. *Vierteljahrshefte für Zeitgeschichte*, vii, 1959, no. 9, p. 200 (reports of 23–24 August 1919).
[11] Hitler to Gemlich, 16 September, 1919: ibid., no. 12, pp. 203–4.

his gift of oratory and became one of its main speakers. The party began to attract much larger audiences, The meeting which Hitler addressed on the Treaty of Brest-Litovsk in November took place in a beer hall which was completely filled. 'Unfortunately' only twenty to thirty workers were present, but 'very many students, officers, tradesmen and soldiers'.[12] Another meeting held during December was attended by about 300 people from every social group, civilians as well as soldiers. Apart from Hitler it was addressed by an Austrian National Socialist and by a member of the right-wing white-collar workers' union, the *Deutschnationaler Handlungsgehilfenverband*. Hitler proudly pointed out that the party had started with two, then seven, then nine men and that it was growing from day to day. Again his speech was strongly anti-Semitic. One of his hearers, a young student, the son of members of the anti-Semitic Fritsch circle in Leipzig, wrote to his parents that he had joined the German Workers' Party after hearing Hitler speak. He had been informed at the meeting that Hitler was a building worker; but he did not believe this, for like that 'only a trained man can speak'. He thought that the party thus aimed at winning over workers. 'They are all rather nice people with reasonable views. They are strongly opposed to Marxism. . . .'[13]

There is no doubt that many students and youngsters joined the party, many soldiers and officers, who could not or would not return to a civilian life, many whose existence was threatened or destroyed, such as ex-servicemen, small tradesmen and craftsmen, but also members of the professions and artists. An original membership list of the German Workers' Party has survived which lists 193 members, most of them with their occupations. It gives ten students, twenty-two soldiers and officers, four doctors, five engineers, four journalists, three writers, three sculptors, three directors, four factory owners, one professor, one teacher, one architect, one composer, and one publisher. There were nineteen *Kaufleute*, but it is difficult to say whether these were businessmen or tradesmen, three shopkeepers, and sixteen white-collar workers (mainly bank and post office employees). Five members gave their profession as 'master' of a craft; the forty-six who gave theirs as painter, locksmith, gardener, baker, joiner, mechanic, smith, shoemaker, etc., were either craftsmen or workmen and represented the working-class element; it amounted to

[12] Ibid., no. 14, p. 206 (meeting of 13 November 1919).
[13] Heinz Zarnke to his parents, no date: Hauptarchiv der NSDAP, NS. 26, no. 107, Bundesarchiv Koblenz.

twenty-five per cent of those whose occupation was listed.[14] It was a rather motley crowd but seems to represent a fair cross-section of the Munich population of the time, looking more respectable than has often been thought, with a clear preponderance of the small people and the lower classes. The number of those coming from the middle class proper was apparently rather small, but it is difficult to identify them from this list with its vague and general descriptions.

In 1919 Hitler's role within this party was still a modest one. In the membership list he was simply described as a 'painter'. Harrer continued as president, also at the meetings, and Drexler as chairman. But there could be no doubt about Hitler's usefulness as a speaker, and his ambitions were aroused. People far above him in the social scale, Dietrich Eckart and Captain Röhm, took an interest in him; they introduced the much younger man—he was then thirty years old—into bourgeois society and arranged for him important political contacts, far above the reach of a mere lance-corporal. In March 1920 he was discharged from the army and became a professional politician. His meteoric rise had begun.

Hitler and the National Socialists

When Hitler joined the German Workers' Party it had a committee which was elected by the members, and this committee debated political issues and took its decisions by a majority vote, like any other party or group. During the years 1920–21 Hitler established his complete control over the party and became its undisputed Leader, while its founders either left or were relegated to the background. Following the Austrian example—close contacts were established with Dr Walter Riehl in Vienna—the words 'National Socialist' were added to the party's name, so that it became the 'National Socialist German Workers' Party' or N.S.D.A.P. Following an Austrian suggestion the swastika, long known in *völkisch* circles as a symbol of Aryan Germanism, was adopted as the party symbol and flag. In the spring of 1920 it was shown for the first time in black on a white circle surrounded by a red field: preserving the black, white and red of the old imperial flag, transforming it by an approximation to the red flag of the socialist workers, and at the same time emphasizing the link with the Ehrhardt

[14] The membership list has no date but is clearly from this period: Hauptarchiv der NSDAP, NS. 26, no. 111, Bundesarchiv Koblenz.

Brigade and other *völkisch* groups which sported the swastika. There is no doubt that the new flag had a powerful propaganda effect. Hitler always attached great importance to details of propaganda, uniforms, arrangement of meetings, etc. More than twenty years later he still considered it important to tell his companions, in the midst of the second world war, that in Munich he had designed political posters of the most striking red, that lorries completely covered in red and decorated with red flags had been used for propaganda purposes, and that he had told his followers to attend the party meetings without tie and collar and not well dressed, because he wanted to frighten away bourgeois elements and keep the ranks of the movement 'free of frightened rabbits'.[15]

On 24 February 1920 Hitler announced the party programme, the famous Twenty-five Points, to a mass meeting. The first points were those of the extreme nationalists: the union of all Germans, on the basis of the right of self-determination, in a Greater Germany, the acquisition of land and colonies, and the annulment of the peace treaties of Versailles and St Germain, which had deprived Germany of her colonies and territories in the east and west and forbade Germany and Austria to unite. There followed the points directed against the Jews: only those of German blood could be members of the nation (*Volksgenossen*, literally: 'comrades of the people') and of the state; only such citizens should be allowed the right to decide on legislation and the leadership of the state and to occupy official posts; all those who had immigrated after 2 August 1914 should be expelled from Germany immediately. Then came the more specifically 'socialist' points: the abolition of income not earned by work, the breaking of the shackles of interest (Feder's demand), the nationalization of all businesses and trusts which had already been amalgamated (*vergesell-schaftet*), the communalization of the department stores and their leasing to small tradesmen, a land reform, the confiscation of land for the common weal without any compensation, and the prohibition of all speculation in land. To carry out these demands a strong central government and the unconditional authority of a central parliament over the whole of Germany must be established. As in the first Fascist programme of 1919 and in the book written by the Bohemian National Socialist Jung earlier, radical social demands figured prominently in the programme. Among them was one dear to the hearts of the small

[15] *Hitlers Tischgespräche im Führerhauptquartier 1941–1942*, ed. Percy Ernst Schramm, Stuttgart, 1963, p. 261.

shopkeepers and tradesmen, the communalization of the department stores; but others, such as the expropriation of land 'for communal purposes' and the nationalization of certain types of business, can hardly have been popular with the respectable burghers of Munich. Exactly as in the Fascist programme, there also figured a demand for profit-sharing in large industrial enterprises. The programme was not anti-democratic, but envisaged on the contrary an enhanced authority of the central German parliament. One might say it promised something to everybody. Needless to say, the radical social demands were not carried out when Hitler came to power.

The audiences addressed by Hitler steadily grew. In April 1920 he spoke to about 1,200 people in the Hofbräuhaus on the party's programme: the Jews must be treated as aliens; 'it is the Jews who incite all classes and equally the different workers against each other. . . . These parasites now put their stamp on our beautiful German towns. What has become of the town of the kind-hearted Viennese? (Shame!) A second Jerusalem! (Strong applause).' Greater still was the applause when Hitler demanded that a united German Empire from the Niemen to Bratislava, and from Königsberg to Strasbourg, should be created and that 'the November criminals of 1918' must be brought to justice, starting with Erzberger and Scheidemann.[16] Two days later Hitler exclaimed that all Germany was ruled by Jews: they sat in the government and did their shady trading; when they had filled their pockets they incited the workers against each other, 'of course, because the Jew has money in his pocket'. In October, after an electioneering tour in Austria, Hitler reported on the 'incredible state of affairs in German-Austria which has been delivered entirely to the Jews. The Jew sells everything, from the valuable paintings in the museums to whole countries and nations, such as the Germans in Czechoslovakia and Carinthia.' The parties always wanted to preserve law and order, but 'our party must have a revolutionary character. . . . We Germans want to be revolutionary against the alien race which oppresses and exploits us, and we shall neither rest nor halt until this gang has been removed from our fatherland.'[17] In November he fulminated against those who had torn down the epaulettes and cockades of the soldiers returning from the war, had destroyed the black, white and red flag, 'the symbol

[16] Reginald H. Phelps, 'Hitler als Parteiredner im Jahre 1920', *Vierteljahrshefte für Zeitgeschichte*, xi, 1963, no. 4, p. 300 (speech of 27 April 1920).
[17] Ibid., no. 16, p. 322 (speech of 18 October 1920); the previous speech of 29 April, ibid., vii, 1959, no. 19, p. 211.

of our national pride' and had put in its place 'the Jewish flag': now
the same people wanted to deprive the Germans of the last and best
left to them, their honour.[18]

It seems, however, that his violent anti-Semitic propaganda was
received in Munich with a good deal of criticism. Thus in August 1920
the party brought out a poster, signed by Drexler, which tried to answer the following arguments: '"Are there not also good Jews, but
at the same time rascals among the Christians?" "Do you not also see
the Christian usurers, profiteers and exploiters, big capitalists and their
press?" "Is the Jew responsible for the fact that he is not a German
but a Jew?"' In reply to these awkward questions Drexler declared:
'We fight all capital, whether Jewish or German, it if does not consist
of productive work, but of the principle of interest, of income achieved
without any effort of labour. We fight the Jew not because he is the
only carrier of this capital, but because he systematically prevents the
struggle against it and originally founded this system. We fight him not
because he is the only usurer, but because he comprises ninety per cent
of all usurers in only one per cent of the population. . . . We fight him
as an alien race not because he is not German, but because he pretends
to be German. . . . We fight his activity as the racial tuberculosis of
the nations and are convinced that a recovery will only take place after
he has been eliminated.' Drexler also claimed to know that the money
of the German Communists was supplied by Jewish bankers and that
the Socialists and Communists were nothing but the protective
guard of finance capital: only his own party was free from all these
influences. The International had never helped the workers; there was
only an International of gold and profit-making.[19]

By the end of 1920 the party had grown to such an extent that it
required a paper of its own. It thus bought a Munich racialist newspaper, the *Völkischer Beobachter*, which henceforth remained the
party's central organ. It was first published twice a week, and in 1923
became a daily paper. Dietrich Eckart supplied one of the necessary
guarantees of 60,000 marks, but the money came from *Reichswehr*
funds; the loan was probably arranged by Captain Röhm. The paper
was soon eagerly read in extreme right-wing circles all over Germany.
Two former navel officers and members of the Ehrhard Brigade who a

---

[18] *Vierteljahrshefte für Zeitgeschichte*, vii, 1959, no. 31, p. 226 (meeting of 24
November 1920).
[19] Poster of 13 August 1920; speeches of 6 February and 19 May 1920: Hauptarchiv der NSDAP, NS. 26, no. 82, Bundesarchiv Koblenz.

few months later were to murder Erzberger were completely captivated by it. One of them pronounced it was 'brilliant', and the other urged his brother to subscribe to it because it was the only German paper that looked at political events from the angle of the Jewish question and 'sets to work really to my heart's delight'.[20] Another member of the Ehrhardt Brigade reports that the National Socialist movement in Frankfurt received a strong impetus from two former naval officers sent from Munich, who organized meetings and recruited many members, but that the strong rivalry between the different leaders had very bad results.[21]

The Ehrhardt Brigade helped the National Socialists in another important way: to organize an efficient, para-military formation to protect their own meetings and to break up those of their rivals. As soon as the party organized meetings not merely in the backrooms of public houses, but in large halls, the danger existed that these meetings might be broken up by political enemies or disturbed by hecklers. From the outset Hitler was determined not to suffer any such interruption. Stewards were organized—mainly former soldiers, sometimes even active soldiers—to remove by force any hecklers, a practice common also in other political parties. From these modest beginnings there developed a new para-military formation, renamed the *Sturmabteilung* (Stormtroopers) or *S.A.* after a great successful battle in the Hofbräuhaus in November 1921. Hitler asked Captain Ehrhardt to lend him for this formation officers of his brigade; several former naval officers became the organizers and trainers of the *S.A.* which was soon a highly efficient military force, organized in companies, with its own cavalry, artillery and technical detachments, and its weapons stored safely away.

Many other para-military associations existed in Bavaria at that time, such as the former Free Corps *Oberland*, the *Reichsflagge*, or *Bayern und Reich*. All were commanded by former officers, and some by active officers of the *Reichswehr*. The latter also supplied the funds and often the weapons with which these private armies were trained and equipped. All were preparing for the day when they would be summoned to save the fatherland, be that from the foreign foe, the French or the Poles, or from the internal one, the Marxist government

[20] Carl to Heinrich Tillessen, 2 March 1921, and Heinrich to Werner Tillessen, 12 March 1921: *Vierteljahrshefte für Zeitgeschichte*, x, 1962, no. 4, p. 442, no. 6, p. 447.
[21] Autobiographical account of Otto Schroeder: Hauptarchiv der NSDAP, NS. 26, no. 528, Bundesarchiv Koblenz.

and parties. But from the outset Hitler considered his *S.A.* a political, and not a military, formation, which was to conquer the streets and was subject to his orders; none of the others were so closely connected with a political party. By the end of 1922 the Munich *S.A.* had perhaps 700 members; outside Munich there were another 300–400 men, mainly in the area of Landshut where they were commanded by Gregor Strasser, a former lieutenant. This was not yet a considerable force, compared with the other para-military associations, but it was to grow quickly in 1923. It then acquired a new commander in the person of ex-captain Hermann Göring, a flying ace of the world war. With his men Hitler, in September 1921, stormed the platform of a meeting which was to be addressed by a speaker of the Bavarian League, and the meeting broke up in disorder. The attempts of political adversaries to disrupt the Hitler meetings were successfully defeated by the *S.A.*

Rival Groups and Leaders

The Munich German Workers' Party was not the only right-wing extremist group founded in 1919. About the same time the engineer Alfred Brunner from Düsseldorf founded in several north and south German towns groups of the 'German-Socialist Party' (*Deutsch-sozialisten*). Both parties subscribed to the same *völkisch* ideology, and the common root of both was the secret 'Germanic Order' which had been founded before 1914. But many of the German-Socialists were more radical and more socialist in their outlook—their members addressed each other with the 'comrade' of the working-class movement—and they had more radical ideas on land reform and other economic issues. Most important were the groups of the party in Bavaria, at Augsburg, Munich and Nuremberg. The latter was founded in November and soon had some 300 members; among them was Julius Streicher, who had returned from the war as a lieutenant. The founding meeting took place in the restaurant 'Germanenhalle'; the meeting held that 'true socialism can only flourish on a *völkisch* basis and that the causes of all misery lie in our wrong land legislation, the asocial Roman law, our wrong financial system, and the political equality of those alien to our race and people. . . .'[22] The Munich group soon had about 400 members.

[22] Handwritten notes dated Nuremberg, 24 November 1919, in Nachlass Streicher, AL. 9, Bundesarchiv Koblenz.

At Easter 1920 the new party held its first conference at Hanover, which was attended by representatives of about a dozen local groups. But all those in north Germany—Berlin, Bielefeld, Düsseldorf, Duisburg, Frankfurt, Hamburg, Hanover, Leipzig, Kiel—were still very small and had hardly started any public propaganda. The Munich leader, S. H. Sesselmann, reported that an agreement had been reached with the German Workers' Party and that the town had been divided into districts for propaganda purposes. He emphasized: 'We are completely to the Left and our demands more radical than those of the Bolsheviks. . . . We are national and *völkisch*, national but not pro-capitalist. . . .'[23] In May—shortly before the Reichstag elections—Streicher addressed election meetings at Zeitz and Leipzig in Saxony; he emphasized the 'systematic and purposeful seduction of our nation by people alien to our country and race' and 'the terrible moral and economic misery' this had caused; in each town about fifty new members then joined the party.[24] Two days before the elections Streicher once more appealed to the 'brothers' of the Socialist and Communist parties; but in the elections of 6 June his party polled only 2,000 votes in Nuremberg, a failure which it attributed to lack of funds.

Two issues occupied the party's attention during the following months. One was Streicher's violent anti-Semitic propaganda in his weekly paper *Deutscher Sozialist*. The Bielefeld group wrote to him that the members complained about his exclusive concern with the Jewish question; they were not opposed to its discussion, so as to win the masses, but things looked apparently very different in south Germany; the demand that Jews be taken into protective custody must disappear; he should write more on economic issues and less on the Jewish question.[25] Even members of the party committee attributed the party's stagnation to Streicher's exaggerated anti-Semitism and advised him strongly to change his approach. The other issue was the relationship to the Munich National Socialists who, under Hitler's forceful leadership, were developing into a strong party but had no influence outside Munich. Sesselmann, the German-Socialist leader in Munich and co-founder of the party, tried to bring about an

23 'Bericht über den Parteitag der "Deutschsozialistischen Partei" Erste Tagung am 24., 25. und 26. Ostermond 1920 in Hannover', Hauptarchiv der NSDAP, NS. 26, no. 109, ibid.
24 *Deutscher Sozialist*, no. 1, 4 June 1920: Nachlass Streicher, AL. 8, ibid.
25 Deutschsozialistiche Partei Bielefeld to Streicher, 10 July 1920: Nachlass Streicher, AL. 72, ibid.

agreement with Hitler. But the latter refused to give up the name of his own party and declared that the German-Socialists nowhere made any propaganda among the masses and had not achieved anything.[26] His negative opinion seems confirmed by a report about the party's activities in Berlin: its first meeting had been attended by about twenty-five, its second by about forty people; the Berlin workers simply did not come although the party concentrated its efforts on them, rather than on bourgeois circles.[27]

The differences between the two rival parties were discussed at Salzburg in August 1920. At the end of 1919 the Austrian National Socialist leader Dr Riehl established an 'inter-state chancery' for the different National Socialist groups, and the first international meeting of German, Austrian and Bohemian National Socialists took place at Salzburg in the following August. It was agreed that the German-Socialists should concentrate their efforts on Germany to the north of the Main, except Nuremberg where they were particularly strong, and the Munich National Socialists on the area to the south of the Main. But this did not terminate the differences between the two parties. Early in 1921 a member of the 'Germanic Order' wrote to the German-Socialist leader at Kiel that the Munich National Socialists now had more than 2,500 members and about 45,000 followers; within a year they had held forty-five mass meetings; could any German-Socialist group rival these efforts? The writer had been in touch with other 'Brethren of the Germanic Order' at Bremen, Cologne and Wilhelms-haven: all were of the opinion that Hitler's party was the party of the future and was entitled to demand that the other parties should join it; it was also in some respects more radical than the German-Socialists.[28]

These issues were once more debated by the third party conference of the German-Socialists held at Zeitz in March 1921. It was attended by representatives from many more districts, as well as by Drexler for the Munich, Dr Riehl for the Austrian, and Rudolf Jung for the Bohemian National Socialists. The conference decided to unite these groups under the name 'German National Socialist Party'; as Hitler refused to give up the term 'Workers' Party', the Munich group was allowed to retain it. It was also laid down that the united party should

[26] S. H. Sesselmann to Streicher, 13 July 1920: ibid.

[27] Report by Arno Chwatal, 29 September 1920: ibid.

[28] Dietrich to the German-Socialist leader at Kiel, Wriedt, 8 February 1921, quoted by Georg Franz-Willing, Die Hitlerbewegung, Hamburg and Berlin, 1962, p. 103.

have a chairman from the ranks of the German-Socialists, with a second chairman from those of the Munich National Socialists, and equally two party committees, the first in Berlin, the second in Munich. To all this Drexler and the others agreed for the sake of unity. But Hitler, who was not present at Zeitz, was livid with rage, for he considered the German-Socialist leaders incompetent and bourgeois. After severe internal conflicts he succeeded in having the agreement cancelled. For this reason the Munich National Socialists were not represented at the second 'inter-state conference' held in Austria in August 1921. Hitler was clearly determined not to accept any other leadership but his own.

There the matter did not end. Drexler and his friends—probably disliking Hitler's personal ambition and his growing influence in the Munich party—used his temporary absence from Munich in the spring of 1921 to establish closer contacts with yet another *völkisch* group which had been formed at Augsburg by a teacher, Dr Otto Dickel, and called itself *Werkgemeinschaft Augsburg des Abendländischen Bundes* ('Community Group Augsburg of the Occidental League'). There seems to have been strong rivalry between the *Werkgemeinschaft* and a local National Socialist group founded at about the same time. When Hitler addressed his group at Augsburg in May 1921 Dr Dickel spoke in the discussion against him—an unpardonable sin. The *Werkgemein-schaft* grew during the following months and established itself else-where in Bavaria; one of those who joined it was Julius Streicher in Nuremberg. He left the German-Socialists who objected to his exclusive emphasis on anti-Semitism. Dickel had published a book, *Auferstehung des Abendlandes* ('Resurrection of the Occident'); but this was strongly criticized by Hitler, who clearly disliked both the man and his views. Dickel, however, attended all the meetings of the Augs-burg National Socialist group, became a party member, and was even invited to address party meetings. There was nothing unusual in this: many members of the small *völkisch* groups which sprang up all over Germany in the early 1920s belonged to several of them at the same time.

While Hitler was in Berlin in June 1921, where he met the leaders of other *völkisch* groups, Drexler and the Munich leaders negotiated with the Dickel group at Augsburg—apparently without informing Hitler whose dislike of Dickel was known to them. They aimed at some coordination between the overlapping groups: a committee was to be established, with its seat at Augsburg—another unpardonable sin in Hitler's eyes as it would not be controlled by him, and akin to the proposal of March that a general National Socialist committee should be established in Berlin. When Hitler returned to Munich in July he reacted strongly and resigned from the party. Among his reasons for this step he mentioned the negotiations which the party leaders had conducted at Zeitz and at Augsburg, and the invitation extended to Dr Dickel to address party meetings: actions contrary to the principles of the movement. Hitler also stipulated the conditions under which he was willing to rejoin the party: any attempt at bringing about a unification with the German National Socialist Party must be given up; there could be no unification with such groups, but only their subordination to the Munich party; its seat once and for all was to remain in Munich; an extraordinary meeting of the party members must be called immediately; its agenda was to be the resignation of the present committee, and the election of Hitler as the first chairman; he was to have 'dictatorial power' to appoint an action committee of three, which was to purge the party of the alien elements that had penetrated into it.

This time, however, Drexler was not willing to accept Hitler's ultimatum without any opposition. As Hitler had resigned from the party, Drexler used the opportunity to expel some of Hitler's closest associates, especially Hermann Esser, a former Marxist and an ardent admirer of Hitler. The Hitler faction meanwhile went ahead with the preparation of the extraordinary meeting which was to be held on 29 July. On the 25th Drexler took the singular step of informing the police that the invitations to a meeting on the 26th did not come from the party leaders because Hitler had resigned and Esser been expelled. Drexler also told the police that two currents existed inside the party: his own which was in favour of legal and parliamentary methods, and Hitler's which advocated force and revolutionary ways. According to a police report about the meeting Hitler's speech contained 'hardly anything but the [incitement to a] violent fight against the Jews if the opportunity should present itself. According to my personal view and feeling Hitler, with the adventurers from Upper Silesia present at the meeting, in the case of a Jewish pogrom would be merely the leader of a Red Army as we have had it in 1919, to rob, murder and plunder the Jews. . . .'[29]

---

[29] Quoted by Franz-Willing, op. cit., p. 116. Ibid., pp. 107–15, a detailed discussion of the events of July. 'The adventures from Upper Silesia' refers to the Free Corps men who had fought the Poles there.

Three days later, on the 29th, the extraordinary meeting of the party members took place. It was attended by about 1,200 members, presided over by Esser (in spite of his expulsion) and addressed by Hitler. It ended with his complete victory and the acceptance of his conditions. He was unanimously elected first chairman, and Drexler was relegated to the post of honorary president. The new party statutes which were adopted simultaneously established the effective dictatorial powers of the first chairman. Hitler had achieved his goal. Drexler's influence was eliminated; in future the party had only one leader. The decisive step in the formation of a Fascist party was taken. Yet the National Socialist party even in 1922 was strong only in Munich—where it had some 6,000 members—and in a few other Bavarian towns. At the following general members' meeting, on 31 January 1922, delegates from ten other Bavarian towns were present, but from only three in north Germany, none of them very important.

Dickel in his turn did not give up the hope that an agreement with Hitler might be reached. In early September 1921 he wrote to Streicher that he was expecting visitors who were still working for unification. But he considered this only feasible if Dietrich Eckart were eliminated, 'because he is the centre of infection and the supporter of Hitler's megalomania and if Hitler submits to the verdict that he can be active as an agitator, but as nothing else. . . .' In Dickel's opinion Hitler's motives were purely personal and hurt vanity: even before the negotiations started he had declared in the most abrupt form he would know how to prevent any unification.[30] Clearly, Hitler, after the victory over his Munich rivals in July, was less than ever willing to accept any compromise. His reply to Dickel after their meeting was Dickel's expulsion from the National Socialist Party because he had declined to recant and because 'a formidable abyss' separated his views from 'those of the leaders and founders of the party', i.e. Hitler's. At the same time the expulsion of Esser and two other followers of Hitler was revoked as having taken place 'without cause'.[31] Hitler's tactics were equally successful with regard to his other rivals, the German-Socialists. The party dissolved itself in the autumn of 1922, and its members then joined the National Socialists. The same did Julius Streicher with his Nuremberg group; his association with Dickel had only lasted for

[30] Otto Dickel to Streicher, 3 and 5 September 1921: Nachlass Streicher, AL. 13, Bundesarchiv Koblenz.
[31] Rundschreiben der NSDAP, no. 4, Munich, 10 September 1921: Hauptarchiv der NSDAP, NS. 26, no. 97, ibid.

about twelve months. With his violent anti-Semitism he soon became one of the party's most effective speakers, and later Hitler's all-powerful *Gauleiter* in Franconia.

Another German racist organization, also founded in 1919, was the *Deutsch-Völkischer Schutz- und Trutzbund* ('German Racialists' Defence and Offence League'). Its manager was a former officer, Alfred Roth, who as a young man had met Schönerer and become one of his followers; he also joined the Reich Hammer League of Fritsch and closely cooperated with him. The *Schutz- und Trutzbund* was a daughter organization of the Pan-German League, which had been founded long before 1914 and from which it received valuable support. At its foundation it declared that it was opposed to the rule of an alien minority, for Germans could be helped only by Germans. It soon established groups in many German towns, especially in the north; but in the south it cooperated closely with the National Socialists. As early as August 1919 Dietrich Eckart spoke at one of its meetings on the subject of 'the loan capital, its international power and the fight against it'. Later Hitler, whose fame as a speaker soon spread, was used to address meetings. In the early post-war years the *Schutz- und Trutzbund* with its large membership was the main promoter of anti-Semitic propaganda outside Bavaria, but its programme did not contain the radical social demands of the National Socialists and German-Socialists. In East Prussia it was considered as the vanguard of the movement for German regeneration. When it was dissolved by the authorities in 1922 its members were advised to join the National Socialists. As the *Schutz- und Trutzbund* was not a party and did not dispute Hitler's leadership, no rivalry developed in this case.

After the dissolution of the *Schutz- und Trutzbund* a proper *völkisch* party was founded, the *Deutschvölkische Freiheitspartei* ('German Racialist Freedom Party'). The founders were mainly extreme right-wing politicians who seceded from the German Nationalist Party, which in their opinion was too tame in its struggle against the Jews, men such as Albrecht von Graefe and Reinhold Wulle with whom Hitler had negotiated as early as 1920. Other founder-members were General Erich Ludendorff of world war fame, whose name was associated with every rightist venture and who hated Jews and freemasons equally, Theodor Fritsch of the Hammer League, and Count Ernst zu Reventlow, an old Pan-German and *völkisch* writer. In north Germany, where the National Socialists had no influence, the *Freiheitspartei* soon gained a substantial following; but this was much more bourgeois and less proletarian than that of Hitler in Munich. What mattered most of all to the *Völkische* was the liberation of Germany from its internal *and* external enemies, from the shackles of the Treaty of Versailles, from the French who occupied the Rhineland and fostered separatist movements there. What mattered most to Hitler was not nationalism, but the fight against the Jews and their friends and protectors, the Marxists and democrats. At the time this seemed merely a difference in emphasis which few people noticed, but it was to be very important in the future.

Hitler wanted power, power within his own party, and ultimately power in the state, while the *Völkische* felt much too weak to aspire to any such goal, unless they had powerful allies, be that the army or the Bavarian government. Their respectable and bourgeois leaders, although some of them later joined the National Socialist Party, adopted a contemptuous attitude towards the Austrian agitator who had risen from the depth of the people and spoke a dialect which sounded somewhat comic to Prussian ears; at best he was a useful tool, a 'drummer' to arouse the masses. The Austrian 'painter' on the other hand heartily returned this contempt, a contempt for all bourgeois politicians or intellectuals who always talked but never acted, and were unable to win over the masses; they should be taught their trade by a man of the people. He adopted the same attitude towards the intellectuals within his own party, men such as Gottfried Feder or the Baltic German Alfred Rosenberg who became the editor of the *Völkischer Beobachter*. Only his patron Dietrich Eckart, who had launched him into society and staunchly defended him during the crisis of the summer of 1921, came into a different category. With him he flew to Berlin in March 1920 to establish contacts there with nationalist circles. Eckart had introduced him to important people in Munich, such as the publisher Lehmann, the piano manufacturer Bechstein or the Bruckmann family, and he—last but not least—got Hitler the money to buy the *Völkischer Beobachter*: these services Hitler never forgot. His name was to occupy the place of honour at the end of *Mein Kampf*.

1923, the Decisive Year

Having secured control of his party and relegated its founder to a purely ornamental role, Hitler became far more self-confident. This tendency further increased after Mussolini's successful march on

Rome in October 1922: what was possible in Italy must be possible in Germany too, a 'national uprising' must be proclaimed, and its flag be carried to Berlin. His tone against 'the November criminals' if any thing became wilder still. 'We must call to account the November criminals of 1918', he told a mass meeting. 'It cannot be that two million Germans should have fallen in vain and that afterwards we should sit down as friends with traitors at the same table. No, we do not pardon, we demand—Vengeance!' And some months later: 'In the near future, when we have gained power, we shall have the further duty of taking these creators of ruin, these clouts, these traitors . . . and of hanging them on the gallows where they belong.'[32] That was after the French and Belgians, in January 1923, had marched into the Ruhr because Germany had allegedly defaulted on some Reparations payments. In reply the German government proclaimed a policy of passive resistance, while nationalists and former free corps soldiers from all over Germany flocked to the Ruhr to organize sabotage and a more active resistance. But on the day after the beginning of the French action Hitler proclaimed in a Munich beer hall: 'Our slogan is not: down with France, but down with the traitors to the fatherland, down with the November criminals!'[33]

Hitler strongly opposed any participation of his followers in the resistance to the French in the Ruhr. He did not want to transfer his party's centre of activity to the north. He had no use for the 'war of liberation'—the name of the wars of 1813 against Napoleon—which the nationalists were preparing against the French with the help of the army: such a war would only strengthen the position of the government which Hitler wanted to overthrow. But at that time his authority was insufficient to prevent the participation of members of his own party in the fight against the French. One of them, the former lieutenant and free corps officer Schlageter, was caught and executed by the French; he soon became the hero of all the nationalists. But the disarmed Germany of 1923 was unable to fight the French, and the passive resistance proclaimed and financed by the government above all resulted in depriving the German mark of its remaining value. By the autumn one dollar was worth 4,200,000,000,000 marks; at the end of October 1922 it had still been worth 4,500 marks, and a year earlier 200. The catastrophic fall in the value of the currency in 1923 meant that

---

[32] Speeches of 18 September 1922 and 13 April 1923: *The Speeches of Adolf Hitler*, ed. Norman H. Baynes, London, 1942, vol. i, pp. 53, 107.
[33] Hanns Hubert Hofmann, *Der Hitlerputsch*, Munich, 1961, p. 71.

speculation reached dizzy proportions, that all who were paid wages or salaries suffered severely, for these could never keep in step with the fall in the value of the mark, that all who received pensions or depended on fixed incomes suffered even more and had to sell their last belongings. The very foundations of society were undermined. The working classes increasingly turned towards the Communists; they became particularly strong in central Germany, where Red governments were established with their support in Saxony and Thuringia. The middle and lower middle classes, the disinherited and uprooted more and more turned towards the extreme Right.

In this situation Bavaria and its government assumed a vital role. The government since 1920 was much more to the Right than elsewhere in Germany and held its protecting hand over the many local para-military associations and over many right-wing leaders and activists who were sought by the German authorities for their participation in political crimes. When extremist organizations—such as the National Socialist Party—were dissolved in other parts of Germany they continued unmolested in Bavaria. The para-military units were preparing for the march into Saxony and Thuringia, which might then be continued to Berlin to instal a nationalist government. Since August 1923 the central government was a coalition under a moderate conservative, Gustav Stresemann, who was supported by the Social Democrats. The Bavarian division of the army, commanded by General von Lossow, closely cooperated with the para-military units on whose manpower it would have to rely in case of a mobilization. Several *Reichswehr* officers were at the same time leaders of para-military associations, and Captain Röhm and others actively supported them with funds and weapons.

These para-military associations actively intervened in internal Bavarian politics and did not hesitate to act against the local authorities. When the left-wing parties as usual wanted to celebrate Mayday by a demonstration through the streets of Munich, the para-military units planned to prevent this by force. They issued orders for a mobilization of their men who were to form an 'emergency police', without any notification of the Bavarian government. The police president of Munich summoned their leaders on 30 April and told them that no emergency police could be formed without his orders. They replied that on the next day serious rioting was to be expected, hence the emergency police should be called up. Their leader, Zeller, addressed his district leaders and informed them that the 'patriotic fighting units' had finally decided to attack the socialist processions 'with light and heavy weapons, cannon and minethrowers', indicating the strength of their armaments. He also declared that he would call up the emergency police in any case and thus forced the police president to consent to this measure 'so as not to leave the field entirely to the enemies of the government'. Their plan was to shut off whole streets and blocks and then to deal with the Reds caught inside the barriers without any inter-ference from outside. For the same purpose, Göring, the new com-mander of the Munich *S.A.*, secured weapons for his men with the help of Captain Röhm. But the Bavarian government objected to the call-up of the emergency police and the order was cancelled during the night to 1 May.[34] The *S.A.*, however, received their weapons and had to be surrounded and disarmed by troops and police. The question was how long the Bavarian government would be able to control the forces which it had fostered and abetted during the past years.

On 26 September the Stresemann government decided to break off the passive resistance to the French as its continuation threatened the economic life and the very existence of Germany. On the same day the Bavarian government appointed Dr von Kahr as *Generalstaatskommisar* with dictatorial powers. On the following day the *Völkischer Beo-bachter*, now a daily paper, published an article 'The Dictators Stresemann and Seeckt' which contained violent attacks on the chan-cellor as well as the commander of the army. Thereupon the German government forbade the printing and circulation of the paper and en-trusted the Bavarian General von Lossow with the execution of the order. But he referred it to von Kahr and declined to carry out the order even when it was repeated by the defence ministry in Berlin. Thereupon the German government decided to relieve von Lossow of his duties and to have him discharged from the army. Kahr declared he could not accept this and declined to receive any further orders from Berlin. On 22 October the Bavarian division was ordered to take a new oath of loyalty to the Bavarian government, a step to which General von Lossow agreed; his officers decided to stand unitedly behind him. There was now an open conflict between Berlin and Munich.

What the Bavarian nationalists and para-military associations now desired was the march into Saxony and Thuringia, and thence to

---

[34] All details are from a letter of the Munich police president Nortz to the public prosecutor Dresse of 23 May 1923: Hauptarchiv der NSDAP, NS. 26, no. 104, Bundesarchiv Koblenz.

Berlin, the proclamation of a new German government with dictatorial powers, a true national government in place of the Stresemann government which had betrayed the German interests. For this purpose the Bavarian division decided to enlist volunteers from the nationalist and para-military organizations: every regular battalion was to be supplemented by two, formed by their men. When addressing the nationalist leaders General von Lossow insisted that the only possibility was, not a separation of Bavaria from Germany, but 'the march to Berlin and the proclamation of the national dictatorship'; 'we all have only one aim, to liberate Germany from Marxism under the black, white and red banner'.[35] The order for the 'autumn manœuvres', according to which the units of the Bavarian division were to be trebled, was issued two days later, on 26 October. Everthing seemed to be set for the great event.

In Munich there was enormous enthusiasm for the nationalist cause when it became known that an open conflict existed between Munich and Berlin. The young officers and cadets of the infantry school, where all future infantry officers of the army were trained, 'showed a childish enthusiasm for Bavaria and the *völkisch* movement, sang the Ehrhardt song all the time, and adorned themselves with black, white and red cockades', the colours of the former Empire. The few young officers and cadets who remained loyal to their oath and refused to obey the orders of the Bavarian government were called by their comrades 'Red dogs who sympathize with the Jewish government', and 'traitors to the national cause'.[36]

The enthusiasm for the swastika and the black, white and red banner pervaded civilian circles. On the evening of 22 October Hitler addressed a mass meeting of the 'patriotic' associations. A young woman present at the meeting told her parents: 'You have no idea what silence reigned when this man spoke, as if the thousand listeners could not breathe any more; for minutes there are shouts of exultation in the hall when he full of wrath scourges the deeds of those who since the revolution have ruled our people, and of those who always prevented him and his followers from settling accounts with the November leaders. . . . Adolf Hitler is permeated by such a firm faith in the honesty of his nationalist convictions that he unwittingly transmits

---

[35] Ernst Deuerlein (ed.), *Der Hitler-Putsch*, Stuttgart, 1962, no. 61, p. 258; ibid., no. 68, pp. 277–80, the order of 26 October for the 'autumn manœuvres'.
[36] Lieutenant Leist to Lieutenant-Colonel von Hammerstein, 22 October 1923: *Vierteljahrshefte für Zeitgeschichte*, v, 1957, p. 95.

this faith to his listeners. God may grant that he prepare the way for better times and gather many comrades under the swastika. Every group is represented. Between workers and simple officials there sit officers, between stormtroopers students and old-age pensioners, all embracing the great idea that Hitler personifies for them. . . . Every human being, in the present troubles of his soul which coincide with the economic misery, seeks support and finds this support in a man who will not disappoint him: thus one can understand the fervour created by his appearance. . . .'[37] At about the same time the German Embassy in Bucharest reported that the Transylvanian students returning from Germany 'all carried their Adolf Hitler in their hearts'.

The November Putsch

In October the military preparations for the march to the north were proceeding apace. Ehrhardt with his men put himself at the disposal of the Bavarian government. His units were concentrated on the northern frontier in the area of Coburg, disguised as an emergency police to protect the Bavarian frontier against Communist attacks from Thuringia. Ehrhardt's units were armed by the Bavarian police and numbered about 1,200–1,500 men. Most of the other para-military associations did likewise and they arranged between them in which direction and by what routes they would advance northwards. But when weeks passed and the Bavarian government did not give the expected signal, dissatisfaction began to spread among their troops. The men felt that they were led by the nose, they urged that a decision must be taken, and increasingly blamed their own leaders for their passivity. Ehrhardt strongly complained that much valuable time was being lost and that the Bavarian government lacked the courage for decisive action.[38]

When the commander of the Bavarian police, Colonel von Seisser, went to Berlin to negotiate there with the army leaders and political friends Hitler told him that he would wait until the colonel's return, but then he must act: 'there is no more time. The economic misery drives our men so that either we must act, or our people will go over

[37] Anna to her parents, 22 October 1923: Hauptarchiv der NSDAP, NS. 26, no. 513, Bundesarchiv Koblenz.
[38] All details are from a declaration of Oberlandesgerichtsrat Ernst Pöhner of 9 December 1923: Hauptarchiv der NSDAP, NS. 26, no. 120.

to the Communists.' Lieutenant Brückner, the commander of the *S.A.* regiment Munich—a force that was now about 1,500 men strong—begged Hitler to strike soon, for 'we had many unemployed in the *S.A.*, men who had staked their last suit, their last pair of shoes, their last penny to be trained as soldiers': their misery must be brought to an end.[39] The uprooted former soldiers who swelled the ranks of the *S.A.* and other para-military units could not be held back any longer, at a time when the mark had become completely valueless, when there was mass unemployment and a severe economic crisis.

Colonel von Seisser, however, returned from Berlin at the beginning of November without any promise of help from the north-German army or nationalists, and it became more and more evident that the Bavarian government would not take any action without a promise of support, or without being pushed from outside. This is precisely what Hitler decided to do, trusting that this push would induce the hesitating Bavarian government to break with Berlin and to proclaim the 'national revolution'. This would then be carried to Berlin by the para-military units aided by the Bavarian army and police; a 'national government' would be formed under General Ludendorff, the hero of the first world war, in which the Bavarian leaders—Kahr, Seisser, Lossow—would sit side by side with Hitler and other nationalists; a 'national army' would replace the *Reichswehr*. The *S.A.* leaders all over Bavaria were informed and their units mobilized; so were the small National Socialist groups in other German towns. On 6 November *Generalstaatskommisar* von Kahr told the leaders of the para-military units that there were two ways of establishing a 'national dictatorship': the normal one was doubtful, but all preparations had been made for the abnormal one; action would begin when everything was ready, and *he* would give the orders.

On 7 November it became known in Munich that Kahr was going to address the assembled Munich notables in a large meeting at the Bürgerbräu the following evening. Was this to be the signal for the long-awaited event, or would it be postponed once more? In any case, Hitler decided to act. The Munich *S.A.* regiment received orders to surround the Bürgerbräu hall; units from inside and outside Munich —not only *S.A.*, but also from *Bund Oberland* and other para-military organizations—were to reinforce them and to occupy the public buildings. All were to receive weapons from the hidden arms depots.

[39] Quoted by Franz-Willing, op. cit., p. 136; Konrad Heiden, *Der Führer*, London, 1944, p. 149.

This plan was carried out. After Kahr had begun to address the over-crowded meeting the *S.A.* occupied the entrance to the hall, a machine gun was carried inside, an excited Hitler at the head of his faithful pushed his way through, jumped on a chair and fired a shot into the ceiling. The hall was occupied by his armed men. Kahr, Lossow and Seisser were asked to go with Hitler into the adjoining room where he outlined his programme to them: proclamation of a 'national government' under Hitler, with Ludendorff in charge of the army. Ludendorff was quickly fetched and added his entreaties to those of Hitler: 'Now we'll do it, Lossow.' The latter in correct military atti-tude replied: 'Your Excellency's wish is an order for me.' Seisser con-curred. The revolution was launched.

Other armed units occupied public buildings and strategic points. The *Reichskriegsflagge* under Röhm occupied the war ministry with-out encountering any resistance; guards were posted and the telephone service was maintained by its men in cooperation with the army. The cadets of the infantry school were summoned by the former Lieuten-ant Roßbach, a famous free corps leader, and marched to the Bürger-bräu under the swastika flag, where Hitler addressed them amidst wild scenes of enthusiasm. Meanwhile Lossow and Kahr had left the hall. Then three Bavarian generals, junior in rank to Lossow, and opposed to his constant wavering, succeeded in persuading their commanding general to change sides once more, against Hitler and his tactics of political blackmail. In the Bürgerbräu too, about midnight doubts began to arise as to the attitude of the *Reichswehr*, and Hitler sent an emissary, Major Siry, to Lossow to ascertain his course. But he was informed by Lossow, Kahr and Seisser that they considered a word of honour enforced at pistol point null and void. When he in-sisted that a battle between the army and the National Socialists must be avoided at all cost, Lossow replied: 'One does not negotiate with rebels.'[40] The emissary was put under arrest.

On the morning of 9 November recruiting bureaux of the National Socialists and other para-military units were opened in the various districts of Munich. Ministers and 'hostages' were arrested by the stormtroopers. Speakers addressed the crowds at street corners and found enthusiastic support. The expected reinforcements arrived from outside, but equally those of the army. One battalion commander reported to his superior officer that his unit stood ready 'enthusiastically

[40] Report by Major Siry on events of 8-9 November 1923, no date: Nachlass Traub, no. 9, Bundesarchiv Koblenz.

for the battle of liberation under Adolf Hitler'[41]; another unit was informed only on arrival that it had not been summoned to Munich for this purpose. The leaders in the Bürgerbräu decided in the course of the morning to march through the streets to rally the population. But at the Odeonsplatz in the centre of Munich the marchers met a police cordon, and when they refused to disband the police fired. Fifteen people were killed by the shots. Hitler was saved by the death of the man with whom he had walked arm in arm, for the other was shot through the heart and in falling pulled Hitler down. That was the end of the 'Hitler *Putsch*'. This term, however, is quite incorrect, for Hitler did not aim at power for himself, and not even for his party (which was much too weak outside Bavaria); he wanted to start the national revolution, in cooperation with the many other organizations which had the same aim, and with the Bavarian *Reichswehr* and police, exactly as Mussolini's *fasci* had marched on Rome together with the Nationalists and the help of the army. Even on 9 November the *S.A.* cooperated closely with the *Reichskriegsflagge*, the *Bund Oberland*, and similar units, and among the fifteen dead were several of their men, facts never mentioned in the later propaganda.

When the shooting became known there were violent demonstrations in Munich for Ludendorff and Hitler, and against Kahr. The university students demanded his resignation. 'Down with Kahr!' was the general slogan of the excited crowds.[42] Policemen and soldiers were attacked and spat at. In the elections of April 1924 the *Völkische Block* polled 105,000 votes in Munich and became the strongest local party. In the whole of Bavaria it received 512,000 votes, seventeen per cent of the votes cast. Hitler's spell was not broken by the failure of the *Putsch*.

During the preceding weeks Hitler and nine of his associates were tried by a Munich court for attempted treason. They were sentenced to short terms of 'honourable' detention; Ludendorff was acquitted; his drive home was a triumphal progress. At the trial Hitler was careful to preserve good relations with the army which he would need one day. 'When I heard that it was the police that had fired I had the happy feeling: at least it was not the army which has soiled its honour; the army stands as untarnished as before. One day the hour will come when

[41] Major-General von Unruh to Hitler, 11 November 1936: Hauptarchiv der NSDAP, NS. 26, no. 76, ibid.
[42] The student Rudolf Lechle to his parents, 14 November 1923: Hauptarchiv der NSDAP, NS. 26, no. 116, 32, ibid.

the *Reichswehr* will be on our side, officers and men. . . . One day the hour will come when these wild troops will grow to battalions, the battalions to regiments, the regiments to divisions, when the old cockade will be lifted from the mire, when the old flags will wave in front of us. . . .'[43] He was not burning his bridges.

What seems somewhat strange in these events is how Hitler, in spite of his low social origin, his wild manners and his lack of any constructive programme, could influence and sway not just the crowds, but middle-aged and experienced men, such as the judge of the Bavarian high court, Theodor von der Pfordten who was killed at the Odeonsplatz, or the generals Ludendorff and von Lossow. It was in vain that Ludendorff's confidant, the former Colonel Bauer, wrote to him a few days before the *Putsch*: 'What is lacking are capable leaders and unity. . . . But even men such as Hitler, Graefe, Wulle have no clear programme and are in addition unteachable. . . .' Three months earlier Bauer had sent a long report to Ludendorff from Vienna about the Austrian National Socialists and their relations with Munich which sounded an equally warning note. Bauer had just come from a meeting of the Austrian National Socialists at Salzburg which had been attended by 'quite a lot of people, the large majority youths of seventeen to nineteen years. . . . What I missed altogether were older, more sensible people and politicians. Of the decisions taken one is of special importance, that they do not want to take part in the coming elections in Austria. . . . The second decision, which seems more questionable, is that the Austrians are to accept the military-dictatorial leadership of Hitler. I discussed this at length with Captain Göring, the leader of Hitler's *S.A.* The impression which I received is quite exceptionally bad. In the first place I doubt very much whether he and his subordinates are capable of creating a militarily useful organization. Secondly, these people completely overestimate the strength of their own movement, and in particular forget entirely that it is madness today to undertake something which could not be countenanced by France. . . . In my opinion it must be stated clearly that the Austrian National Socialists come under Austrian orders in all purely Austrian matters, and it would only be natural if they remained under my orders as hitherto. For *German* matters, they would, of course, be available . . .'; but even for these Bauer refused to accept any orders from Hitler or

---

[43] Quoted by Heiden, op. cit., p. 167; Hofmann, *Der Hitlerputsch*, p. 255. Political offenders had to serve their sentences in a disused fortress where they enjoyed considerable privileges.

from Göring.[44] Yet Ludendorff refused to heed the warnings: it was only some years later that he finally broke with Hitler.

If Hitler could influence some very senior officers there is no doubt about the fascination which his appeal had for the young lieutenants and cadets, and for the soldiers of the world war. Their world had been the Hohenzollern Empire and the war, and that world had disappeared: as they believed, it had been destroyed by the November criminals. Hitler promised them vengeance, a national rebirth, a Germany strong and free, cleansed of all alien influence. In Italy this national appeal was powerful enough although Italy was one of the victorious powers: it was far stronger in a country that had been defeated and humiliated. Among Hitler's followers and supporters the number of soldiers and former soldiers was very large, and the Bavarian *Reichswehr* played a decisive part in his phenomenal rise. So did Bavarian particularism, the dislike of Berlin and of Marxism, the shock of the Munich Soviet Republic. But the pupil of political officers had outgrown his teachers. He was no longer content to be 'the drummer', the auxiliary of great generals and right-wing politicians; he was the leader of a mass party who could sway the crowds. The government which he proclaimed in the Bürgerbräu on 8 November 1923 was *his* government, in which Ludendorff was relegated to the post of minister of defence. The drummer had become the band-leader. At his trial in March 1924 Hitler proclaimed: 'Who is born to be a dictator is not pushed but he wills; he is not pressed forward, but pushes forward himself. . . . Who feels called upon to rule a nation has no right to say: If you want me or fetch me I work with you. It is his duty to do so. . . .'[45]

Mein Kampf

The months which Hitler spent in the fortress of Landsberg on the Lech—he was released on parole at the end of 1924—he used to dictate the first volume of *Mein Kampf* ('My Struggle'), a mixture of auto-biography and history of the National Socialist movement with an exposition of his ideology and bitter attacks on his many enemies. The first volume was significantly called 'a reckoning'; the second followed two years later. The work, in spite of its turgid language, bad style and

[44] Colonel Max Bauer to Ludendorff, 20 August and 7 November 1923: Nachlass Bauer, no. 81, Bundesarchiv Koblenz.
[45] Hofmann, op. cit., p. 254.

many repetitions, became the bible of National Socialism, a bible such as Italy did not possess. As Hitler's basic ideas remained unchanged throughout his later career, some of them might be mentioned here.

There is, in the first instance, Hitler's violent anti-Semitism which had meanwhile been reinforced by his reading of the *Protocols of the Elders of Zion*, the story of the alleged Jewish world conspiracy which was imported into Germany from Russia. 'How much the whole existence of this people rests on a continuous lie is demonstrated in an incomparable manner in the *Protocols of the Elders of Zion*, hated so infinitely by the Jews. They are said to be based on a falsification, the *Frankfurter Zeitung* time and again moans into the world: the best proof that they are genuine. What many Jews may do subconsciously that is here demonstrated consciously. But this is the point. It is quite immaterial from which Jewish head these revelations come; what matters is that they uncover the essence and the activity of the Jewish people with an almost horrid certainty and expose them in their inner connexions as well as their ultimate aims. . . .'[46] The most dreadful example of the Jew's lust for world domination was 'Russia, where he killed or let starve about thirty million people in truly fanatical ferocity and in part by inhuman torture, so as to secure to a gang of Jewish literati and stock exchange robbers the rule over a great nation. . . .' It is the Jews, too, 'who bring the negro to the Rhine, always with the same crooked design and clear aim of destroying through the bastardization which must result from it the white race hated by them, to hurl it from its cultural and political heights and to make themselves its masters. . . .'[47] The Jew's 'ultimate goal is the denationalization, the promiscuous bastardization of other peoples, the lowering of the racial level of the highest peoples, and the domination of this racial mish-mash through the extirpation of the *völkisch* intelligentsia. . . . Hence the result of Jewish domination is always the ruin of all culture and finally the madness of the Jew himself. For he is a parasite of nations, and his victory signifies his own end as much as the death of his victims. . . .'[48] This was a truly apocalyptic vision, a theme of ruin and destruction as it occurred in the Germanic sagas and the Wagnerian operas which Hitler loved so much.

This view equally influenced Hitler's ideas in the field of foreign

[46] Adolf Hitler, *Mein Kampf*, 97th ed., Munich, 1934, p. 337.
[47] Ibid., pp. 357–8.
[48] *Hitler's Secret Book*, New York, 1961, p. 213. This book was written in 1928, and published for the first time in 1961.

policy. To him, 'France is and remains by far the most horrible enemy. This nation, which is increasingly subject to negroization, is tied to the aims of Jewish world domination and thus presents a lurking danger to the existence of the white race of Europe. For the adulteration by negro blood on the Rhine in the heart of Europe corresponds as much to the sadistic and perverted desire for vengeance of this chauvinistic hereditary enemy of our people, as to the icy-cold deliberation of the Jew to start thus the bastardization of the European continent at its centre and to deprive the white race of the basis for a superior existence by infecting it with a lower humanity. . . . For Germany, however, the French danger means the obligation . . . to stretch out the hand to those who, equally threatened as we, do not want to suffer and to countenance France's lust for domination. In Europe there will within the foreseeable future only be two allies for Germany: England and Italy. . . .'[49]

The colonial and trade policy of the pre-war years should be abandoned in favour of a policy of territorial expansion, a policy as it had been pursued by the Teutonic Order and the German colonists of the Middle Ages. 'We start there where they stopped six centuries ago. We halt the eternal movement of the Germans to the south and west of Europe and direct our sight to the lands in the east. . . . But when we talk today about new land and soil in Europe we can think in the first place only of Russia and the states bordering upon it and subject to it. . . .', for Russia is 'ripe to collapse. . . . Germany will be a world power or she will cease to exist. . . .'[50] What was essential was the acquisition 'of sufficient living space for our people for the next hundred years', and this could be found 'only in the east'.[51] Within hardly more than a decade this policy would be carried out in practice, not only against Russia, but also against Czechoslovakia and Poland.

The leading German political parties, the Centre and the Social Democrats, were considered traitors by Hitler. The leaders of the Centre 'were fonder of any Pole, any Alsatian traitor and Francophile than they were of the German who did not want to join such a criminal organization. Under the pretext of representing Catholic interests this party even in peacetime lent a helping hand to harm and ruin the major bulwark of a real Christian world view, Germany, in all possible ways. . . .' The Social Democrats, too, 'betrayed and sold out Germanism

[49] *Mein Kampf*, pp. 704-5.
[50] Ibid., p. 742.
[51] *Hitler's Secret Book*, p. 145.

in the old Austria in the most shameless way at every opportunity
that offered itself. They always stood on the side of the enemies of our
people. The most important Czech arrogance always found its defender in the so-called German Social Democracy. Every oppressive
act against Germany had their approbation. . . .'[52] Needless to say,
Jews were the 'leaders of Social Democracy'; 'starting with the editor,
only Jews' wrote in the Socialist press. 'I took all the Social Democratic pamphlets I could lay my hands on and looked for the names of
their authors: Jews. I remembered the names of almost all their
leaders; they were for the largest part also members of the "chosen
people". . . '. [53] It was indeed all very simple, so simple that even the
slowest-witted German could be made to understand it. Complicated
political or economic developments were reduced to a magic formula,
to a conspiracy, to a devilish plan in which people could believe: they
became a matter of faith.

There were—then and later—many other nationalist parties and
organizations in Germany. They too were opposed to the Treaty of
Versailles and to the system of parliamentary democracy; they too
were—less violently than the National Socialists—anti-Semitic. Yet
they would never have been able to accomplish what Hitler did. Their
leaders were too bourgeois and too cautious, and so was their policy;
they could not fascinate the masses. Their members and voters came
from the middle and the lower middle classes, not from the working
class. Their programme in the field of foreign policy was almost exclusively the undoing of the Treaty of Versailles, the restoration of the
frontiers of 1914. Hitler was not only much more ambitious and much
more extremist. His *Raumpolitik* was by its very nature quite different
from the policy of the nationalists. He wanted to incorporate with
Germany wide areas in eastern Europe which were not inhabited by
Germans and to resettle them with Germans. He later did not hesitate
to sacrifice the existence of certain German minorities in eastern Europe
to his wider schemes and plans of power policy. His racial policy often
disregarded German interests, and the German minorities were
merely the convenient vehicles of this policy. Hitler did not only want
to remould the Germans, but the whole of Europe, in the image of
racial phantasies which knew no bounds.

[52] Ibid., pp. 57, 62.
[53] *Mein Kampf*, pp. 64–5.

4 | National Socialism: the Road to Power

Years of Reorganization

In the autumn of 1923 the German mark was stabilized; the inflation which had ruined Germany was at last brought under control. Stresemann, first as chancellor and later as foreign minister, rightly considered that the key to a recovery was the establishment of better relations with France, and he succeeded in bringing this about during the following years. In August 1924 the Dawes Plan was signed which for the first time regulated the vexed question of the German Reparations payments to France and other western powers. Soon the Ruhr and parts of the occupied Rhineland were evacuated by their armies. American loans began to flow into Germany, and her economic recovery was swift. The years 1925–28 were the heyday of the Weimar Republic; prosperity was restored and the parliamentary institutions seemed to be accepted by the majority of the electorate. Indeed, no observer of the political scene in 1928 could have prophesied that five years later Hitler would be in power and parliamentary democracy in ruins. While the *Völkische* and National Socialists still polled nearly two million votes or six and a half per cent of the total in May 1924, by December this was reduced to 900,000, and in May 1928 to 800,000 votes, a mere two and a half per cent of the votes cast in the country as a whole. The voting strength of the Communists equally declined, while that of the moderate parties increased.

While Hitler was imprisoned at Landsberg in 1924 the National Socialist movement went through a severe crisis, the aftermath of the defeat of November 1923. In many parts of Germany the National Socialist Party was dissolved by the authorities after the *Putsch*. General Ludendorff, advised by Hitler's former lieutenant Gregor

Strasser, now wanted to amalgamate the party with the north German *Deutschvölkische Freiheitspartei*, led by von Graefe, an extreme right-wing politician. As on previous occasions Hitler opposed any merger, but demanded that he be the sole leader of the new party and that the National Socialist programme be accepted by it. In June 1924 he resigned the leadership of his party as he did not want to engage in politics during his imprisonment, and desired to delay all decisions until he had been released. In August the National Socialists held a conference at Weimar which led to open clashes between the rival factions so that Ludendorff left the hall in disgust. Some of the leaders favoured a union with the *Deutschvölkische Freiheitspartei*, while some hotly opposed it, and still others only advocated it provided that Hitler remained the undisputed leader. In the end Esser and Streicher founded a rival party, the *Großdeutsche Volksgemeinschaft* ('Pan-German People's Community'), which openly opposed the united *völkisch* party and remained absolutely loyal to the silent Hitler. Röhm, released from prison, attempted to unite the paramilitary associations and the *S.A.* in yet another organization, the *Frontbann*, which was to remain outside these faction struggles and to become the nucleus of the new movement. Röhm alone was to be responsible for the organization and leadership of the *Frontbann*, but in political matters it was to accept Hitler's guidance. Other National Socialist leaders bitterly opposed the new venture. Röhm always believed in the 'primacy of the soldier' who should occupy the place above the politician in a movement which aimed at the seizure of power[1]—an idea that was anathema to Hitler. Clearly, the events of 1923 had reinforced Röhm's ingrained suspicion of all politicians; he was willing to recognize Hitler as 'a reliable comrade', but demanded the right to oppose him when he disagreed with him.[2]

The year 1924 presented a picture of severe crisis and disintegration in the *völkisch* camp. But a nucleus loyal to Hitler survived, especially in Bavaria. At the end of the year there were sixty members at Berchtesgaden, fifty-five at Traunstein, forty-eight at Freilassing, and twenty-five at Brannenburg, all small places in Upper Bavaria. Among these 188 faithful a large percentage—over twenty-five—were employees and officials of the government, the railways and the post office. The remainder were drawn from a large variety of occupations, among which only the tradesmen (*Kaufleute*) formed a group of about

[1] Ernst Röhm, *Die Geschichte eines Hochverräters*, 7th ed., Munich, 1934, p. 349.
[2] Ibid., 1st ed., Munich, 1928, p. 297.

twelve per cent.[3] Between the small *völkisch* groups there were bitter conflicts, for example at Magdeburg between the *Deutschvölkische Freiheitspartei* and the *Großdeutsche Volksgemeinschaft*, in which the 'Germanic Order' also became involved; the commander of the garrison, Colonel Etzel, remained loyal to the National Socialists.[4] A similar struggle was waged at Bremen. Ehrhardt and the officers of his Brigade, on the other hand, were bitterly disappointed by the events of November 1923. One of them, Friedrich Wilhelm Heinz, sharply criticized the inept leadership of Hitler and Ludendorff and declared in a meeting at Frankfurt it would have been better if they had been shot at the Odeonsplatz; thereupon a dozen of the faithful left the hall as a sign of protest. In Frankfurt too the movement was now completely 'leaderless'.[5] The breach between Ehrhardt and Hitler was never healed.

After Hitler had been released from Landsberg the National Socialist Party was refounded early in 1925. Once more he addressed his followers in the Bürgerbräu cellar: 'To make a struggle intelligible to the broad masses, it must always be carried on against two things, against a person and against a cause. Against whom did England fight? Against the German Emperor as a person, and against militarism as a cause. Against whom do the Jews fight with their Marxist power? Against the *bourgeoisie* as a person, and against capitalism as a cause. Against whom, therefore, must our movement fight? Against the Jew as a person, and against Marxism as a cause. . . .'[6] He considered it necessary for psychological reasons to have only one enemy, the Jews; his opinion had not changed. He insisted that his orders must be obeyed unconditionally and that the regional leaders must be appointed by him. He rejected Röhm's plan of the formation of the *Frontbann* and demanded that it be incorporated into the National Socialist Party so that he would be entitled to dismiss obnoxious leaders. Thereupon Röhm offered his resignation to Hitler, but did not receive any reply. A break between the two men resulted which was to last for several years. The *S.A.* was reformed according to Hitler's plan, but was unreliable and disunited;

---

[3] The complete membership lists of these four groups are in Hauptarchiv der NSDAP, NS. 26, no. 88, Bundesarchiv Koblenz. They show roughly the same social picture as the Munich members' list of 1919, discussed above, p. 94.

[4] The above according to the recollections of former Lieutenant Karl Georg Peters of 1940: ibid., no. 514.

[5] This according to the recollections of Otto Schroeder of 1937: ibid., no. 528.

[6] Quoted by Heiden, op. cit., p. 207.

a personal bodyguard was thus formed to protect Hitler. It wore black uniforms and soon became the *S.S.* ('Security Guards'); it remained a small force.

Hitler was forbidden to speak in most parts of Germany, and few local leaders were available to organize the movement according to his wishes; nor was Hitler's authority recognized by them all. In March 1925 Gregor Strasser was appointed the party's leader in northern Germany; as he had used the months during which Hitler was imprisoned to create a party organization in the north and to unite the different splinter groups, his appointment was largely a recognition of the existing situation. Therefore, Strasser's position in the north was virtually autonomous. Helped by his more radical brother Otto, he built up his own organization, founded newspapers, and appointed local leaders. Often these were the leaders of existing *völkisch* groups which now merged with the National Socialists; in other cases, the leaders were elected or confirmed by the party members. The programme of the Strasser wing was vague, but in a sense it was more socialist than Hitler's—or rather it tried to go back to the original socialist demands of the Twenty-Five Points, which the party leaders in Munich no longer took very seriously. A programme drafted in the autumn of 1925 envisaged that the large estates were to be divided into peasant farms of 30–120 acres; these were to be granted to peasants in the form of a hereditary lease by the Reich government; the estate owners were to be allowed to retain 600 acres, also in the form of a hereditary lease; any alienation, sale or mortgaging of these properties was to be prohibited. The Reich government was to acquire shares to the value of thirty per cent in large industrial undertakings, and the employees another ten per cent; a further nine to eleven per cent was to be vested in public authorities, but the administration and leadership were to remain entirely private. Small enterprises, employing fewer than twenty workers, were to be grouped in compulsory guilds. It was also envisaged that the employees were to receive their wages 'to a large extent in kind'.[7] The clauses about the compulsory guilds and payments in kind show how hopelessly utopian this economic programme was, and how far removed from true socialism. Even in later years, after his expulsion from the National Socialist Party, Otto Strasser continued to preach a 'Germanic Socialism', based on hereditary leaseholds and guilds.

[7] The Strasser programme is published by R. Kühnl in the *Vierteljahrshefte für Zeitgeschichte*, xiv, 1966, pp. 324–33.

In the field of foreign policy the Strasser programme demanded the restoration of the frontiers of 1914, the uniting of all the Germans of central Europe in one Great German Reich (including Austria, South Tyrol and the Sudetenland), and a colonial empire in central Africa which was to be carved from Belgian, French and Portuguese colonies. But some of the Strasser papers sponsored the rights of the young nations against the capitalist west; and some of their followers dreamt of an alliance with Soviet Russia, to wage the war of liberation against the Treaty of Versailles. One of Strasser's ardent supporters was the young Dr Joseph Goebbels, then a party functionary in his native Rhineland, where conditions were vastly different from those in rural Bavaria. Goebbels believed that Strasser was 'ready for any radicalization of the idea' and wanted to use him as 'our battering ram against the party bosses in Munich', whom Goebbels considered senile (*verkalkt*). He was looking forward to the struggle which was bound to ensue between them and the younger generation. The radicals held that the socialist liberation must come first, and the national liberation would then follow 'like a storm'. This was 'a question of the generations. Old or young! Evolution or revolution! Social or socialist! For us the choice is not difficult.' As to Hitler, he was wavering, but would, so Goebbels hoped, join the younger group.[8]

In November 1925 Strasser called together the north German party leaders at Hanover and explained to them his basic ideas. Goebbels and another local leader were given the task of working out a more detailed programme. In the eyes of Hitler these steps amounted to an open revolt. In January 1926 Goebbels wrote in one of the Strasser papers: 'We do not achieve anything if we defend the interests of property and education. We achieve everything if we mobilize hunger, despair and sacrifice for our aims. . . . I believe in the socialism of the proletariat.'[9] He considered the continuous clashes between National Socialists and Communists 'terrible' and planned to meet leading Communists. One of his close associates, Karl Kaufmann, the later *Gauleiter* of Hamburg, declared in replying to a Communist that, if Germany signed a pact with the western powers, 'the N.S.D.A.P. would fight shoulder to shoulder with the K.P.D. against the social-democratic crooks'. Another west German party leader, the teacher Bernhard Rust, proclaimed that he 'had more sympathy with the

[8] *Das Tagebuch von Joseph Goebbels 1925–26*, ed. Helmut Heiber, Stuttgart, 1961, pp. 27, 30 (11 and 30 September 1925).
[9] Ibid., p. 53, n. 1.

Communists than with any Social Democrats or the so-called black, white and red leaders of Germany'.[10] The *NS-Briefe* ('National Socialist Letters') which Goebbels edited served as a rallying point for the radicals and anti-conservatives among the National Socialists, but also—as Goebbels put it—as 'a weapon against the senile bureaucrats in Munich'.[11]

The issue on which the fight with Munich was joined aroused strong political passions in the Germany of that time: whether the former ruling houses—the Hohenzollerns, Wittelsbachs, etc.—should be paid vast sums in compensation for the rights and properties which they had lost, or should be expropriated. The political Left, Social Democrats and Communists, strongly agitated for their expropriation without any compensation. The bourgeois parties and the government equally strongly opposed this as an interference with the right of property; hence the Left moved for a referendum which left the decision to the voters. The Strasser papers and the radical north German leaders, loyal to their principle of siding with the working class, came out in support of the referendum, but Hitler denounced it as a 'Jewish swindle'. In his opinion, the National Socialists must defend private property, for otherwise how could they hope to win over the farmers and artisans, the white-collar workers and lower grade civil servants who were frightened by the spectre of Communism? Two years later he took special pains to explain away the seventeenth point of the party programme, which demanded the expropriation of land without any compensation 'for communal purposes', by declaring that it was, above all, directed against Jewish land speculation.

On 25 January 1926 Strasser once more assembled the north German party leaders at Hanover to gain their support for a more outspoken socialist line and for the referendum against the former ruling houses. Hitler sent Gottfried Feder to protest against this move and to enjoin party discipline. But all the north German leaders present, except only Robert Ley from Cologne, sided with Strasser and expressed their confidence in him. One of them was then sent to Munich to explain there the different conditions of the industrial areas of the north, where anti-capitalism had a real meaning. Hitler countered these moves by summoning a conference of all the party leaders to Bamberg in Bavaria, where he would be certain of much stronger support. Goebbels still hoped that Hitler could be lured on to a more socialist platform: his native Elberfeld was to 'become the Mecca of German Socialism', he wrote, and 'nobody believes any longer in Munich'. At Bamberg on 14 February Hitler spoke for several hours: Germany's task was the destruction of Bolshevism, which was a Jewish invention, and Italy and Britain were her natural allies. With regard to the main current issue, the compensation of the former princes, he emphasized that the right of property must not be undermined; right must remain right, and that of the princes too. Esser, Feder, Ley and Streicher agreed. Strasser spoke badly and hesitatingly in the discussion which was very brief. Goebbels considered Hitler's views 'ghastly' and 'horrible'— he himself desired an anti-capitalist alliance with Soviet Russia—but did not speak.[12] The meeting ended in a complete victory for Hitler and his cautious policy. It was the last time that there was an open discussion of principles within the party. Henceforth there was only one policy, that of the Leader.

During the same month, February 1926, Hitler addressed in a private meeting the leaders of trade and industry at Hamburg, men who stood politically on the Right but were not inclined to any extremist views. Hitler's theme was the rebirth of Germany as a strong power: this could only be achieved by the extirpation of Marxism; if this was not accomplished the country could not recover, as little as a human being could be made healthy if it was not healed from tuberculosis. It had been the same in Italy; there the problem had been solved, 'not thanks to the genius of one man who realized the danger, but thanks to the understanding of that part of the Italian nation which learned that any flowering of the economy, trade, etc. is ridiculous as long as this poison prevails'; that was the question which was decisive for the future of Germany, too. The Jews and anti-Semitism were never mentioned throughout the speech. Hitler was always able to adapt himself to his audience. To these leaders of trade and industry he also made one admission which was psychologically highly significant: 'The cuirassier Bismarck was venerated. Why? The broad masses love the man because they are feminine; they want to be led, and do not want to have someone leading them who says: perhaps it can be done this way, perhaps that way, perhaps one can do it differently too.

[12] Ibid., pp. 59–60 (11 and 15 February 1926).

The masses desire the man with the cuirassier boots who says: this is the right way!'[13]

The victory gained at Bamberg in February was consummated in May. A general meeting of the party members—similar to that of July 1921 which had given Hitler control of the Munich party—declared the Twenty-Five Points immutable and adopted new statutes. The Munich local group was declared the 'bearer' of the party, and its leadership *eo ipso* identical with that of the whole party. The first chairman of the party—Hitler—was indeed elected, but only by the members of the Munich group where his personal influence was paramount. Once elected he had dictatorial powers to appoint and dismiss the party's provincial leaders, the *Gauleiter*, as well as the chairmen of its main committees (for propaganda, organization, internal investigations, etc.). The latter, together with the first chairman, the secretary and the treasurer, formed the central party committee. As most of its members were appointed and dismissed by the first chairman, his will in effect prevailed throughout the organization, to a much larger extent than did Mussolini's during the early years of Fascism. The first chairman was not bound by any majority decisions, not even of the Munich local party; he had the final decision in cases of expulsion and dissolution of party branches. It was a completely centralist structure, obedient to Hitler's will. Since July 1921 it had been law in the Munich party—now this system was transferred to the whole of Germany. It was significant too that Germany was treated as if it were a mere dependency of Munich, the 'capital of the movement', and the Munich party as identical with the party as a whole. Within fifteen months of his release from prison Hitler had staged a magnificent come-back. In future no one was to doubt that he was the undisputed leader of the party.

One local leader who recognized this even before the May meeting was Joseph Goebbels, who had remained strangely silent at Bamberg in February but still wrote about the Munich 'swine'. In April he visited Munich and met Hitler several times. The result was a complete conversion to Hitler's ideas on collectivism and individualism, the land question and nationalization, which was to be limited to certain trusts and fields, such as transport. Goebbels' doubts were allayed. He was willing to recognize Hitler's 'political genius'. 'Adolf Hitler, I love you because you are great and simple at the same time', he con-

[13] Quoted by Werner Jochmann, *Im Kampf um die Macht*, Frankfurt, 1960, pp. 101–4, 110–11.

fided to his diary. Soon there was even more fulsome praise: 'He is a genius, the automatically creative instrument of a divine fate. I stand before him deeply shaken. Thus he is: like a child, dear, good, merciful; like a cat, cunning, clever and astute; like a lion, roaring, great and gigantic.'[14] The reward soon came. In the autumn of 1926 Goebbels was appointed *Gauleiter* of Greater Berlin. There, at the political centre of the Strasser brothers, he would be able to counteract the political influence of his former allies whom he had deserted.

In Berlin at that time violent conflicts were raging not only between the followers and opponents of Strasser, but also between the leaders of the party, of the *S.A.*, and of the local districts. Their meetings led to heated discussions, which often became purely personal, and blows were exchanged between the rival factions. The local leaders disregarded all orders from the *Gauleiter* and the party's work suffered severely. All this Goebbels was to remedy; above all, he was to carry the party propaganda to the Berlin workers who hitherto had not been influenced by it; the capital was to be 'conquered' by the brown battalions. The mistake of 1923, to try to conquer it from Munich, was not to be repeated. The fortress must be taken from inside.

In Austria too, Hitler's influence grew after his release from Landsberg. Many local groups acclaimed him and joined the movement directed from Munich. Thus for some time there were two organizations: the older, more independent one which had been led by Dr Riehl and was—after his resignation—led by Karl Schulz, and another one which recognized Hitler as the Leader. In 1926 a conference of Austrian National Socialists was held at Passau, with Hitler as the chairman; there the majority accepted his unconditional leadership and the Twenty-Five Points as the party programme, now declared immutable. Hitler then appointed Friedrich Jancovic, a retired colonel, as leader of the Austrian National Socialists and ordered a purge of those still favouring autonomy for the Austrian party. In effect, it soon was controlled by Hitler like any party unit in Germany, while it continued to have its own party directorate, first in Vienna, later at Linz. The German party structure was copied in Austria, with local leaders on the *Kreis* and *Orts* levels, and with the special formations of the Hitler Youth, the *S.A.* and the *S.S.* Those who favoured Austrian autonomy within the party were either expelled or forced to resign. Hitler was now in complete control, and his party

[14] *Das Tagebuch von Joseph Goebbels 1925–26*, pp. 72, 74 (13 and 19 April 1926); p. 92 (24 July 1926).

was no longer limited to Bavaria, but was beginning to strike root all over Germany and Austria.

It was still a small party, but it was growing. There were 27,000 members in 1925, 49,000 in 1926, 72,000 in 1927, and 108,000 in 1928. It was thus able to gain new members at a time of growing economic prosperity, at a time too when it did not gain any new votes in elections. If this seems rather strange the explanation is partly that the National Socialists during these years succeeded in absorbing most of the many racist and *völkisch* groups that had existed in Germany for decades, including some of their prominent leaders, Theodor Fritsch and Count Reventlow. Many of the older party members later recorded proudly that before they joined they had been members of Fritsch's Hammer League, of the *Deutschvölkischer Schutz- und Trutzbund*, of the *Deutschvölkische Freiheitspartei*, or of a *völkisch* gymnastic club. In spite—or because—of this, the line separating the National Socialists from the *Völkische* was emphasized more strongly than before, and even violence was used against the latter. When their leader von Graefe, an old associate of Hitler, addressed a meeting at Frankfurt an explosive charge was hurled through the air, a terrific noise set in, and the police had to clear the hall. The National Socialists had achieved their aim: to prevent the meeting of their 'dangerous' *völkisch* rivals from taking place.[15]

Many others who joined the party during these early years had been members of a free corps, of *Oberland*, of *Wiking*, or another paramilitary organization. Indeed, in a limited sample of 124 members who joined between 1925 and 1927 forty-four per cent had belonged to a free corps or a para-military organization. Many who joined were extremely young, schoolboys, students, etc. These youngsters and the former soldiers were attracted by the dynamism of the movement, by its fanaticism and rejection of any compromise, the untold opportunities for 'heroic' deeds, the constant clashes with political enemies. During these years it was not the party organization but rather the *S.A.*, the party's strong arm, that was characteristic of the movement as a whole.

In the person of Franz Pfeffer von Salomon, a former captain and free corps leader in Westphalia and the Baltic countries, a participant in the Kapp *Putsch* and the sabotage actions in the Ruhr, the *S.A.* received a new forceful leader who personified these traits, especially the ten-

[15] Proudly related in 1937 by a National Socialist deputy, Adalbert Gimbel: Hauptarchiv der NSDAP, NS. 26, no. 532, Bundesarchiv Koblenz.

dency to beat the political adversaries by breaking up their meetings and by conquering the streets. His hatred was directed against the Weimar Republic which in his opinion had destroyed a more beautiful and better past and the glory of the soldier. Under him, the *S.A.* was trained to dominate the streets; 'the street was our trench', as one of his comrades put it later.[16] Thus the ideology of the world war, of the trenches, was transferred to the battles of the *S.A.*, and youngsters who had been schoolboys during the war could show their mettle together with the 'front soldiers'. 'Without youth nothing can be organized, not even the distribution of leaflets', a leader of the *Deutschvölkische* in Hamburg confided to one of the local National Socialists.[17]

At this time, too, the *S.A.* received—instead of the windcheaters it had worn in common with other para-military organizations—its distinctive uniform: brown shirts, brown trousers, and brown caps, a dress inspired by the Fascist Black Shirts. In place of the military salute the *S.A.* adopted the Fascist salute with the outstretched right arm. Instead of the military units into which the *S.A.* had been divided in Munich (companies, battalions, etc.), the *Sturm* ('Storm') became the basic unit. All these were signs that the line separating the *S.A.* from the para-military organizations was to be drawn much more sharply, that it was to be the strong arm of a political party, and not to enjoy any autonomy as it had done under Göring and Röhm; for under them the *S.A.* only too often had cooperated with organizations whose aims were akin to those of the National Socialists.

Hitler wanted, above all, to emphasize the dividing line, to make his movement the dominant factor among the welter of *völkisch* and extreme right-wing groups and parties, and to push his rivals to the wall. As he expressed it himself in an open letter to von Graefe in 1926: 'I was once the drummer and will be the same in the future; but I shall drum only for Germany, and not for you and your likes, so help me God!'[18] The experience of Munich, where Hitler had closely cooperated with Ludendorff and other extreme right-wing leaders, was not to be repeated. For most of the members and leaders of the National Socialists in northern and western Germany, on the other hand, the party represented a continuation of the old anti-Semitic and *völkisch* groups of which they or their parents had been members: for Hitler probably another reason to underline the difference. The members

[16] Recollections of Paul Then of 1937, relating to Crefeld in the Rhineland: ibid.
[17] Albert Krebs, *Tendenzen und Gestalten der NSDAP*, Stuttgart, 1959, p. 43.
[18] *Völkischer Beobachter*, 19 March 1926.

came largely from the lowest groups of the middle classes—artisans, tradesmen, lowest-grade civil servants, white-collar employees—and felt threatened alike by the development of capitalism and of the working-class movement. The middle classes proper were almost totally absent, as were the industrial workers.[19]

In September 1926 the new *Gauleiter* of Berlin, Dr Goebbels, wrote: 'We do not believe and shall never believe in a union, a combination of groups which more or less agree on this or that, but we believe that the strongest will prevail. . . . The problem of Germany is not the union of the nationalists, but destruction of Marxism and thus the fulfilment of nationalism. The new nationalism will be formed by the workers, by the youngest Germans. It will be socialist, or it will never be. There is no question of union. There is only fight, until the one triumphs and the other lies smashed in the dust. . . .'[20] The new *Gauleiter* was as self-confident as his Leader; but in 1926 there were few indications that their self-confidence was justified. Yet the fast progress of the party during the economic crisis of the 1930s would have been impossible without the patient spade-work of the mid-1920s.

The Gathering Storm

The general election of 1928—held at the height of post-war prosperity—brought a significant victory to the moderate and republican parties. The leading republican party, the Social Democrats, polled over nine million, the Catholic Centre three and three-quarter million, and the two liberal parties more than four million votes. Together these four parties received fifty-five per cent of the votes cast, which gave to the 'Great Coalition' under a Social Democratic chancellor a safe majority in parliament. The right-wing opposition was severely reduced: the Nationalists to fourteen and the National Socialists to two-and-a-half per cent of the votes cast, together 5·2 million votes. This irreconcilable opposition to the republic further included the Communists whose vote amounted to three and a quarter million votes, or more than ten per cent of the total. In retrospect it seems symptomatic that even at the height of prosperity twenty-seven per

[19] This is the analysis of the former Hamburg *Gauleiter* Albert Krebs, op. cit., p. 41. It was equally true of Berlin and other large north-German towns.
[20] Article in *Nationalsozialistische Briefe*, 1 September 1926.

cent of the voters thus expressed their rejection of the Weimar Republic. Also symptomatic was the very large number of parties which participated in the election without being able to gain a significant share of the votes, e.g. an Economic party, an Agrarian party, two Peasant parties, a Hanoverian party, etc. This abundance of parties— under a system of proportional representation—and the resulting 'horse-trading' invited much criticism in a country which had no real tradition of parliamentary government.

The giant among the parties was the Social Democratic Party; but its electorate was almost purely working-class and it lacked any dynamic leaders. Most of them were of working-class origin, honest, hard-working, loyal to the republic and to democracy, but with a very limited horizon, middle-aged, unable to take any big decisions or to arouse any enthusiasm, even among their own followers. The same was true of the other moderate parties: not a single statesman emerged during the whole history of the Weimar Republic, capable of steering a firm course through troubled waters, or of inspiring the youth of the country with democratic ideals. On the contrary, it is remarkable to what extent the middle classes and the intellectuals remained alienated from, and hostile to, the republican régime, either hankering after the glory of the Hohenzollern monarchy, or in some cases, criticizing it from the Left. In the secondary schools the young were educated not in the spirit of democracy, but in—at best—complete indifference towards it, of bitter hostility to France, the hereditary foe, to the Treaty of Versailles and the system it had established in Europe. And that was at a time when Gustav Stresemann followed a policy of reconciliation with France and led Germany into the League of Nations and to Locarno. Not even the fact that, since 1925, the former commander-in-chief, Field-Marshal Paul von Hindenburg, was the president of the republic did bring about a reconciliation of the middle and lower middle classes with the new order. They disliked the 'upstart' Social Democrats who dominated the government of Prussia and, at times, that of Germany, and they feared the working classes, although the Social Democrats were moderate enough and the Communists no longer a serious danger.

There was so little that was attractive about the Weimar Republic and its pedestrian leaders. A number of corruption scandals, in which Jewish financiers—Barmat or the Sklarek brothers—were involved, did not make it more attractive. Although these were isolated cases, they became—in the eyes of the republic's enemies—symbols of a

picture of general corruption in higher circles. They were also immediately exploited by these enemies. When the mayor of Berlin, who had
accepted presents from the Sklareks, returned to the city from an
official journey he was received by a howling mob that had been mobilized by the National Socialists, and soon after he was forced to resign.
Cases such as these provided the National Socialists—and the Communists—with live ammunition for their attacks on the 'system' of
Weimar, on the *Bonzen* ('bosses') enriching themselves at the expense
of honest workers, on the Jews and profiteers fattening on the country.
Much more effective during the years of prosperity, however, was the
propaganda spread by the big right-wing newspaper concerns—
especially the Scherl publishing house, which owned hundreds of
small provincial papers—and by hundreds of 'patriotic' clubs and
ex-servicemen's associations against the republic and its institutions,
against reconciliation with France, and for a strong revived Germany
that would break the 'shackles of Versailles'.

This vicious and systematic propaganda reached many millions and
made them susceptible to National Socialist slogans. It fulminated
against the foreign policy of Stresemann and subjected him and other
leading politicians to constant personal attacks: a factor that contributed to his untimely death in October 1929. A violent nationalism
soon engulfed much of Germany, a nationalism bitterly hostile to
other nations and races, and to any creed of pacifism or internationalism.
This nationalism, endemic in Germany since the days before the world
war, had grown tremendously on account of the military defeat and
the onerous conditions of Versailles: it did not abate later although
Germany was again an important power and played a leading part in
the League of Nations and in international politics. It was certainly a
major factor in the rise of National Socialism. Another was the widespread contempt of parliament, commonly referred to as the *Quassel-
bude* ('twaddling shop'), and of the ministers and deputies. On all
these issues National Socialist propaganda only differed in degree, but
not in principle, from that of the Nationalists, and could reckon with
support among large sections of the population.

This was also demonstrated in the course of 1929 when the German
government accepted the Young Plan which obliged Germany to pay
Reparations to its former enemies for another fifty-eight years but
lifted some of the restrictions of the earlier Dawes Plan. Against this
settlement the Nationalist leader Alfred Hugenberg, who was also the
head of the Scherl publishing house, launched a violent campaign.

A national committee was formed which was joined by the leaders of the *Stahlhelm*, the large nationalist ex-servicemen's organization, by Dr Schacht, the president of the central bank, and by Adolf Hitler. The committee drafted a law 'against the Enslavement of the German People', which repudiated any payments to foreign powers based on the provisions of the Treaty of Versailles and threatened any minister signing such a treaty with the penalty of treason. This bill, in the form of a popular initiative, was signed by 4,135,000 voters, just over ten per cent of those entitled to vote, but rejected by parliament. As the bill had received over ten per cent of the vote, it had to be submitted to a referendum; in December 1929 5,839,000 voters supported the referendum, about fourteen per cent of the electorate, a few hundred thousand more than had voted for the two extreme right-wing parties in the previous year. This showed how many Germans could be moved by a purely irrational nationalism, the chief aim of which was to discredit Germany's foreign policy and to dishonour the members of the government. Above all, the campaign for the first time provided Hitler with a national platform. Every speech of his was carried prominently by the Hugenberg press; he was provided with ample funds by his allies and attracted the attention of many millions. 'The unknown lance-corporal' of the world war became a figure on the national stage, and his power of vituperation proved highly superior to that of his colleagues. Some Ruhr industrialists, such as Kirdorf and Thyssen, now made large contributions to the party funds.

Certain local issues were exploited with the same vigour, and often with considerable success. In Schleswig and Holstein, in the extreme north, the peasants were hit hard by competition and economic changes; many got into debt, and cattle or stock were often seized by the authorities on account of accumulated debts or tax arrears. In 1928 a tax strike started among the peasants of certain districts, especially on the west coast. This soon became a radical opposition movement, a widespread refusal to pay taxes from the 'substance' of the farm, a dogged determination to prevent seizures and compulsory sales by the authorities. Activists from many parts of Germany—members of the dissolved Ehrhardt Brigade and other free corps prominent among them—flocked to the area. Under their guidance primitive bombs were manufactured and used against official buildings. Violent demonstrations were organized and seizures prevented by force. In 1929 many peasants and several of the leaders were arrested and tried, but the authorities were for some time unable to suppress the movement.

This was directed against the parties and the régime as such—a movement of exasperated farmers as they have occurred in many European countries—and ideologically it had close links with National Socialism, but it was not controlled by them. When it collapsed the National Socialists became its heirs, for the traditional conservative and agrarian organizations had been very much weakened; a radicalism gained ground which could easily be directed into National Socialist channels. In this area as well as in Lower Saxony the National Socialists, long before 1933, achieved a dominant position in the countryside. In April 1932 Goebbels noted: 'In Schleswig-Holstein we alone play the tune. This province is already in our possession.'[21]

If in this case the National Socialists were able to use very real grievances of the peasants, they did not hesitate either to revive for propaganda purposes the tale of Jewish ritual murder. When in a village near Würzburg a small boy was found murdered in 1929 this propaganda assumed such proportions that a mass meeting was organized in Würzburg to counter it. It was to be addressed by a clergyman, a rabbi, a university professor, the mayor of the town and left-wing leaders. But they were prevented from speaking by the local *S.A.* who shouted 'hear, hear' after every word and sang their battle songs until the police closed the meeting.[22] In near-by Nuremberg the *Gauleiter* of Franconia, Julius Streicher, edited the *Stürmer* ('The Attacker') which soon gained fame by its vitriolic assaults on the Jews and their alleged sexual crimes. The many volumes of correspondence addressed to the paper bear witness how many Germans took it seriously, and believed at least partly in its veracity.[23] A new line of propaganda was developed by the Berlin *Gauleiter*, Dr Goebbels, when the American film 'All Quiet on the Western Front'—based on the famous novel by Erich Maria Remarque—was shown publicly in 1930 after certain cuts had been made at the request of the military authorities. To prevent the performances Goebbels and his youthful disciples not only molested people in the audience but let loose white mice to cause panic in the cinema. The authorities capitulated, and the Highest Board of Film Censors revoked the permission for a public showing of the film.

Within the party Hitler's authority was increasing, and the remnants of local autonomy were eliminated. What had been meetings to discuss

[21] Joseph Goebbels, *Vom Kaiserhof zur Reichskanzlei*, Munich, 1934, p. 80.
[22] Proudly related in 1937 by the *S.S. Standartenführer* N. Scharf: Hauptarchiv der NSDAP, NS. 26, no. 530, Bundesarchiv Koblenz.
[23] The correspondence is preserved in the Streicher papers, ibid.

political and propaganda issues became summonses where orders were given out. Decisions were no longer taken by vote—as had been the practice in earlier years—but from above. If previously the local functionaries had been elected by the members, this too came to an end; local as well as regional leaders were now appointed from Munich. In 1929, for example, the Hamburg *Gauleiter* was removed and replaced by Karl Kaufmann by an order from the centre, as Goebbels had been moved to Berlin three years earlier. Occasionally, meetings of the top leaders were held to discuss certain important questions, but no proper discussions took place. As a participant in such a meeting held at Munich in October 1928 recollects, most of those present simply waited for a decision by Hitler; but he 'pulled a bored or mocking face; he spoke only very seldom. It was quite clear that his opinion of the "twaddle" was very low, and thus he achieved after a time that a paralysing apathy reigned among the participants.'[24] There was no longer anyone inside the party who disputed Hitler's unlimited authority. Even Gregor Strasser accepted it for the time being and became, as the chief of the central office of organization, one of the party's most influential leaders. His brother Otto, who continued to adhere to a Germanic form of Socialism, was forced to leave the party with a handful of adherents, to form a splinter group, the 'Black Front'. To one of the doubters Hitler shouted in 1930: 'What is Socialism? A Jewish invention to set the German people by the ears!'[25] And in the *Sunday Express* he wrote at about the same time: 'Our adopted term "Socialist" has nothing to do with Marxian Socialism. Marxism is anti-property; true Socialism is not.'[26]

Yet to the party members, especially in the large towns, anti-capitalism was not just a slogan devoid of any meaning. As the former *Gauleiter* of Hamburg reports, 'any attack on capitalism and plutocracy found the strongest echo among the local functionaries with their lower middle-class origin'.[27] This applied even more strongly to the unemployed who began to join the movement in large numbers, and to the 'German proletarians under the red storm banner', to whom Dr Goebbels appealed in Berlin. Many young students and young army officers were particularly attracted by the mixture of nationalism and socialism for which the National Socialists stood. They were

[24] Krebs, op. cit., pp. 131–2.
[25] Ibid., p. 46.
[26] *Sunday Express*, 28 September 1930.
[27] Krebs, op. cit., p. 47.

longing for radical solutions of the problems of Germany, for something new and revolutionary that would end the 'system'; this should be neither reactionary nor Communist, but German-socialist. These ideas were never clearly defined, but they affected wide circles of the academic and other youth. Their adherents were not necessarily in favour of National Socialism as a party; but this in the long run proved the strongest magnet among the many groups which professed similar aims, yet were too weak to have any chance of success.

In the army, young officers from the oldest noble families were drawn towards National Socialism, in opposition to the strictly conservative generals of the *Reichswehr*. In 1929 Lieutenant Henning von Tresckow (who later became prominent in the conspiracy against Hitler) spoke in the officers' mess at Potsdam in favour of the National Socialist slogan, 'The Breaking of the Shackles of Interest'. In the Potsdam regiments which continued the traditions of the Prussian guards such slogans found a ready echo, especially among the young lieutenants, as they had done in 1923 among the cadets of the Munich infantry school. In 1929, too, three lieutenants of an artillery regiment at Ulm sent out a leaflet to dozens of brother officers: all officers who were in favour of 'the national revolution' should combine, 'so that the *Reichswehr* does not fire on a national uprising of the people, but joins this revolt and becomes the nucleus of the future people's army of national liberation'. The lieutenants were convinced, so they declared in the autumn in a conference with leading National Socialists, that a part of the army would not oppose the National Socialists if they used violence against the Young Plan or to seize power in Germany; 'certain units will even join the movement'.[28]

Soon after the young officers were arrested. In September 1930 they were tried for treason by the highest German court and sentenced to short terms of 'honourable' detention in a fortress. At their trial they proudly proclaimed that the war of liberation always remained the army's last goal and that under no circumstances must the army be used against 'the last national movement'. It became clear that the army was no longer united, that many of the younger officers were in search of new revolutionary ideals. As to the senior officers, at least one of them—Colonel Ludwig Beck (who later led the conspiracy against Hitler)—openly celebrated the National Socialist election

[28] Richard Scheringer, *Das große Los unter Soldaten, Bauern und Rebellen*, Hamburg, 1959, pp. 179, 194. Scheringer, one of the accused, soon after became a Communist.

victory of September 1930 in the officers' mess; but this was certainly not the rule among the senior officers. A movement which was so strongly nationalist and so clearly advocated the rearmament of Germany was bound to find much sympathy in the army and navy which had adopted an attitude of cool neutrality towards the Weimar Republic.

At the trial of the three lieutenants Adolf Hitler was heard as a witness and pronounced, to loud cheers from the gallery: 'I can assure you that, when the National Socialist movement is victorious in its fight, then there will be a National Socialist court of justice, and [the revolution of] November 1918 will be avenged, and heads will roll.'[29] Thus the 'legal' way would be preserved and heads would roll 'legally', for Hitler was determined not to be driven into a repetition of the Munich venture of 1923. This trial was held only a few days after the elections of September 1930 which brought to the National Socialists their first great triumph in Germany as a whole. They polled 6·4 million votes—18·3 per cent of the total— and gained 107 seats in parliament (as against twelve in 1928). The only other parties which made some gains were the Communists and the Catholic Centre. All other parties lost severely, most of all the right-wing parties whose followers were beginning to desert to the National Socialists. The economic crisis had set in, the number of unemployed mounted quickly, and the future was to lie with those who stood for extremist solutions.

The Crisis

From 1930 onwards Germany was in the grip of an economic crisis which lasted much longer and was in some aspects worse than the inflation crisis of 1923. Unemployment figures rose steeply, from 2,258,000 in March 1930 to 5,670,000 in December 1931 and 6,128,000 in February 1932. More than half of their number did not receive any regular benefits but so-called 'welfare' support, which was quite insufficient to maintain a family. Hundreds of thousands of young workers never saw a factory or a workshop from inside. It was in particular from the ranks of the unemployed that the *S.A.* during these years recruited a private army of about 300,000 men. Over sixty per

[29] *The Speeches of Adolf Hitler*, ed. Norman H. Baynes, London, 1942, vol. i, p. 191.

cent of its members were permanently unemployed: in Hamburg, for example, 2,600 out of 4,500. Many of the unemployed *S.A.* men were housed in *S.A.* 'barracks' where they received shelter and food. But there was also a large academic proletariat, thousands of students without any hope of future jobs and without any money to pay for their maintenance. In the universities the National Socialists made particularly rapid headway. Many joined the National Socialist students' organization, many more voted for it. At the congress of the German and Austrian students held at Graz in 1931 the National Socialists obtained a clear majority; so did they at the universities of Erlangen, Breslau, Jena, Rostock and Greifswald. The students' parliaments of many other universities were dominated by a coalition of National Socialists and right-wing corporations. Both equally cooperated in disturbing the lectures of professors disliked for their pronouncedly left-wing views or in beating up left-wing and Jewish students. Political clashes became a daily occurrence in some of the universities, as well as in the streets of the large industrial towns, where political predominance was hotly contested between National Socialists, Communists and Social Democrats, or rather by their para-military organizations; political adversaries were ruthlessly attacked and beaten up. Naturally, the *S.A.* thrived in this atmosphere of violence and attracted many of the young toughs and professional brawlers who loved a good fight for its own sake.[30] It also attracted many ardent nationalists and anti-Communists, especially from the younger generation, as well as former soldiers and officers, eager to fight Marxism and the Reds. After bloody street battles with the Communists in the town of Altona one former officer wrote enthusiastically to a brother officer: 'For us National Socialism is an idea, a faith, a religion; the party organization as seen by us is a form of transition and at the same time the means for the unification of the German nation. If left-wing radicalism is not opposed within the next fortnight by energetic measures of the powers of the Reich and the states we will have civil war. . . .'[31]

Although law and order were at times seriously threatened and the police often had to intervene against rioters—these were as often

[30] Their autobiographical reports, many hundreds of which are preserved in the Hauptarchiv der NSDAP, give an excellent picture of the atmosphere of violence on which the *S.A.* thrived in the years before 1933.

[31] Ludwig Karl Strieder to Major Düvert, Altona, 20 July 1932: Reichswehrministerium, Wehrmachtsabteilung, Geheim-Akten, O.K.W. 881, World War II Records Division, National Archives, Washington, D.C.

Communist as National Socialist—there was no breakdown of public authority as it had occurred in Italy before the march on Rome. There were no punitive expeditions such as the Fascists organized by the hundred, no burning and destroying of Socialist or trade union property, no enforced resignations of Socialist mayors or other officials. Until July 1932 the Prussian police remained firmly under Social Democratic leadership and acted as efficiently against the extreme Right as against the extreme Left. The army nowhere fraternized with the Brown Shirts and many soldiers equally disliked their proletarian character and their military incompetence. The army leaders were determined to prevent the coming into being of a rival army in the form of a Brown-Shirt militia as it had happened in Italy. This dislike of the S.A. in higher army circles was reinforced by the fact that most of the S.A. leaders came from the free corps and were, in the eyes of very conservative generals, dangerous revolutionaries and adventurers who could not be trusted and in some cases had a very unsavoury past.

What spirit animated the S.A. in Berlin was shown by two mutinies which broke out within six months of each other. In August 1930 enraged S.A. men stormed the party headquarters and threatened the *Gauleiter* who was forced to ask the police to protect him. Hitler had to intervene in person and succeeded in restoring his authority by assuming himself the position of Highest S.A. Leader. In future he was entitled to appoint and dismiss all S.A. leaders who had to take a personal vow of loyalty to him. Captain Pfeffer von Salomon resigned his offices. A few months later Captain Röhm was recalled from Bolivia by his old protégé Hitler and made chief of staff of the S.A. The S.S. became a stronger force under its own *Reichführer*, Heinrich Himmler, who as a young man had taken part in the Munich *Putsch* and then become Gregor Strasser's secretary.

This reorganization, however, did not bring to an end the rebellious tendencies within the S.A. They were, above all, directed against Hitler's official course of 'legality'. Röhm's deputy in east Germany, the former free corps leader Captain Walther Stennes, refused to accept this course and aimed at removing Goebbels from his post of *Gauleiter* and gaining greater independence for the S.A. Hitler once more intervened and in April 1931 had the unreliable S.A. leaders removed by the loyal S.S. Many hundred S.A. men left or were expelled in Berlin alone and soon combined with Otto Strasser's revolutionary National Socialists. But the secessionist movement remained small and isolated. Its appeal to the 'Workers, Peasants and Soldiers'[32] found no echo among the masses. In the *S.A.*, on the other hand, the idea remained widespread that Hitler's legal way was impractical, as it was reported to Röhm on several occasions. The unemployed and many others distrusted all legal tactics and wanted to see action, action at any price. They were desperate, and became more desperate the longer the crisis lasted.

One thing, however, Hitler achieved by his professions of legality: they were taken at their face value in some very high quarters. Several months after Stennes' expulsion the minister of defence, General Groener, enquired from the undersecretary of state in the Prussian ministry of the interior, Abegg, whether his office was giving any money to Stennes. Abegg replied that unfortunately he could not do so as he had no funds, but that Stennes should be supported. Groener declared this would be absolutely wrong because Hitler was the man of legality: 'he must be supported against the others who are all wild men'. The amazed Abegg asked whether the general believed a word of what Hitler said, but Groener repeated: 'He is a man of legality. We must do nothing against him. We must support him.'[33] In a conference of the military leaders held in January 1932 Groener after a meeting with Hitler declared that the latter was 'modest and determined to eradicate the revolutionary ideas', that he 'wants the best', that 'Hitler's intentions and aims are good'.[34] The *Reichswehr* now accepted recruits who belonged to the National Socialists, and soldiers were allowed to attend meetings where the swastika was displayed. Such support from the highest quarters was of inestimable value to the party.

Very tangible support also came from other quarters. In January 1931 Hitler at length expounded his aims to the agrarian leaders and the Brandenburg noblemen. Many of them disliked the losses of votes by the Agrarian League to the National Socialists. But when Hitler had finished one of them got up and said: 'In the name of all present I request not to enter into a discussion. The solemnity of the hour that we have experienced must not be disturbed. The Agrarian League declares to give up all opposition to the Nazis, and on the contrary will enter into close cooperation.'[35] Henceforth the *Landbund*—an old

[32] This, significantly, was the title of Stennes' newspaper.
[33] Quoted by Heiden, op. cit., p. 337.
[34] Conference in the defence ministry on 11 January 1932: quoted by F. L. Carsten, *The Reichswehr and Politics*, Oxford, 1966, p. 334.
[35] Letter of Dr Hermann Gmelin of 4 February 1931: Hauptarchiv der NSDAP, NS. 26, no. 513, Bundesarchiv Koblenz.

associate of the Pan-German League—supported Hitler. So did the Nationalist Party which stood closest to the agrarian interests. In July 1931 Hitler and Hugenberg met and issued a statement that they would in future cooperate for the overthrow of the 'system' of Weimar.

In October the National Opposition held a large meeting at Bad Harzburg which was attended by the right-wing party leaders, those of the *Stahlhelm* and other para-military organizations, and well-known political figures, such as the leader of the Pan-German League, Claß and the former army chief, General von Seeckt. But there was a good deal of friction. The *Stahlhelm* contingents were much more prominent than the *S.A.*, and Hitler abruptly left before their march past. The leader of the National Socialist parliamentary deputies, Wilhelm Frick, tried to pacify the doubters among their ranks, who were critical of the cooperation with the bourgeois nationalists, by pointing to the example of Mussolini: as he had done the National Socialists would at first have to form a nationalist coalition, but they would demand to be its leaders and would not give up any of their aims. In January 1932 Hitler addressed a still more important audience: the assembled industralists of the Rhine and Ruhr area at the Industry Club in Düsseldorf. The speech, which stressed the prime necessity of restoring a sound national body politic in Germany, made such 'a deep impression on the assembled industralists' that 'a number of large contributions flowed from the resources of heavy industry into the treasuries of the National Socialist party'.[36] Thus the report of Fritz Thyssen who had arranged the meeting, and who had joined the party in the previous year.

Thanks to this support, and thanks to the ever-worsening economic conditions, the National Socialist party grew quickly. At the end of 1929 it had 178,000 members, by the end of 1930 about 380,000, and by the end of 1931 more than 800,000. Thirty-eight per cent of these members were under thirty years of age, far more than in any other party. Among them there were fewer manual workers in proportion than in society as a whole, but more white-collar workers, civil servants, farmers and independent businessmen. As before, these social groups with their *petit-bourgeois* standards and resentments were particularly attracted by the party. But above all, it was the victims of the crisis, not only the unemployed, but the disinherited in general who flocked to the party and provided it with enthusiastic audiences at carefully

[36] Fritz Thyssen, *I paid Hitler*, London, 1941, p. 132.

staged monster meetings. There rousing military tunes were played, the serried banners and standards were carried into the hall by giant Brown Shirts, until finally the speaker himself appeared amid shouts of 'Hail!'. Searchlights illuminated the platform and the speaker whose voice was often drowned by thunderous applause. This atmosphere gradually affected those who had come out of curiosity or vague sympathy; they were drawn into the vortex of excitement and frenzy, of chiliastic hope and deep hatred which pervaded the meetings. Hundreds of thousands of Germans hoped ecstatically that this movement, and above all its Leader, would free them from their misery and suffering, and would establish a 'Third Reich' of power and of glory, a Germany stronger than Bismarck's Second Empire, from which the Communist and Socialist menace had been banished for ever.

This propaganda, more than that of any other party, stretched to the smallest towns and into the last villages. In Protestant north Germany Lutheran clergymen were often used to address such meetings. The National Socialists realized that nationalism and religion, preferably combined, were the most popular topics apart from the iniquities of the 'system'. 'The attributes which made the Nazis respectable were their intense nationalism, their manipulation of religion, and the support given by the conservatives'; thus the picture drawn by a student of the political scene in a small town near Hanover.[37] There, as in many other small places, it was hatred of the Social Democrats that drove the inhabitants into the arms of the National Socialists: in this small industrial town the Social Democrats were the dominant political force, and they preached Marxism and the class struggle. The Communists were too weak to count, and there were hardly any Jews. Thanks to the support of many highly respectable people— among them the local judges, the headmaster and several teachers of the secondary school, and high officials of the railway directorate—the National Socialists managed to poll there twenty-eight per cent of the electorate in 1930 and sixty-two per cent in July 1932, in both cases far above their national average. The middle-class parties virtually disintegrated; yet the town's leading Nationalists were pleased by the National Socialist successes, and the Nationalist newspapers gave them editorial support. But the membership of the National Socialist

[37] William Sheridan Allen, *The Nazi Seizure of Power—The Experience of a Single German Town*, Chicago, 1965, p. 133. The observations made in this interesting study of one small town apply equally to many others.

organizations remained rather small: before 1933 the *S.A.* had about fifty and the party only about forty members in the town.

As to the regional distribution of National Socialist influence, Schleswig and Holstein with their agrarian crisis throughout these years remained the area with by far the highest National Socialist poll. It was followed by other agrarian areas, such as Hanover-Brunswick, Mecklenburg, Pomerania, Silesia, East Prussia, but also by some industrial areas in Saxony and Thuringia, where economic misery was particularly strong. All these were situated in Protestant north Germany. The only south-German mainly agrarian and partly Protestant, partly Catholic areas falling into this group were the Palatinate and Franconia, districts hit severely by the agrarian crisis. Those areas where the National Socialists polled considerably less than their national average were mainly Catholic districts in the south and west of Germany, partly industrial, partly agrarian, but also Protestant Württemberg with its liberal tradition, and the large cities of Berlin, Hamburg, Leipzig, Düsseldorf and Cologne. There is no doubt that the Catholic districts resisted the lure of National Socialism far better than the Protestant ones, and the large towns and industrial areas better than the small towns and the countryside, although National Socialist propaganda concentrated on the working-class quarters and the large towns. The Catholics were often frightened by the National Socialists' neo-paganism. In general it seems that in areas with a mixed religious population—such as Franconia and the Palatinate—the Protestants were particularly prone to fall for National Socialist propaganda. Curiously enough, in the same areas the post-war successors to the National Socialists have gained their most substantial successes, in comparison with the rest of the country, especially in certain towns. Thus patterns of political behaviour tend to outlive even the cataclysm of 1945.

Semi-Dictatorial Government

From 1930 onwards Germany was no longer ruled in a parliamentary way but by a government which relied on the confidence of the old president, Field-Marshal von Hindenburg, and issued 'emergency decrees' which were later submitted to parliament for its approval. The chancellor was Heinrich Brüning, the leader of the Catholic Centre party, whose name had been suggested to the president by the all-powerful General von Schleicher, the grey eminence of the army, who enjoyed the full confidence of the president. Brüning's government and its emergency decrees were tolerated by the Social Democrats, the largest party in parliament, to prevent the establishment of an openly right-wing government. This form of government thus depended on close cooperation between the president and the chancellor, and the president was eighty-five years old in 1932, and easily influenced by his entourage. Moreover, his term of office was running out in the same year and a re-election became necessary.

The National Socialists put forward Hitler, who had just been made a German citizen, as their candidate, and the Communists their own leader. It was symptomatic of the sad state of democratic politics in Germany in the last year of the Weimar Republic that the parties pledged to its defence against the extremists of the Right and of the Left could find no better candidate than the ancient field-marshal, who seven years before had been elected as the candidate of the Right against the leader of the Centre party. 'To keep Hitler out' the moderate parties, including the Social Democrats, voted for Hindenburg, the loyal servant of the House of Hohenzollern and symbol of arch-conservatism. Although they did so, Hindenburg just failed to gain an absolute majority in the first ballot in March 1932 while Hitler polled 30 per cent. Thus a second ballot became necessary: now Hindenburg obtained fifty-three per cent of the total, but Hitler's share rose to almost thirty-seven per cent, while the Communist candidate gained only ten—a clear proof how much stronger was the danger from the Right than that from the Left. The elections also showed how precarious was the position of the Social Democrats whose main slogan was the defence of democracy—a democracy that rested on the issuing of emergency decrees and the protection of an ancient president who was no democrat.

How fickle this protection was became clear only a few days after the re-election of the president. The minister of defence, Hindenburg's old comrade General Groener, wanted to dissolve the *S.A.* who were responsible for much of the political violence which occurred in Germany every day. Groener was strongly pressed to do so by the ministers of the interior of the leading German states, and was supported by the army leaders and the chancellor. The order was issued under the presidential signature on 13 April. But only two days later General von Schleicher reported to his chief 'that there was a storm brewing in the house of the president and in the defence ministry against the emergency decree'. From Potsdam the Crown Prince added his voice to that of his friend Schleicher and wrote to Groener: 'I can only consider the decree a grave mistake and a very serious danger to internal peace. It is incomprehensible to me how you as the minister of defence can help to destroy the wonderful material that is united in the *S.A.* and *S.S.* and receives there a valuable education. . . .'[38] In fact there was a crisis of the government, as it depended on the confidence of the president and of the army command, neither of which any longer had confidence in General Groener. In May he was forced out of office after Schleicher had threatened with the collective resignation of the leading generals. The whole affair fatally weakened the Brüning government and shook Hindenburg's confidence in his chancellor who throughout had loyally supported Groener. Schleicher wanted to bring the National Socialists into the government and give them a share in political responsibility. This, however, could not be achieved with Brüning as chancellor; at the end of May he too had to resign as the president withdrew his confidence from him. The new chancellor, Franz von Papen, was the candidate of Schleicher.

Papen was meant to accomplish the 'miracle' which Brüning had failed to accomplish: to 'tame' the National Socialists and to bring them into the government. But before this could be attempted a price had to be paid: parliament was dissolved after less than two years, and new elections were held in July. They brought a new triumph to Hitler: his party polled 13,750,000 votes and became, with 230 deputies, by far the strongest party in parliament. The Communists gained moderately and now had eighty-nine deputies. For the first time the two extremist parties together held more than fifty per cent of the seats, hence no government could be formed which had a majority. The Papen government—popularly called the 'government of the barons'—was only supported by the Nationalists who polled a mere six per cent of the total and had thirty-seven deputies. Thus a government which still commanded a parliamentary majority had been replaced by one which enjoyed hardly any popular support. Even before the elections a last bastion of democracy was destroyed. The government of Prussia, the largest German state, which was dominated by the Social Democrats, was deposed by military action, and Papen was appointed state commissioner for Prussia by a presidential decree. The Prussian police— which in contrast with the army was a loyally republican force and well able to protect democracy—passed under different command. The will

[38] Quoted from the Groener papers by Carsten, op. cit., p. 344.

of the republican mass organizations to defend democracy, if need be
by arms, was further paralysed.

Before the fall of Brüning and the elections which enormously
strengthened his hand Hitler had been extremely anxious not to offend
Schleicher and not to disturb their good relations. The two men met
frequently, and Schleicher openly voiced his dislike of the chancellor.
When a National Socialist paper nevertheless attacked Schleicher
Hitler intervened sharply. The culprit was not only removed from his
post as editor of the *Hamburger Tagblatt* but also expelled from the
party. Hitler told him that such an attack was bound to destroy the
confidence of the army in the *N.S.D.A.P.*; he alone was responsible
for the party's policy; no editor was to have an opinion of his own, nor
permitted any independent line.[39] After the elections Schleicher and
Papen still tried to win Hitler over to a policy of cooperation, by
offering him the post of vice-chancellor and the Prussian ministry of
the interior, which controlled the police. Hitler, however, demanded
no less than the office of chancellor and six other ministerial posts,
which would have given him complete control of the government. He
also talked wildly about mowing down the Marxists, about three days'
freedom of the streets for his *S.A.*, and demanded complete power for
himself.

Thus the attempts of the Papen government to 'tame' the National
Socialists broke down in the course of August. During the same month
a Communist of Polish origin was trampled to death by five National
Socialists. When the murderers were sentenced to death by the court
at Beuthen Hitler sent a telegram to them: 'My comrades! In the face
of this monstrous blood sentence I feel myself tied to you by bonds of
unlimited loyalty. From this moment, your liberation becomes a
question of our honour, the fight against a government under which
this was possible, our duty!'[40] There was to be open war. What Hitler
wanted was total power, and not just a slice of the cake; and his followers were just as wild and reckless as their Leader.

Wild were also the dreams of German expansion to which Hitler
regaled some of his visitors. To achieve a 'decisive ascendancy over
all the European nations', he informed one of them, a nucleus must
first be created from Austria, Bohemia and Moravia, western Poland

[39] Diary entries of Albert Krebs of 19–20 May 1932: Nachlaß Krebs, no. 1,
Bundesarchiv Koblenz.
[40] A slightly different translation in *The Speeches of Adolf Hitler*, ed. N. H.
Baynes, vol. i, p. 166.

and the Baltic states; the areas bordering on Germany in the east 'will be colonized with German peasants. The Czechs and the Bohemians we shall transplant to Siberia or the Volhynian regions. . . .'[41] Another follower was told: 'One day we shall command over enormous areas, be responsible for the security of vast spaces. Can we do that with a hundred thousand, or with three hundred thousand men? We will mobilize the millions! . . .'[42] These remarks were, above all, directed against the army leaders whom Hitler considered complete ignoramuses with their talk of professional soldiers and a small mobile army. Yet the surprising thing about his wild prophecies is that the dreams became a terrible reality in the course of the second world war. Phantasy and reality were strangely mingled in his mind.

How reckless Hitler's followers became when all the hopes of gaining power seemed frustrated by the opposition of the government was shown in the autumn of 1932. A strike of the Berlin transport workers broke out in November against the advice of the trade unions. It was led by the Communists, but the National Socialists joined in, so as to prove their determined opposition to the forces of 'reaction'. For some days there was chaos in Berlin. The united front of Red and Brown attacked drivers willing to work and the policemen who tried to protect them, poured cement into tramway points, damaged the rails, pulled down high-tension cables, and engaged in sabotage on a massive scale. The police found it extremely difficult to restore order. Many respectable people got frightened by the spectre of Bolshevism which seemed to unfold itself: they had voted for Hitler to protect them from Bolshevism, not to bring it closer. In the elections held a few days after the strike the National Socialists suffered a significant defeat—their first for many years—and lost two million votes and thirty-four seats in parliament. Most other parties lost too, but the Communists made further gains and now had 100 deputies, compared with 196 of the National Socialists. The number of unemployed, which had been well over the six million figure during the winter 1931–32, had declined too and stood at 5,100,000 in the autumn. For the first time there were signs that the economic crisis had passed the high-water mark. Was this to be the beginning of the end for Hitler? Characteristically enough, however, Hitler himself attributed the defeat in the November elections not to any objective factors, but largely to 'the unfair behaviour' of the Strasser clique and Gregor

[41] Hermann Rauschning, *Hitler Speaks*, London, 1939, p. 46.
[42] Krebs, op. cit., p. 145.

Strasser's 'eternal work of undermining and sabotage';[43] thus he succeeded in finding a culprit, a traitor within his own ranks.

The Seizure of Power

The elections of November 1932 brought not only a defeat for the National Socialists but also for the Papen government which still had hardly any parliamentary support. Papen therefore requested from the president far-reaching powers to change the constitution and to rule without parliament. But he met with the opposition of Schleicher, his minister of defence, who did not want the army to become involved in the defence of so unpopular a government and feared that Papen would bring the army on to the streets 'against nine-tenths of the nation'. This situation must be avoided at any cost, and a *kriegspiel* was arranged in the defence ministry to prove that the army would not be able to cope with a general strike and sabotage by the combined Reds and Browns. That in such a situation the army would be supported by the trade unions and millions of others was not taken into account. The *kriegspiel* served its purpose: Papen was forced to resign, and General von Schleicher, rather unwillingly, had to become chancellor. His plan was to cooperate with the trade unions as a 'social' chancellor, and to win over to his policy of social reform some 'moderate' National Socialists. After a renewed attempt to negotiate with Hitler had broken down, Strasser was offered a ministerial post.

Yet the attempt to split the National Socialists failed completely. Schleicher's only success was that on 7 December Strasser resigned all his party offices and went abroad 'on leave'. But he made no attempt to rally the opposition in the party and did not accept any office under Schleicher. Hitler assembled his faithful, addressed them at length and renewed their obligations of loyalty to him. They solemnly promised to carry on to the end against all obstacles, and Hitler took over most of Strasser's functions himself. That there was a deep crisis within the party, a danger that it might fall to pieces, is confirmed by Goebbels' diary. On 8 December he noted: 'In the organization there is a severe depression. The financial worries make any purposeful work impossible.' And two days later: 'The financial situation of the *Gau* Berlin is hopeless.' Earlier in the same month he considered 'the

---

[43] Goebbels, *Vom Kaiserhof zur Reichskanzlei*, p. 199 (under 8 November 1932); ibid., pp. 191-2, on the transport workers' strike of 2 November.

situation in the Reich catastrophic.' On the 15th he wrote: 'It is high time that we come into power. For the time being, however, there is not the slightest chance.'[44]

At Christmas Goebbels still considered the future 'dark and gloomy', but a few days later the picture suddenly changed. On 4 January 1933 Hitler met Papen in the house of the banker von Schröder in Cologne, and a reconciliation between them was effected. Papen—after his curt dismissal four weeks earlier—had become a bitter enemy of Schleicher; and the government still depended entirely on the confidence of the old president, who had to sign its 'emergency decrees'. Yet the one chancellor whom Hindenburg had really liked was Papen; as he had not even evacuated the premises of the chancery the two continued to meet daily. Now it was Papen's turn to play the game at which Schleicher seemed such a master, the game of back-stairs intrigues. The alliance between the National Socialists and the Nationalists was renewed. The meetings with Hitler were continued in Berlin later in January, and they were also attended by the son of the president, Colonel Oskar von Hindenburg, and the president's undersecretary of state, Dr Otto Meißner. It was through them that the old field-marshal was finally won over to the plan of making Hitler chancellor. They were the link in the chain forged by Papen.

Schleicher who was informed about the negotiations approached the president and requested from him powers similar to those which Papen had desired: to dissolve parliament and the two extremist parties, the Communists and National Socialists, and to rule without parliament for the time being. The president, however, well remembering the intrigues against Papen and Schleicher's part in them, refused to grant him the desired powers. What Hindenburg would have liked was another Papen government, but this was sharply opposed by the army leaders who still feared that they would have to defend it against the large majority of the nation. Two of the leading generals approached the president on 26 January to warn him of the dangers of such a course; but he—as it seems, misunderstanding the cause of their anxiety—declared: 'You will not think it possible, gentlemen, that I should appoint this Austrian lance-corporal chancellor.'[45] Yet only four days later the Austrian lance-corporal was the chancellor of Germany, appointed by the president who had held out against him. There were only two

[44] Goebbels, op. cit., pp. 217–19, 223, 225, 229.
[45] This remark was reported by both generals, von Hammerstein and von dem Bussche-Ippenburg: Carsten, op. cit., p. 391.

other National Socialists in the cabinet, Frick and Göring, hemmed in by as many as nine Conservatives and Nationalists: it was the situation of the Mussolini government after the march on Rome. But any hope that the non-National Socialists would be able to contain the flood was doomed. Their old-fashioned and cautious tactics which lacked popular support were no match for the fervour and the dynamism of a revolutionary mass movement. What had taken years to achieve in Italy, the unlimited dictatorial power of one party, took only a few months in Germany.

On the evening of 30 January when the formation of the Hitler government was announced a wave of enthusiasm and frenzy swept over Germany. Torchlight parades were organized in every town which were joined not only by the *S.A.* and the National Socialists, but also by the *Stahlhelm* (whose leader became a member of the government) and similar nationalist organizations. For hours the masses marched through the Wilhelmstraße and acclaimed Hitler who stood at the window of the chancery surrounded by his closest collaborators, a few windows from where President Hindenburg stood. After a succession of weak and more and more unpopular governments Germany had a strong government with a broad popular basis; at the November election forty-two per cent of the voters had voted for the two parties which combined on 30 January. This was not a majority, and the government still depended on the confidence of the old president. But already at its first meeting it decided to dissolve parliament and to hold new elections, so as to obtain from the electors a verdict in its favour and to convert the forty-two per cent into a majority. As the government controlled the means of power and the resources of the state, it had far-reaching possibilities of influencing the result of an election. Control of the army was guaranteed in the person of the new minister of defence, General von Blomberg, an old enemy of Schleicher; he was influenced in favour of National Socialism by his chief of staff and by his divisional chaplain who were ardent admirers of Hitler.

There was no opposition to the establishment of the Hitler government. As the new chancellor was appointed legally by the president and as this appointment was welcomed by millions of nationalists and law-abiding Germans, any resistance could only have come from the Left. But the German Left was itself deeply divided. The Communists issued a call for a general strike—such as had overthrown the Kapp 'government' of 1920—but no one obeyed the call. For years the Communists had called the Social Democrats 'Social Fascists' who differed only in degree from the 'National Fascists': how could the so often maligned Social Democrats now combine with their Communist enemies? Nor would they take any action on their own initiative—they had not even done so when the Prussian government was overthrown by Papen's *coup d'état* six months before. The power of resistance of the German working-class movement was broken by years of slump and unemployment, by trying to defend a republican régime which was no longer democratic and did not arouse any enthusiasm among the masses. Although thousands of their followers ardently hoped for a signal from Berlin which would summon them to arms, the Social Democratic leaders decided on doing nothing. In their opinion the party had weathered the storm of Bismarck's laws against the Socialists: it would equally weather the new wave of persecution and emerge triumphantly. Many hoped against hope that Hitler would be as little able to solve the problems of Germany as his predecessors and then be replaced by another chancellor. Few people realized that the National Socialists, once entrenched in power, could only be removed by an earthquake. In a military sense any resistance was hopeless against the combined forces of the *S.A.*, the police and the army, which would have stood united against the Left, indeed would have welcomed this opportunity of settling accounts for the 'shame of November 1918'.

Göring, now the minister of the interior of Prussia and thus in control of the police, actually made all the preparations required for such a fight. Hundreds of civil servants were removed and replaced by National Socialists. He ordered the police to avoid any action against the *S.A.* and the *Stahlhelm*, but to show no mercy to the 'enemies of the state', and to make use of their firearms if necessary. On 22 February an 'auxiliary police' of 50,000 men—40,000 from the *S.A.* and the *S.S.*, and 10,000 from the *Stahlhelm*—was formed who were to support the regular police against the opposition. A Secret State Police (*Gestapo*) was established to cope with the enemies of the régime and carry out arrests of political suspects. Thus even before the Reichstag building went up in flames the machine of terror which was to crush all opposition went into action. In many parts of Germany the *S.A.*, whose hour of vengeance had finally arrived, took the law into their hands and carried out indiscriminate arrests and beatings.

On the evening of 27 February—six days before the elections—the Reichstag was ablaze. It is now generally held that it was not the National Socialists who set it on fire, or at least that this cannot be proved. It still seems difficult to understand how one half-crazy former Dutch Communist, Marinus van der Lubbe, could have accomplished this feat without any help. In any case, it was the National Socialists who benefited from the deed. During the same night thousands of prominent Communists, Socialists and Radicals were arrested, including many members of parliament. Thousands of other victims were rounded up and carried away to the S.A. barracks where they were inhumanly treated; many were beaten to death. The opposition papers were suppressed, and opposition activities made impossible. On 28 February a decree 'for the protection of nation and state' was promulgated which abolished the basic democratic rights of personal liberty, freedom of the press, of public meetings and association, and of free speech and permitted searches, confiscations and the censorship of mail. Treason, arson, sabotage and poisoning became liable to the death penalty; so did attempts on the life of the president, a member of the government or a high official, and armed rioting. All this was ostensibly directed against the Communists, but could without any difficulty be extended to other enemies of the régime.

In this atmosphere of terror the elections were held on 5 March— the last time that a parliament was elected in a seemingly democratic way. The National Socialists polled forty-four per cent of the total and their Nationalist allies another eight. This gave them a bare majority of fifty-two per cent, but not the two-thirds majority required for a change of the constitution. The Social Democrats virtually retained their strength, and even the Communists only declined slightly and still had eighty-one deputies; the Catholic Centre gained a few seats. Thus the three principal opposition parties emerged hardly weakened from the election, but the National Socialists made further inroads on the bourgeois parties. The new parliament was ceremonially opened on 21 March in the Garrison Church of Potsdam where the Prussian kings were buried, the shrine of the past greatness of the House of Hohenzollern, to symbolize the union of the forces of the old Germany with those of the new. They were also symbolized by the old field-marshal in full-dress uniform and many other active and retired generals, and by Adolf Hitler who appeared in a morning coat, and not in his party uniform. The 'Day of Potsdam' served to allay many fears and apprehensions in Germany.

Two days later parliament met in the Kroll opera house. The building and the surrounding streets were filled with uniformed S.A. and S.S. men to intimidate the deputies. The Communists had been deprived of their seats, and many Social Democrats too were prevented from attending. An Enabling Act was put before parliament 'to eliminate the distress of nation and Reich'; it gave full powers to the government to legislate for a period of four years without consulting parliament, and even to change the constitution. The Act was passed by a majority of 441 to 94 votes. It became the basis of the establishment of the Third Reich and was renewed by decree when it expired in 1937. Only the Social Democrats voted against the Enabling Act. Their leader, Otto Wels, made a dignified speech in which he pledged his party to the eternal principles of humanity, justice, freedom and socialism, which no Enabling Act would be able to destroy. If his party had not offered any resistance to the establishment of dictatorship, at least it did not lose its honour. All the other parties—including the Centre—voted for the Enabling Act. Parliamentary government was at an end, or rather it had died a slow death: from 1930 onwards it was gradually replaced by 'presidential' government, and very few regretted its demise. All this, moreover, was accomplished 'legally', by using the machinery provided in the constitution.

Gleichschaltung

What happened in Germany during the spring and summer of 1933 is best described by the term *Gleichschaltung* ('Coordination','Streamlining'), which meant that everything, from bowling clubs to bee keeping, was brought under National Socialist control. The army, through the new minister of defence, led the way. On 1 March General von Blomberg proclaimed that there was 'one party on the march. Thus the attitude of remaining "above party" loses its meaning and there is only one course: support without any reservation!' Three months later Blomberg repeated to his commanding generals that 'there remains only one thing: to serve the National Socialist movement with complete devotion'.[46] The army was to benefit enormously from the rapid rearmament which started quickly. About the same time the state governments were brought into line. Prussia was controlled by Göring. For the other states Reich Commissars were appointed to take over the government; their diets were dissolved at the end of March. Then a local National Socialist—often the *Gauleiter*—was appointed *Reichsstatthalter* (Reich Governor) of the state in question with full

[46] General von Blomberg addressing the divisional and corps commanders on 1 March and 1 June 1933: Carsten, op. cit., pp. 395, 397.

powers to dismiss and nominate officials. Thus Germany ceased to be a federal state. Prussia, Bavaria, Saxony, etc., lost the powers which they had possessed for centuries.

Next it was the turn of the trade unions. The first of May was proclaimed 'National Labour Day' and celebrated throughout the country with the full support of the trade union leaders. But on the following day the houses and offices of the Free Trade Unions all over Germany were occupied by the *S.A.*, the unions dissolved and their leaders arrested; many were put into concentration camps with thousands of other opponents of the régime. In June the Christian Trade Unions suffered the same fate. In their place the 'German Labour Front' was established which all employers and employees were forced to join—not in separate Syndicates as in Italy but in common organizations. Although the 'German Labour Front' took over the property of the trade unions it did not exercise their functions as there was no longer any collective bargaining or working-class action: its aim was to preserve industrial peace and to promote schemes of social welfare. The houses, newspapers and property of the Social Democrats were equally seized; in June the party was dissolved as 'subversive and hostile to the state'. The Nationalist Party, whose ministers sat in the government with the National Socialists, tried to promote a Green Shirt movement to rival Hitler's Brown Shirts and in doing so attracted many opponents of the National Socialists, but also their wrath. At the end of June the Nationalist offices were occupied by the police. The party then 'voluntarily' dissolved itself and its leader, Hugenberg, resigned from the government: in contrast with Italy where the Nationalists joined the Fascist Party. Early in July the remaining parties—the Centre, the People's Party, and the Bavarian People's Party—also dissolved themselves. It was then enacted that the National Socialist Party was the only political party in the country; any attempt to maintain or to form another party became punishable by penal servitude or imprisonment. Germany was a one-party state.

The same process was carried through in every field of national activity. Cultural life was controlled by the setting up of a National Chamber of Culture, with subordinate chambers for fine arts, music, theatre, literature, radio, films, and the press. Anyone working in any of these fields was obliged to join the chamber in question, from which all Jews and opponents of the régime were excluded, thus depriving them of their livelihood. Even earlier the books of all authors obnoxious to the régime—whether Jewish, or left-wing, or simply 'decadent'—

were burnt by crowds of enthusiastic students. The lectures of Jewish
and left-wing professors were made impossible by well organized disturbances. The universities and the civil service were purged by a law
'for the restitution of a professional civil service'. Jewish students were
excluded from the examinations. Jewish doctors, lawyers, etc., were in
many cases prevented from carrying on their professions. A boycott
of all Jewish shops was proclaimed by Streicher on a nation-wide scale
on 1 April 1933. All clubs and associations, however non-political their
purpose, were brought under National Socialist control and their by-
laws reframed according to the 'leadership principle'.

The opposition did not dare to raise its head. People opposed to the
régime could only meet clandestinely and in small groups, and even
then they risked immediate arrest and a period in a concentration
camp. The tales of horror about what happened inside these camps
which soon spread were one of the most effective weapons of the
dictatorship. Many thousands of opponents of the régime were simply
too frightened to do anything. But many thousands of others continued to work for the Communist and Social Democratic parties in spite
of all intimidation and persecution; most of them were soon arrested or
had to flee the country. After a few years there existed only minute
remnants of the proud German working-class movement.

Opposition also continued in a different field. Certain sections of the
Protestant churches continued to resist all attempts of the 'German
Christians' backed by the government to 'coordinate' the Church and
to bring its teaching and doctrine into line with the principles outlined
in *Mein Kampf*. This was the only field in which a vigorous and semi-
legal resistance continued throughout the years of the Third Reich, in
spite of the persecution of many Protestant clergymen. All opponents
of National Socialism were ruthlessly dealt with by the *Gestapo*, which
soon became a very efficient police force, feared throughout the
country.

There remained one problem, that of the *S.A.* After the initial wave
of terror had passed its men had no function in the state. Its leaders
confidently expected that, with the rapid expansion of the army, they
would be taken over into the officer corps with a rank corresponding
to theirs in the *S.A.* The army leaders were equally determined to
prevent this and to preserve their monopoly of the 'bearers of arms'.
The *S.A.* leader, Captain Röhm, had always demanded 'the primacy
of the soldier above the politician';[47] but in the new state the politicians

[47] Ernst Röhm, *Die Geschichte eines Hochverräters*, 7th ed., Munich, 1934, p. 349.

clearly had the upper hand, and the soldiers were still the stuffy conservative generals, not the revolutionary leaders of the free corps whom
Röhm favoured. Among his men there were soon mutterings about a
'second revolution', not to be directed against Hitler, but against the
conservatives and 'reactionaries' who surrounded him. The army
began to take military precautions which were reciprocated by the S.A.
Tension increased visibly in the course of June 1934, but it is certain
that Röhm did not prepare a *Putsch*. He sent his men on leave and
retired to a hotel at Wiessee in Bavaria where he expected a visit from
Hitler. But Röhm's opponents, above all Himmler, the leader of the
S.S., and some army leaders, succeeded in convincing Hitler that he
was planning a *Putsch*. Hitler decided to side with the stronger battalions and against his old friend and protector, one of the very few
men towards whom he used the familiar 'thou'.

Himmler was entrusted with putting down the 'revolt' in Bavaria,
Göring with its suppression in Prussia. Everywhere it was the S.S.
that carried out the purge against its comrades of the S.A. During the
night to 30 June and in the early hours of the morning the surprised
S.A. leaders were taken from their beds, arrested and shot without any
trial, many of them in the S.S. barracks at Lichterfelde near Berlin.
But Göring and Himmler used the opportunity to settle their accounts
with many other enemies. General von Schleicher, Hitler's predecessor
as chancellor, and his wife were shot in their house near Berlin.
Prominent Conservative and Catholic leaders suffered the same fate;
so did Gustav von Kahr, who had 'betrayed' Hitler in 1923, Gregor
Strasser, who had defected in December 1932, and Major-General von
Bredow who had been Schleicher's right-hand man. It has never been
established with certainty how many were murdered, but the figure
certainly ran into hundreds. It was the famous 'night of the long
knives' of which the S.A. men had dreamt for years, but it was the
S.S. which used the long knives; it thus triumphed over its rivals and
soon became the most powerful force in Germany. If the army leaders
hoped to eliminate the danger threatening them from the S.A., they
helped to create a much more formidable rival to their own power in
the S.S., which developed into an army of its own, its power permeat-
ing the whole state. The purge of 30 June, by eliminating the enemies
and the potential enemies of the régime, completed the National
Socialist 'revolution'. Adolf Hitler was in complete and undisputed
control of the whole country.

His amazing success was, above all, due to the economic crisis which drove millions of desperate Germans into his camp, a crisis such as had not occurred in Italy ten years before. It was also due to the expert organization and the propaganda efforts of the National Socialists which no other party could rival, to their violence, dynamism and unscrupulousness in attacking the system and its representatives, in mobilizing the masses and rousing the rabble. There still remains the question how a great nation and many of its leaders could have been taken in and won over by such methods and such aims. Undoubtedly, it was Hitler's nationalism that helped to win many who deeply resented the Treaty of Versailles and desired to restore Germany's position in the world; and it was his anti-Semitism that attracted those looking for a convenient scapegoat for all the ills of Germany. It has to be remembered that a fervent nationalism and a strong anti-Semitism had been endemic in Germany since the nineteenth century, although in less violent forms.

While Socialist or Communist propaganda in favour of the class struggle and international solidarity never influenced people outside the working classes, National Socialist propaganda always used themes which evoked a sympathetic echo in millions of people, and adapted itself with great skill to different audiences. In the conditions of the great crisis it played successfully on middle-class fears of Communism and on their dislike of the republican régime. Not particularly attractive to anyone, the republic was burdened with the acceptance of the Treaty of Versailles and with the inflation of the mark, which largely expropriated the middle and lower middle classes, with the signing of the Dawes and Young plans which, in nationalist eyes, perpetuated Germany's 'enslavement' and could be made responsible for the economic decline. Thus the republic found few determined defenders. There was no frontal assault, but its foundations were undermined and sapped by a process of attrition. It was an irony of history that the constitutional guardianship of the republic in the decisive hour was entrusted to the ancient paladin of the House of Hohenzollern. Thus the fortress surrendered without a shot being fired, exactly as Rome had surrendered to Mussolini ten years before.

Varieties of Fascism in Eastern Europe

Mussolini and Hitler were men of the people, of comparatively low social origin, and during their youth both went through periods when they were virtually down and out. They both knew the lower classes and could speak their language, coarse and primitive. These factors were vital to their success; they made them the symbol of the social aspirations of the masses. For a member of the upper classes or of the intelligentsia it would have been much more difficult to become a people's tribune, the mouthpiece of popular passions and hatreds. Yet, strangely enough, in most other European countries the Fascist leaders came from the upper classes, even from the wealthy aristocracy—José Antonio Primo de Rivera or Sir Oswald Mosley; or they were professional officers—Ferencz Szálasi or Vidkun Quisling—or senior civil servants—such as Vilho Annala in Finland. Several came from comfortable middle class and professional families, had studied at the universities and obtained degrees and positions, for example Anton Mussert in Holland, Léon Degrelle in Belgium, and Corneliu Zelea Codreanu in Rumania. Indeed, to some of them their social origin proved a serious handicap of which they were keenly aware, while others would try to overcome this handicap by super-radical demands and actions. If Hitler and Mussolini expressed their contempt for all intellectuals and all theories and often relied on their intuition or inspiration, rather than on their knowledge, the Fascist leaders with an academic background and training were no more intellectual in their political activities than the two successful dictators. None of them made a serious attempt to develop a Fascist philosophy or spent much time on any theoretical pursuit. What ideology or theory they had was usually taken over from Italy—above all the idea of the corporative state—or from Germany—above all racism. The rise of the National

Socialist movement and the seizure of power, and even more so the later existence of a powerful and expansionist National Socialist state, had strong repercussions in many European countries; it encouraged the growth of similar movements elsewhere, and Germany often supported them directly or indirectly.

Finland : from Anti-Bolshevism to Fascism

Among the smaller European countries two had particularly close ties with Germany, from the days of the first world war to those of the second: Finland and Hungary. There was not only the comradeship in arms and the close ties between the national armies; there also was the traumatic experience of civil war between Reds and Whites, the threat of a Communist revolution, and the resultant violent anti-Communism which was shared by the three countries. Indeed, of the three it was Finland which was the most seriously threatened, partly by its geographical position in close proximity to the Soviet Union, partly by the existence of a strong and left-wing labour movement with a radical revolutionary tradition. This went back to the years of the Finnish struggle for independence and of the first Russian revolution in 1905. In Finland—which was part of Tsarist Russia—this revolution became a national struggle in which all social classes participated, a struggle for the country's constitutional rights against Russian interference and violation of the country's privileges. To preserve law and order armed national guards were formed, but in Helsinki these became proletarian and Red, and White defence units were organized to counteract their influence. The strike movement of the autumn of 1905 became revolutionary and greatly increased the workers' self-confidence. Within two years the membership of the Social Democratic Party increased five times, and in the first elections after the end of the revolution it gained forty per cent of the seats in the Finnish Diet, an enormous success. At the outbreak of the second Russian revolution, early in 1917, the Social Democrats even succeeded in gaining an absolute majority in parliament, 103 out of 200 seats—the first time this happened in any country. The workers had become even more radical and revolutionary.

During the first world war public opinion in Finland was largely pro-German although officially the grand duchy fought on the Russian side. Especially in university circles the opinion was widespread that only Russia's defeat could ensure greater freedom for Finland, and that only Germany could bring this about; the opportunity presented by the war must be used to gain independence. Early in 1915 Finnish agents were sent to Berlin and there they succeeded in winning over the German General Staff to their cause. During the following years about 2,000 young Finns secretly left their country and volunteered for the German army; most of them were students, but young men from other social groups also took part. They were trained at a camp near Schleswig and formed a special 'Jäger' battalion which fought against the Russians on the eastern front—the nucleus of the future national army. The core of the later Finnish officer corps was drawn from the ranks of the Jägers. They were linked to the German soldiers by strong ties of comradeship—ties that were to reappear during the second world war when many young Finns volunteered for the Viking Division of the *Waffen SS*. The Jägers were full of admiration for the German army and its might and became strongly indoctrinated in a pro-German sense.

Meanwhile in Finland the movement for national independence was growing apace. After the outbreak of the Russian revolution Red and White defence units reappeared, on a larger scale than they had done in 1905. A week after the Bolshevik revolution of October 1917 the Finnish Socialists proclaimed a general strike which assumed revolutionary forms. Most of the Russian troops in Finland sided with the Red guards who seemed the masters of the situation. They searched houses, arrested people and engaged in looting. Leading Socialists urged that the country must follow the Russian example, while the moderates lost their influence. In January 1918 the socialist revolution was proclaimed in Helsinki and a revolutionary government formed which was joined by two representatives of the trade unions.

Already during the preceding month, December 1917, the Finnish Diet had announced the independence of the country and authorized the formation of military units. Field-Marshal Baron Gustaf Mannerheim was appointed the commander-in-chief: he was the best known of the Finnish officers serving in the Russian army, and soon his forces took the initiative in the civil war between Reds and Whites. While they were highly successful against the badly organized and armed Red guards in some parts of the country, the most densely populated areas in the south and the capital itself were only freed from the Red danger by the arrival of a German division commanded by General Count von der Goltz. Their arrival was enthusiastically welcomed by all nationalists and anti-Communists. As one of them wrote at the time: 'There they were, the representatives of the world's most illustrious army, of whom we had read for four years, the unshakeable sentries of the Western Front, the crushers of Russia, the conquerors of Rumania, Hindenburg's, Ludendorff's, and above all Emperor William's iron soldiers! . . .'¹ Owing to the superiority of the forces of the Finnish government, the demoralization of the Russian units, and the lack of effective help rendered to the Red guards the civil war was over after a few months, but is was marked by terrible cruelty on both sides and it left lasting scars. About a quarter of those killed on the government side were listed as having been murdered by the Reds, and the rate of casualites was very high. Among the Red guards the number of prisoners executed amounted to about fifty per cent of those killed in battle. The prisoners were put into improvised concentration camps where thousands died, mainly from lack of food and medical care. According to Field-Marshal Mannerheim's testimony the mortality rate in the camps was 'frighteningly high'. The government had decided that all prisoners must stand trial—a procedure which was very lengthy while food was woefully insufficient: 'a measure bound to increase bitterness and hatred and to enlarge the gulf which was dividing our nation into two camps. . . .'² The adherents of the extreme Right, however, looked at the civil war as a glorious victory over Russia: the invincible White army had swept the Red plague from the country and had erected a barrier against Bolshevism. The very ease of the victory created dangerous illusions. Only 125 of the death sentences pronounced against Red prisoners were carried out, but many more were sentenced to varying terms of imprisonment.

When the Finnish Communist Party was formed at the end of 1918 about half the members of the Social Democrats joined it; many party groups and organizations, including that of Helsinki itself, became Communist. In 1920, after a bitter struggle, the Federation of Trade Unions fell under Communist control, and so did most individual unions. In the elections of 1922 the Communists polled 14·8 per cent of the total and received 128,000 votes, proving that they still possessed considerable strength, but this declined somewhat during the following

---

¹ Eino Leino, *Helsingin valloitus*, p. 78, quoted by Marvin Rintala, *Three Generations: The Extreme Right Wing in Finnish Politics*, Bloomington, Indiana, 1962, p. 48. This is by far the most important study of the subject discussed in this section.
² Gustaf Mannerheim, *Erinnerungen*, Zürich, 1952, p. 222.

years owing to energetic measures taken by the government. Meanwhile, in October 1920, peace had been concluded with Soviet Russia; Finland's independence and its historic frontiers were recognized, and in addition she gained the port of Petsamo in the far north with its valuable mines. The large majority of the parliamentary deputies accepted the treaty.

To the extreme Right, however, it was a deep disappointment because the ideal of a Greater Finland was not realized in the treaty. This Greater Finland should include the lands from the Gulf of Bothnia to the Arctic Ocean: Eastern Karelia, Kola, Ingria and Estonia; thus the Finnish nation would be able to fulfil its historic mission as the northernmost guardian of western civilization. The acquisition of Eastern Karelia and Kola alone would have doubled the size of Finland. They were largely inhabited by Finnish-speaking peoples, but in Ingria they were only a minority, and Petrograd was an entirely Russian town. Estonia had become an independent state. While the president of Finland, K. J. Ståhlberg, tried to follow a policy of compromise and of healing the wounds left by the civil war, the extreme Right preached hatred of the president and of the parliamentarians who had accepted the treaty with Russia which it considered shameful. In Eastern Karelia the civil war was continuing in 1921–22, and right-wing activists secretly crossed the frontier to fight the Soviets. When the minister of the interior tried to close the frontier to prevent these illicit crossings he was murdered—a deed that caused as much jubilation among the activists as the murder of Erzberger and Rathenau in Germany at the same time. In Finland, too, the policy of fulfilment of the peace treaty was opposed tooth and nail by the extreme Right.

Early in 1922 three young soldiers who had returned from the war in Eastern Karelia founded an organization of university students and graduates which was devoted to the idea of Greater Finland, the 'Academic Karelia Society'. Its members greeted each other as 'brothers in the hatred of the Russians' and the new member had to swear an oath: 'Under our flag, and to our flag, I swear, in the name of all that is sacred and dear to me, to sacrifice my work and my life to my fatherland, for the national awakening of Finland, Karelia and Ingria, the Greater Finland. . . .'[3] But joining the Society was not easy. During the first year the prospective member had to attend intensive lecture courses and to serve for long hours, and would then become a candidate member; only after that year could he take the

[3] Rintala, op. cit., p. 105.

oath and become a full member. The Society's total membership amounted to only 2,000–3,000. But soon there were many branches in secondary schools, and many graduate members who were teachers, civil servants, clergymen, etc., spread the ideas of the Society. Even bishops and cabinet ministers belonged to it. The Society's leader and his subordinates bore military titles. They had to be obeyed by the other members, and an iron discipline reigned. In the Society's view, the precondition of a territorial expansion was an internal order in which the Finnish language predominated entirely; hence it forcefully attacked the Swedish-speaking minority—about eleven per cent of the country's population. The members also held strongly racialist views— but very different from those of the German National Socialists who, in a racially very mixed country, upheld the purity of the Germanic race. The Finnish racialists believed that, in the struggle for mastery in Europe, not the racially pure nations would triumph, but rather those of mixed origin: while the Scandinavians and the Russians were relatively pure nations, the Finns were of mixed Scandinavian and Baltic stock, hence they were more likely to gain control of northern Europe, and later of Europe as a whole. Thus Finland would emerge as a great power. As there were fewer than three million Finns in Finland, territorial expansion on a large scale was essential; the Estonians were elevated to the rank of a Finnish-speaking people, and should be incorporated with Finland. These ideas had gained ground among the 'Jägers' of the world war, and they deeply influenced the post-war student generation. Above all, it was Eastern Karelia which remained their goal: it must be conquered by force of arms, as indeed it was in the course of the second world war. It was a powerful myth, but it exercised small influence outside academic circles.

On a much wider scale there were the White defence units of the civil war which were not disbanded—as the Free Corps were in Germany— but continued as Civil Guards; this force of about a 100,000 well-armed men existed side by side with the regular army, under their own commander-in-chief. In 1921 he was made subordinate to the president. The Civil Guards were strongly influenced by the rise of Italian Fascism. As early as 1922 the chairman of the Diet's Military Affairs Committee declared: 'People have tried to compare us with the Fascists so that it might be shown how very dangerous the existence of an armed organization like the Civil Guards is to parliamentary life. I must honestly admit that we Civil Guards members are not at all ashamed of that comparison: on the contrary, we recognize willingly and proudly that we are the intellectual comrades of the Italian Fascists. . . .'⁴ What particularly attracted the Civil Guards in Fascism was the violence committed so freely against the Reds in Italy and the success of the anti-Communist crusade; while in Finland Communism continued to preserve its strength and in the elections of 1929 once more polled 128,000 votes, 13·5 per cent of the total, after a slight decline during the preceding years.

Anti-Communism—with the events of the civil war as a very recent memory—continued unabated and was fanned by this Communist success in the elections. In November 1929 a Communist youth group held a meeting in the village of Lapua at which the participants appeared wearing red shirts. They were set upon by the Civil Guards and the farmers, beaten up, stripped of their red shirts, and their meeting was prevented by the infuriated crowd. Within a few days a popular movement came into being, the 'Lapua Movement': it demanded that the Communist Party be outlawed, that its deputies be deprived of their seats in parliament and local government, that their newspapers and meetings be suppressed. A bill to this effect was introduced but met with opposition. Soon the members of the movement took direct action; the Communists' printing presses were smashed; Communist deputies were prevented from attending parliamentary sessions; others were beaten up or kidnapped, the victims being forced to cross the Russian frontier. These victims were not only Communists, but moderates too. Among many others, the retired Finnish president, K. J. Ståhlberg, and his wife were seized by former Jägers who wanted to settle accounts with him on account of his negative attitude towards the Jäger movement; the seizure was planned by the chief of the general staff, Major-General Wallenius, a former Jäger officer. The government was unable to prevent these lawless deeds.

In June 1930 the Lapua Movement presented an ultimatum to the government demanding that all Communist newspapers should be suppressed and all Communist officials be arrested immediately. Three days later a decree banned all Communist publications, and in July the cabinet decided to arrest the Communist deputies, after two of them had been kidnapped from a meeting of a parliamentary committee. Thirteen thousand armed members of the Lapua Movement and the Civil Guards descended upon Helsinki to press their demands, in particular the dissolution of the Communist Party. The march was organized by five high army officers. The government of P. E. Svinhufvud condemned

⁴ Quoted by Rintala, op. cit., p. 154.

'mob action' and the Law of Lapua, but its members participated in the public ceremonies held by the marchers in the capital. There was no disagreement in public: all bourgeois forces seemed united in the fight against Communism. After a general election held in October the anti-Communist laws were finally approved by parliament with the required two-thirds majority; Svinhufvud threatened to resign if they were rejected, and only the Social Democrats opposed them. Yet the Lapua Movement was not satisfied with this success. It now turned against the Social Democrats, and its methods became ever more violent. Its leader, Vihtori Kosola, considered himself chosen by God to lead the Finns and in his dress and manner began to imitate Mussolini.

The Lapua Movement aimed at the destruction of all parties and of parliament itself. Its leaders declared that no one would weep at the parties' grave; the power of the trade unions must be destroyed, the expenditure on social legislation and public education be reduced, and equal voting be abolished. But the Movement's primary aim—the outlawing of the Communists—had been achieved while its violence increased; thus popular support which had been very strong in 1930 began to subside. The leaders realized that they could no longer rely on it to gain power and turned to the alternative, a *coup d'état*. The revolt began at the end of February 1932 with the breaking-up of a Social Democratic meeting held at Mäntsälä in southern Finland. Rebel forces took over this community and declared they would destroy Social Democracy even if they must first destroy the power of the state which supported and protected it. At first they demanded the resignation of the minister of the interior and of the provincial governor, but on the following day that of the entire cabinet and the formation of a new one obedient to the Lapua Movement, 'free from party aims and depending . . . upon the support of the nation's patriotic elements'. The loyalty of many army officers, former Jägers, was doubtful and many Civil Guards officers openly supported the revolt, but Svinhufvud, who had meanwhile been elected president of Finland, took strong action. He issued a personal appeal to the nation to stop the revolt. A state of emergency was declared, the army was mobilized, the Civil Guards were ordered to return home and the basic freedoms declared suspended. The Lapua units were dispersed and the leaders arrested, ironically enough on the basis of the anti-Communist laws voted in 1930. Within a few days the revolt was crushed. A court decision declared the Lapua Movement dissolved. But its enemies, too, especially the minister of the interior and a provincial governor, were removed from office, while the commander of the Civil Guards retained his post.

A few weeks later, however, in April 1932 the 'People's Patriotic Movement' was founded so that the sacred flame of Lapua should not die. It aimed at 'the formation of a broad White front . . . to annihilate all that which is Red. This action will be directed not only against Communism, but also against that Socialism which seeks to destroy the patriotic, religious and nationalist spirit. . . .'[5] The new movement, exactly like the Academic Karelia Society, also made a firm stand against the Swedish minority and its language, as well as against liberalism which it considered a dying force. In its place it sought to create a new social and political order. There should be a strong central authority, and the government should no longer be responsible to parliament. Finland was to become a unilingual country; the nation and the fatherland were to be the highest values to which all others would have to be subordinated. A corporative state was to be created and parliament to be transformed in a corporative sense. Economic planning was to be introduced, every citizen to be guaranteed work by the state, and social justice was to reign. The entire Finnish race was to be united in a Greater Finland. The movement adopted as its leader the leader of the dissolved Lapua Movement, Vihtori Kosola, who was soon released from prison. But the real leader was a senior civil servant, Vilho Annala, and his closest associate the professor of criminal law at Helsinki university, Bruno Salmiala. The members wore black shirts and trousers with a blue tie, a uniform similar to that of the dissolved Lapuas.

The programme had a close affinity with that of the Academic Karelia Society, especially in the Greater Finland idea, and was more clearly pro-Fascist than the Lapua Movement had been. The new movement greatly admired the two successful European dictators and adopted the Leadership principle in deference to them. Its leaders overlapped with those of the Academic Karelia Society, a prominent member of which became the commander of the youth organization of the People's Patriotic Movement. This was modelled on the Hitler Youth and the Balilla, the Fascist youth organization, whose example it tried to emulate. Like the Academic Karelia Society, but unlike the Lapua Movement, the new party was above all a party of the educated and the students. It was supported by the large majority of the students,

[5] Quoted by Rintala, op. cit., p. 222.

by very many civil servants, and by about half the Lutheran clergy. In the parliamentary elections of 1936 more than ten per cent of its candidates were clergymen, and another twenty per cent professors or teachers. But the party also enjoyed popular support: in the elections of 1936 it polled 98,000 votes, or 8·3 per cent of the total. This was the high-water mark of its influence, for in 1939 it only gained 6·6 per cent of the votes, hardly more than it had done in 1933. It thus lost six of the fourteen parliamentary seats which it had obtained in 1936; and this was the last time it participated in an election. For a time it even succeeded in winning over the Conservatives to a policy of cooperation and electoral alliance, but this came to an end in 1935 on account of Conservative opposition. It thus seems that, even if the war had not broken out in 1939, the party's strength had passed its peak. The war brought the final undoing of the Greater Finland conception and of violent anti-Communism in general; but not before the Finnish army, commanded by former Jäger officers, had triumphantly marched in 1941 into Petrozavodsk, the capital of Eastern Karelia.

Thus a powerful tradition influenced the upper ranks of Finnish society from the days of the first world war to those of the second. It was above all anti-Communist and expansionist; but later—under the influence of the German and Italian prototypes—it became strongly Fascist and authoritarian. It also posed, at least in 1931–32, a strong threat to the existence of a democratic government although it did not succeed in overthrowing it. Viewing the movement as a whole it was apparently too intellectual and too academic to achieve this goal, and the Greater Finland idea too far removed from reality to be able of fulfilment. As there were hardly any Jews in Finland, the movement developed an anti-Swedish tendency, but it could hardly aspire to the goal of removing the strong and influential Swedish minority from the country. The movement overreached itself, and this brought about its defeat.

Revisionism and Anti-Semitism : the Hungarian National Socialists

Hungary—like Finland and Germany—in 1919 went through the traumatic experience of civil war and a short-lived Communist régime, followed by one of White terror. The revolution which in the autumn of 1918 swept away the Habsburg king brought to power a liberal government under Count Mihály Károlyi; but his government was unable to halt the dismemberment of Hungary by her neighbours who coveted the parts inhabited by a Slav or a mixed population, and whose rapaciousness was abetted by the victorious Entente powers. Thus Count Károlyi, who was a sincere democrat, was forced to resign in March 1919 and to hand over to a coalition of Socialists and Communists headed by the Communist journalist Béla Kun. His doctrinaire and terrorist methods of government succeeded in converting the large majority of the Hungarians into fierce anti-Communists—exactly as were the Bavarians by the short-lived experiment of the Munich Soviet Republic. No Soviet aid ever reached Béla Kun, but, acting on the orders of the Entente, Rumanian troops invaded Hungary and occupied Budapest. The Soviet Republic collapsed in August and its leaders fled the country. The Red terror was replaced by a régime of White terror. At Szeged in the south Admiral Miklós Horthy formed the 'Szeged Committee' which employed 'order detachments' to cleanse the country of Bolshevism. When the Rumanians occupied Budapest these forces transferred their activities to the west of Hungary which remained unoccupied. When the Rumanian forces finally withdrew from the capital in November Horthy's army moved in. Wherever it went pogroms were organized, Jews were killed and Communists hanged; special courts were set up which sentenced Communists or suspected Communists to death or to long terms of imprisonment.

These events spelled the death of the Left as a political force in Hungary for a quarter of a century. Although the existence of a Social Democratic Party was tolerated by the Horthy régime it only exercised influence in Budapest and a few other towns and never posed a threat to the government. The Communists were persecuted and led a very precarious underground existence, from which they emerged only when the Red Army entered Hungary in 1944. Moreover, the Communists suffered from the handicap that their leaders—and those of the party reformed in exile—were almost all Jews. While there had been comparatively little anti-Semitism in Hungary before 1918—indeed the Hungarian Jews were quickly Magyarized—the events of 1919 created a strong anti-Semitic movement. Jews formed five per cent of the population of Hungary, but they were predominant in certain fields: half the lawyers and 60 per cent of the doctors were Jewish according to the census of 1920, 53 per cent of the 'independent' people engaged in trade, and 80 per cent of those in finance and banking; among the white-collar workers, 39 per cent of those in industry, 44 per cent of

those in finance, and 48 per cent of those in trade were Jewish. Jews
were very prominent in journalism and the arts. It was easy to blame
the events of 1918–19 on the Jews: they had made profits during the
war but had evaded military service, they had stabbed the 'victorious'
army in the back, they had established the Red terror, for 'it was in-
conceivable that peasants and workers—true Hungarians—could have
been responsible for these revolutions. . . .'[6] Not only the Communists, but also the Social Democrats and Liberals were considered to
be under Jewish influence and hence 'non-Hungarian'. As one close
observer of the Hungarian political scene has put it, 'to the younger
generation of the Hungarian middle class and petite bourgeoisie, as to
the Szeged generation proper, the Jewish question loomed quite
fantastically large'.[7] This widespread anti-Semitism was to facilitate
the growth of National Socialist ideas. But among the conservative
ruling class, largely drawn from the Magyar nobility, it was a limited
and non-racial anti-Semitism, much more akin to that of the conservative Nationalists in Germany than to that of Hitler.

In the peace settlement of 1919 Hungary fared worse even than
Germany or Austria. The old kingdom had been very large and the
ruling Magyars had only been a minority of the population. At Trianon
the position was reversed. Hungary lost 63·5 of her former population
and was left with only 7,600,000 people. They were nearly all Magyar-
speaking: the only sizeable minority left in Hungary were the German-
speaking 'Swabians', who numbered about half a million. But 3,200,000
Magyars were left outside the frontiers of the new state, most of them
in Rumania (in Transylvania) and in Czechoslovakia (in Slovakia and
Ruthenia). This treatment at the hands of the Entente powers caused
deep resentment in Hungary and a widespread desire to bring about a
revision of the 'unequal treaty' whenever this would be possible—the
same feelings dominated Germany on account of the Treaty of Versailles. Thus the bonds which had united the two countries in the first
world war remained in force, even during the years of the Weimar
Republic, and received new vigour and strength after Hitler had
seized power in Germany. But even before that date Hungary found
a strong supporter of her revisionist claims, directed against the 'Little

---

⁶ István Deák, 'Hungary', in *The European Right*, ed. H. Rogger and E. Weber,
Berkeley and Los Angeles, 1965, p. 370.
⁷ C. A. Macartney, *October Fifteenth—A History of Hungary 1929–1945*, Edinburgh, 1956, vol. i, p. 78. This is the only detailed study of Hungary during the
inter-war period: it contains a wealth of material on Hungarian politics and is based
on the recollections of many participants.

Entente' of Yugoslavia, Rumania and Czechoslovakia, in Mussolini's Italy which was pursuing revisionist aims of her own. The government established in Hungary, with Admiral Horthy as regent (in place of the absent king) and Count István Bethlen as prime minister, was not a Fascist régime but rather a right-wing Conservative government, with the old nobility still firmly entrenched in power and in secure possession of their large estates. It was perhaps the only feudal régime left in the Europe of the 1920s, under which the majority of the agricultural population lived in abject misery, either possessing no land or tiny holdings insufficient to maintain a family. Yet there was no land reform, and no attempt by the Social Democrats to organize the agricultural labourers, as any such attempt would have been firmly opposed by the government. This situation was to give an opening to the extreme Right.

Exactly as in Germany and in Finland, the large majority of the army officers—as well as many young intellectuals—despised the ideas of liberalism and democracy and were opposed to parliamentarianism. They also developed political ambitions. But in Hungary, which had not had an army of its own—until 1918 there had only been the Austrian-Hungarian Imperial *and* royal army—the army had strongly attracted young men of German stock, and this continued to be the case after 1919. Those who became professional officers were largely Swabians whose trade was soldiering and who admired the German army—as did the Jägers in Finland. 'Far from keeping aloof from all public affairs the army wanted to direct the nation and interfere in everything.'[8] The army became a separate body within the body politic, and staff officers could consider themselves destined to save the nation. The minister of defence for many years—in 1919–20 and from 1929 to 1932—was a former professional officer, also of Swabian origin, Gyula Gömbös, the son of a village schoolteacher. But he was a Magyarized German, a fervent Hungarian nationalist and anti-Semite who believed that the Jews were sapping the country's strength. He took a leading part in organizing the counter-revolution of 1919 and then described himself as a 'Hungarian National Socialist', before that term was used in Germany. He also organized a secret society with a civilian and a military wing and himself as the Supreme Leader to protect the Magyar race and soon became a racial anti-Semite. In 1923 he founded the 'Party of Racial Defence' and was closely involved in the attempts made in Munich to restore the Wittelsbachs, which was to be paralleled in Hungary by the establishment of an extreme right-wing government

[8] Nicholas Kállay, *Hungarian Premier*, New York, 1954, p. 139.

under Gömbös. Indeed, as early as 1921 he had been in touch with leaders of the extreme Right in Munich, who were organizing the German counter-revolution from the south. In later years he discovered the glories of Italian Fascism and began to groom himself for the role of the Hungarian Mussolini, who would rid Hungary of the Jews and freemasons. Under the regent he would assume the position which Mussolini occupied under the king.

In 1929 Gömbös was reappointed minister of defence, but this did not lessen his ardour for the introduction of a Fascist régime. When the economic crisis broke out and agrarian prices fell sharply the Bethlen system collapsed with them. The younger members of the Right were strongly dissatisfied with his policy of compromise and fulfilment of the peace treaty, his lenient treatment of the Jews, and with the parliamentary system as such. It was due to their pressure that Horthy, in October 1932, appointed Gömbös prime minister. He then arranged an enormous demonstration of his followers and the numerous patriotic associations. When he addressed them in Mussolinian fashion from a balcony they replied with carefully rehearsed shouts of 'Long live our Leader!' Yet the new Leader did not abolish parliament and did not make himself dictator, but the government of Hungary continued much as before, with Horthy wielding the decisive influence. During the election campaign of 1935 Gömbös repeated his intention of establishing a one-party and corporative state and a 'unitary Hungarian nation with no class distinctions'. When he visited Berlin in the same year Gömbös signed a secret agreement with Göring in which he promised to establish in Hungary a political system similar to that of the Third Reich. But few actual reforms were introduced, and when Gömbös died in October 1936 Hungary was no closer to Fascism than she had been in 1932.

While Gömbös had strong pro-Fascist leanings he lacked a Fascist party to sweep him into power—a mass movement as distinct from the secret societies—but by the time of his death several Fascist groups and parties had come into being. Indeed, it was one feature of the Hungarian scene that there always were so many rival and mutually hostile Fascist groups: they only coalesced into one party *after* Szálasi had been put into power by the Germans in October 1944. The most radical of these parties was the 'Scythe Cross', founded in 1931 by Zoltán Böszörmény, the son of a bankrupt landowner who had joined the counter-revolution in 1919 as a young man. As his programme he simply issued a translation of the National Socialist programme of

1920: as with Gömbös his inspiration clearly came more from Germany than from Italy. But his movement had a strong local following, especially among the very poor labourers and peasants of eastern Hungary; it advocated land reform and justice for the poor. It thus attracted many who would have been Communists if there had been a legal Communist Party. It was also violently anti-Semitic, the members describing themselves as the 'fateful Death Reapers of the Jewish swine and their hirelings'. The Scythe Cross, however, was a genuine popular movement of the landless proletariat. In 1934 the writer Imre Kovács met the peasants with their banners on which they had inscribed: 'We have had enough!' 'It was on a large estate beyond the Tisza; they were seasonal workers and very poor. . . . "We fight for the Idea", they repeated when I questioned them, but were unable to tell what the "Idea" was about. They hated the Communists and the Gentlemen.'[9] The Scythe Cross' one attempt at political action consequently was a twentieth-century peasant war. They planned to march on 'sinful' Budapest and raze the capital to the ground. But on the appointed day, 1 May 1936, only a few thousand peasants assembled and were easily dispersed. Hundreds were arrested and declared themselves ready to die for the 'Idea'. Böszörmény was allowed to escape to Germany, and the movement was suppressed. The majority of the peasants were and remained loyal to the Regent and disinclined to support political radicalism.

In June 1932 an independent parliamentary deputy, Zoltán Meskó, founded a rival party, the 'Hungarian National Socialist Agricultural Labourers' and Workers' Party'. He appeared in parliament in a brown shirt and sporting a swastika on his lapel. His party's emblem was the Arrow Cross, but at times a green swastika on a brown field, and the brown shirt was later exchanged for a green one. His party was less revolutionary than the Scythe Cross movement and remained entirely loyal to Horthy as the Regent. But it never exercised any mass influence. Many similar parties then came into being, most of them remaining very small, but all to a greater or lesser extent influenced by Hitler. They all welcomed the growth of German power which would help Hungary to achieve a revision of the frontiers drawn by the Treaty of Trianon. A National Socialist Hungary, they hoped, would gain German support, while a democratic Hungary dominated by the Jews would arouse Hitler's wrath. Not that their anti-Semitism was imported: it had strong roots in Hungary, where indeed Jewish domina-

9 Quoted by Deák, op. cit., p. 385, from Imre Kovács' *A néma forradalom*.

tion in industry and finance was a fact, and not just a product of fantasy as it was in Germany. As late as 1939 the Hungarian prime minister, Count Pál Teleki, had to explain to the Germans that a wholesale removal of the Jews would cause a complete paralysis of Hungary's economic life, hence would not be in the interest of Germany. And a later Hungarian prime minister, Miklós Kállay, remembered: 'The Trojan horse inside which the ideology of National Socialism was smuggled into Hungary was anti-Semitism. The Gömbös men in the Party were anti-Semitic. . . . Anti-Semitism was the pivot around which their ideas turned; it was a disease with them. . . .'[10] He assumed that the anti-Semitism of the lower middle classes and of the intelligentsia had economic causes because their social advance was blocked by the Jews—but also by many members of the nobility who retained the higher positions.

Apart from economic causes, however, there was—as in Germany—a strange racialism, a veneration of the great Magyar past, which was cultivated by numerous secret and semisecret societies. The society founded by Gömbös in 1919 adopted queer tribal patterns, trying to revive the memory of the alleged tribes and tribal leaders who had led the Magyars in the ninth century across the Carpathians into Hungary. In the most radical form there developed a new mystical creed of the Turanians who worshipped a War Lord by the name of Hadúr, supposedly an ancient Magyar god, exactly as some ecstatic Germans—led by General Ludendorff—worshipped Wotan. The Turanians attempted to prove that the Magyars were the descendants of the ancient Persians, Hittites, Egyptians and Sumerians and that Jesus himself had been a Turanian. Weird ideas such as these influenced many of the later National Socialists, exactly as the *völkisch* ideology prepared the ground for German National Socialism. But in neither country did these ideas gain mass support. In general it was Germany, not Italy, that provided the inspiration. But, in contrast with Germany, the extreme Right in Hungary often advocated radical social reform, an end to feudalism and capitalism, and the sweeping away of the relics of the past. This, indeed, was vital for a country in which the past was so strongly entrenched. At the same time, it made the Right extremists entirely unacceptable to the ruling class and to its official leader, Admiral Horthy—as did the National Socialists' rabid anti-Semitism and their political violence.

All this applied in particular to the most important of the many

[10] Kállay, op. cit., pp. 33, 39.

National Socialist parties, the Arrow Cross, from the party emblem of two crossed arrows (which, however, it shared with similar groups). Its leader and prophet from the outset to the bitter end was Ferencz Szálasi. He was born in 1897, the son of a professional N.C.O. in the Austro-Hungarian army, served as an officer in the first world war and later became a major on the Hungarian General Staff. In that position he developed the idea of 'Hungarism'—a concept similar to that of a Greater Germany or Greater Finland. But in the case of Hungary this amounted to the restoration of the frontiers of the ancient kingdom with its millions of non-Magyar subjects, 'engirdled by the Carpathians and reaching down to the Adriatic', in which the Magyars were to regain their old dominant position. As Szálasi put it: 'The struggle of the Great Fatherland must be led by the leading people of the Ancestral soil, the Magyar people, as it led it when 1,000 years ago it welded together the God-given unity into a State unity.'[11] This Greater Hungary Szálasi called the 'Carpatho-Danubian Great Fatherland'. It was to be created by the army, which was to occupy a commanding position in the state: 'When the Army sees that in the nation the three pillars of Religion, Patriotism and Discipline have been shaken, then it is the duty of the Army to force the nation back on to these pillars.'[12]

Szálasi developed his ideas while serving on the General Staff, but he was warned to keep off politics, and in 1935 he resigned his commission to become the Leader of the party he founded under the name of 'Party of National Will'. He was convinced that he was destined by providence to lead his country towards the Hungarist goal: 'I have been selected by a higher Divine authority to redeem the Magyar people—he who does not understand me or loses confidence—let him go! At most I shall remain alone, but even alone I shall create the Hungarist State with the help of the secret force that is within me.'[13] The triumph of Hungarism would bring about the reorganization of Europe; while its fall would mean the fall of National Socialism. 'Every Party member *must* accept the ideology of Hungarism and must accept the Arrow Cross Party as the practical instrument for the realization of Hungarism.'[14] Marxism was a dangerous enemy and must be destroyed, but Liberalism was doomed by its own weakness. The Arrow

[11] Quoted by Macartney, op. cit., i, p. 162.
[12] Quoted by Deák, op. cit., p. 394.
[13] Quoted ibid., pp. 388–9.
[14] Quoted by Macartney, op. cit., i, p. 163.

Cross specifically appealed to the workers, and Szálasi made a point of visiting working-class houses, but he never developed a precise social programme. This was largely because he only moved in the higher realms of Hungarist thought and was completely indifferent to practical issues. But he did advocate the planning of agricultural production, the transformation of the rural proletariat into smallholders, and a system of agricultural cooperatives. The economy was to be directed by a National Council of Corporations, the National Bank to be nationalized, and work to become a right as well as a duty, while strikes were to be forbidden. Throughout Szálasi insisted on the constitutional way: he would take power only when authorized by 'the common will of the nation and the Head of the State'; he always remained loyal to the Regent, but he considered the political parties unconstitutional because they did not derive their power from the freely expressed will of the people.[15]

Szálasi's party grew quickly, from about 8,000 members in September 1935 to more than twice that number in April 1937. It was renamed the 'Arrow Cross Party—Hungarist Movement'. But in October 1937 it merged with several other National Socialist groups, including the remnants of the Scythe Cross, under the name of 'United Hungarian National Socialist Movement'. The unity, however, only lasted a few weeks. Meanwhile Szálasi's fame was spreading. In October 1936, after Gömbös' death, the head of Horthy's military cabinet, Lajos Keresztes-Fischer, asked Szálasi to report, for Horthy's benefit, on the political situation. But Szálasi informed him that the army was 'the Messiah which can force the country on to the true road' and must carry out a *coup d'état:* the Regent must act 'at the head of the nation, and with the nation'.[16] Indeed, many junior and some very senior army officers began to sympathize with the Arrow Cross, as they had done in Germany in the years before Hitler came into power. As in Germany, the younger officers wanted urgently to bring about social and political reforms, and these could not be obtained from the governing conservative party. As to other social groups, there is no doubt that—as in other countries—the lower middle classes and the intelligentsia were strongly represented in the Arrow Cross, partly out of opposition to the ruling group, partly out of anti-Semitism. But, in contrast with Germany and Italy, there was a fairly large proportion of industrial workers —according to one (doubtful) estimate half of the party's membership

15 Ibid., i, p. 165.
16 Ibid., i, p. 175.

in 1937, and that in a country which was still very imperfectly indus-trialized. It seems a fair assumption that, in other countries, many of of these workers would have been Socialists or Communists. According to the same estimate, made by a former high party official, seventeen per cent of the party members in 1937 were army officers, a colossal figure, twelve per cent belonged to the professions or were self-em-ployed, and only eight per cent were peasants.

The growth of the Arrow Cross clearly worried the government, at a time when political tension was increasing all over Europe and when Hungary's neighbour Austria had been occupied by the Germans. Hitler's very success was bound to have strong repercussions in a Hungary burning to achieve a revision of the Trianon settlement. In July 1938 Szálasi was put on trial for issuing subversive leaflets and condemned to three years' hard labour and five years' loss of civil rights. In August he was arrested and imprisoned at Szeged. In the eyes of his followers he became a martyr, and his popularity grew. The persecution of the Arrow Cross became more severe, especially after the appointment of Count Pál Teleki, a strong conservative, as prime minister early in 1939. Yet this did not achieve the desired goal, for in the elections of May 1939 the Arrow Cross Party scored a memorable success and obtained 900,000 out of a total of over three million votes. In Budapest it polled twice as many votes as the Social Democrats and only somewhat less than the government party, and its gains were particularly marked in the working-class districts. The illegal Commu-nists had advised their followers to vote Arrow Cross. In consequence thirty-one Arrow Cross deputies entered parliament, accompanied by another eighteen National Socialists, while the government party secured 179 seats and four smaller parties (the Smallholders, the Social Democrats, the Liberals, etc.) a total of thirty-two. Almost one-fifth of the deputies were National Socialists, while the left wing was con-demned to impotence.

By that time Hungary had begun to reap the fruits of political collaboration with Hitler's Germany. After the Munich conference she received the southern parts of Slovakia, an area with a predomin-antly Magyar-speaking population. There followed in 1939, with the progressive dismemberment of Czechoslovakia, the acquisition of Ruthenia, the population of which was mainly of Ukrainian stock. To these gains was added in the following year, again thanks to the good services of Germany and Italy, Northern Transylvania where the population was half Magyar and half Rumanian-speaking. These territorial gains also added a large Jewish contingent to the population in which the Jews now formed well over six per cent of the total.[17] Most of these Jews (in contrast with the native Hungarian Jews) were not assimilated and did not speak Magyar. The government and parliament passed several anti-Jewish laws, restricting the Jewish share in economic life. But these laws were operated in a Hungarian fashion by which the enterprises took on more non-Jewish staff and paid them salaries, but did not require them to do much work. Business then continued as before. Meanwhile the Germans were pressing for the introduction of more stringent anti-Semitic measures, and this pressure was strongly echoed by the Hungarian National Socialists. Anti-Semitic and racial plans, however, were also voiced by other circles. In August 1941 the chief of the Hungarian general staff, General von Werth, composed a memorandum which not only demanded the restoration of the ancient frontiers by a policy of conquest, but also the removal of the Slav, Rumanian and Jewish minorities from this Greater Hungary, which was to be inhabited solely by 'racially pure Magyars'.[18]

In spite of the growth of German influence in Hungary and the alliance formed by the two countries against Yugoslavia and Soviet Russia in 1941, the Arrow Cross movement did not substantially increase during the war years. On the contrary, there were strong fluctuations in its membership and influence. Several deputies left the party; others became strongly anti-German. Many suspected it of serving foreign interests and betraying those of Hungary. At first Count Teleki refused to release Szálasi from prison; but a few weeks after the second Vienna Award—which gave Northern Transylvania to Hungary—he was finally set free, in September 1940. He easily succeeded in rallying his followers and in bringing the fractious deputies to heel; several rival groups placed themselves under his leadership. But friction soon reappeared; eight rival groups were intriguing against each other and against Szálasi; at the end of the year he noted in his diary that his popularity had declined. A few months later, in the summer of 1941, he wrote that 'a fraction of the workers, the crypto-Communists, secedes from the Party. The Party carries through a merciless purge and excludes all those who are unable to fight unequivocally against the

[17] Kállay, op. cit., p. 75, says eight to nine per cent, but that seems to be an overestimate.
[18] Quoted by Martin Broszat, 'Faschismus und Kollaboration in Ostmitteleuropa zwischen den Weltkriegen', *Vierteljahrshefte für Zeitgeschichte*, xiv, 1966, p. 245.

plutocrats, the Marxists and the Jews.'[19] Yet the party gained many new members and is estimated to have had 116,000 at the end of 1940. Three years later Szálasi once more noted 'apprehension' among his lieutenants because 'Party membership had sunk to well below 100,000. Not only the rank and file, but also the Party hierarchy was generally tired and dispirited. Propaganda and organization practically nil. The existing Party hierarchy was unfit to lead a national party.'[20]

It seems extremely unlikely that a movement which was so dis-united and so beset by internal rivalries could ever have come to power by its own efforts. Indeed, it was the Germans who finally deposed Horthy because he attempted to extricate Hungary from the war, and who put Szálasi and the Arrow Cross into power when the Red Army was already on Hungarian soil. Yet Szálasi was by no means a German stooge. A few months earlier, in April 1944, he met the German Pleni-potentiary, Dr Veesenmayer, for the first time and informed him that he would only take office on his own terms; Germany must accept the 'Hungarist Idea' and the rest of his programme, and his party must be given all the key ministries. The same intransigent attitude he adopted towards the other National Socialist groups and those who had seceded from his own party: from them he demanded a complete recantation and the unconditional acceptance of his own authority as the Leader. It was only after the German *coup d'état* of 15 October 1944 that an agreement was reached with the erring sheep and that their leaders were permitted to enter the Arrow Cross Party. Nor did Szálasi approve of the extermination of the Jews carried out on German orders. In the plan of action he drew up in September 1944 he stipulated that they were to be employed inside Hungary on public works until the end of the war, and then were to emigrate from the country. He was honest and sincere; but he was also hopelessly impractical, unable to control his followers and the rival groups, always moving in the higher realms of Hungarist thought, and for these reasons quite unsuitable to occupy the exalted position to which he aspired.

In Hungary several objective factors—the feudal relics in govern-ment and society, the need of social reform, the absence of the Com-munist Party and the ineffectiveness of the Social Democrats, the virulent anti-Semitism and anti-Communism among the lower middle classes—greatly facilitated the growth of a Fascist movement. But this always remained divided and far from monolithic. What Hitler had

[19] Quoted from Szálasi's diary by Macartney, op. cit., ii, p. 42.
[20] Quoted from Szálasi's diary, ibid., ii, p. 199.

achieved in the earlier 1920s—the ruthless elimination of all rival *völkisch* groups—was never accomplished in Hungary. Hence the old régime had to be removed by the Germans, and that was only a few months before the final collapse of Germany and of the new order Hitler had tried to establish in Europe. Szálasi, moreover, lacked the dynamic qualities of other Fascist leaders, their tactical sense as well as their ruthlessness. He was the prophet of the new Hungary and able to impress many humble people; but this was insufficient in terms of the struggle for power. Power was firmly retained in the hands of the old ruling class—until the Germans stepped in and settled the issue.

Anti-Semitism and Anti-Communism : the Iron Guard

If the national structure of Hungary, after the Treaty of Trianon, was extremely simple, that of her neighbour to the east, Rumania, was very complex. As Rumania was one of the 'victor nations' of the first world war (actually she had been defeated by the Germans), she received in 1919—at the expense of Bulgaria, Hungary and Russia—large areas with a very mixed population and possessed strong national minorities. Even according to the official Rumanian figures of 1920 only 70 per cent of the population of almost seventeen millions were Rumanian-speaking. Among the national minorities, the Hungarians of Transylvania were the strongest with more than nine per cent, or 1,500,000 people. The second largest minority were the Jews, over five per cent of the total, or 900,000 people, closely followed by the Ukrainians and the Germans. Most of the Jews lived in the newly gained lands, Bessarabia, Bukovina and Transylvania; and most of these were not assimilated and did not speak Rumanian, but spoke Yiddish. As in Hungary the Jews occupied a predominant position in trade, finance and industry (together with other foreigners); in a country which was dominated by the landlords the native middle classes had developed very late and the Jews had largely taken their place. Many towns of northern Rumania were largely Jewish.

Even before 1914 there had been strong anti-Semitism in Rumania going back to the time when wealthy Rumanian landlords employed Jewish agents to manage their estates and collect the taxes. The Jews were accused of exploiting the peasants and of having a monopoly of trade and industry. They were blamed for the country's ills, and pogroms were organized, as in Tsarist Russia, with the connivance of the government. Among the intellectuals anti-Semitism was preached by A. C. Cuza, who in 1901 became the professor of political economy at the University of Jaşi in the north-east of the country. To him, the solution of its problems was to be found in the expulsion of the foreigners who prevented the native energies from developing, in particular of the Jews. In this sense Cuza wrote for a review, that was founded in 1906 by the famous historian Nicolae Iorga, and attacked Jewish usurers and innkeepers who were ruining the peasants. In 1909 Iorga and Cuza founded the National Democratic Party which spread the nationalist creed among the young. Cuza, moreover, was opposed to liberalism and democracy and at an early stage adopted the swastika as his symbol. But he also campaigned for a land reform to benefit the peasants and for the grant of political rights to the lower classes. He exercised a strong influence on the younger generation, and on the intellectuals in general. One of his most ardent followers was Ion Zelea Codreanu, a teacher in a secondary school at Huşi.

Thanks to the outbreak of the Russian revolution the Rumanians were able to annex Bessarabia between the rivers Prut and Dniester, thus causing an almost permanent conflict with Soviet Russia. From this prolonged stalemate the agriculture and trade of Bessarabia suffered badly, there was widespread disaffection and many peasant risings occurred which were brutally suppressed.The administration was miserable, and a continuous state of martial law had to be maintained in the province. Political unrest, however, was not confined to Bessarabia. The Bolshevik revolution exercised a strong influence on the Rumanian workers; there were many large strikes and fear of a Russian invasion. In the eyes of a fervent young nationalist who tried to organize his school-mates to fight such an invasion, Jewish agitators were leading the Rumanian workers into action. 'Every Jew, whether he was a trader, intellectual or banker, was . . . an agent of the Communist ideas aimed at the Rumanian people.'[21] The young man who started his political activities in 1919 as a fighter against Bolshevism was Corneliu Zelea Codreanu, Ion Zelea's son born in 1899. He was educated in the years of the first world war at a military academy where he learnt the ideas of Order, Discipline and Leadership; already as a boy he avidly read the articles of Cuza which his father had collected.

In the autumn of 1919 the young Codreanu moved on to the Uni-

[21] Thus Codreanu, *Eiserne Garde*, Berlin, 1939, p. 10. The following, ibid., p. 11. Codreanu's autobiography is indispensable for an understanding of Rumanian Fascism, although it represents an idealized picture.

versity of Jaşi where Cuza was lecturing. But he found the workers and his fellow-students under strong left-wing influence; the king, the government and the army were under attack—facts which Codreanu connected with the number of Jews among the students of the university.[22] In this atmosphere Codreanu and his political friends fought their first battles: they beat up political enemies and Jews, expelled them from student clubs and hostels, destroyed the printing machines of hostile papers, forced the academic authorities to start the session with a religious service, and gradually established their control over the students' organizations. From the outset Codreanu's political ideas were distinctly radical. To the leader of an anti-Communist fighting group in Jaşi, the 'Guard of the National Conscience', he pointed out that it was not sufficient to defeat Communism, but that the workers' rights must be defended and national workers' organizations be founded to oppose the selfish and power-hungry political parties. After an attack on the editors of the paper *Opinia* Codreanu was expelled from the university by a decision of the Senate in 1921, but the Faculty of Law refused to recognize his expulsion. When he was elected president of the association of law students the Senate refused to confirm him in office, but this had little effect. All discussions and talks of the association now centred on the Jewish issue, and the lectures of Professor Cuza on political economy, which admonished all Rumanians to attend to 'this most serious problem of our time', were read not once, but several times.

As the official association of the Jaşi students continued to be in the hands of their enemies, Codreanu and his friends in 1922 founded the 'Association of Christian Students' and declared the rival organization dissolved. In their own association they abolished elections and the democratic system and adopted the leadership principle—not from any theoretical considerations, but out of an instinctive rejection of majority rule, which was deeply embedded in their 'blood'. In the following year Cuza and some other professors, among them Codreanu's father, in a solemn ceremony held in the university, founded the 'League of Christian and National Defence'. The flag of the new movement was black with a white circle and inside it the swastika, as a symbol of the anti-Semitic struggle. The League aimed at the exclusion of the Jews from the civil service and the army, the legal and the

[22] According to the figures given ibid., p. 76, over thirty-three per cent of the Jaşi students were Jews, and they strongly predominated in the medical and pharmaceutical faculties.

teaching professions and at the limitation of their numbers in the universities and schools. It opposed all political parties which it considered alien to the national interest, and during the following years it succeeded in absorbing some smaller Fascist groups of students and professors. That at Bucharest called itself the 'Rumanian National Fascio'; its programme was not only strongly anti-Semitic, but also anti-capitalist and demanded that the land should belong to those who tilled it. For the time being Codreanu and his fellow-students worked within the League, in which Cuza's influence predominated.

In 1923 Codreanu and some of his friends were arrested for the first time because they planned to kill 'traitors', responsible for granting rights of citizenship to Jews, as well as leading Jews. While in prison at Vacaresti he occupied himself with working out the plan for an organization of the young to be called the 'Archangel Michael', for in contrast with similar movements in other countries that in Rumania was strongly religious; the later meetings of the Legion were preceded by Orthodox religious services. To enlist Rumania's youth for nationalist action the first 'Brotherhood of the Cross' was founded at Jaşi. Its leader appointed by Codreanu was Ion Mota, a student who had just translated the *Protocols of the Elders of Zion* into Rumanian, and who saw the Jewish spirit at work everywhere. The Brotherhoods of the Cross spread to many secondary schools, and their members were taught discipline and strict organizational principles. In 1925 Codreanu was again in prison, this time because he had shot three police commissars who had manhandled arrested students. But he was acquitted by the jury, the members of which sported the national colours and the swastika. The train on which he returned to Jaşi was decorated with flowers and received at every station by festive crowds, led by the clergy and teachers. A vast crowd awaited it in Bucharest, and Codreanu was carried shoulder-high from the station. In his own opinion this wave of enthusiasm might have carried the League into power, but Cuza did not prove equal to the situation. In the elections of the following year the League polled 120,000 votes, only five per cent of the total, and gained ten seats in parliament. But in the next elections, in 1927, these seats were lost again; the League mustered a bare 50,000 votes and soon split into several groups.

Shortly before the elections Codreanu finally broke with his teacher Cuza and founded his own organization, the 'Legion of Archangel Michael', with himself as the Leader. The first roll-call lasted one minute. Codreanu told the few students present to examine themselves whether they were strong and determined enough to join the new movement; he then appointed sub-leaders to carry out his orders. The Legion had no programme; it was not to be a party and not to engage in politics, but an order animated by a faith. From older members, professors, officers, etc., Codreanu appointed a Senate of the Legion: its members were to hold the highest rank and should render advice but only when requested to do so. The Legion was to defend the Rumanian race against all attempts to destroy its structure and against the politicians who dishonoured and fouled the nobility of the race. To his fanatically loyal followers Codreanu became the 'Captain', the man without whom they could not carry out their 'mission'. 'Him we love; to him we listen. We are at his orders. He is our hope and the hope of the Rumania of tomorrow. We are strong through him. We are feared through him. We shall win through him.'[23]

The meetings of the Legion assumed a strange, semi-religious character. They only lasted for a few minutes and suffered from continuous interference by the police. In December 1929 Codreanu addressed a meeting in the small town of Beres̗ti, and then rode through the villages of the district. In his own words: 'After four kilometres I came to the village of Slivna. The night had fallen. The people awaited me in the street with burning lanterns and torches. At the entrance of the village I was received by the Legionaries. . . . In Comanesti, too, the whole village awaited me with torches and lanterns. The young were singing. . . . From village to village our number grew. Soon we were twenty horsemen. We were all young, between twenty-five and thirty years old. . . . As we were so many we felt that we needed a badge, a uniform. As we had no other possibility we decorated our caps with turkey feathers. . . . The news of our coming spread through all the villages from mouth to mouth. Everywhere we were expected eagerly. Whoever we met on the road asked us: Sir, when will you come to our village? Yesterday the old and the young waited for you until late at night! . . .' When the group returned to Beres̗ti it had grown to about fifty horsemen. 'We assembled and rode singing down in a long column. We were received with enthusiasm. The Rumanians came out of their houses full of joy. They put large buckets filled with water in our path. According to old custom, this was to bring us plenty and luck. We assembled in the yard of Nicu Balan where the meeting

[23] Quoted by Eugen Weber, 'Romania', in *The European Right*, ed. H. Rogger and E. Weber, Berkeley and Los Angeles, 1965, p. 532. Professor Weber's articles on the Iron Guard are by far the most valuable contributions to the subject.

was to take place. Now more than 3,000 people had assembled, but we did not hold a meeting. . . .'[24]

A few weeks later, in January 1930, Codreanu carried his crusading campaign across the Prut into Bessarabia: 'In the evening I had some white linen crosses made, about twenty centimetres long. I attached these to the breasts of the horsemen. I myself was given a small wooden cross which I was to carry in my hand. Thus I confronted the godless Jewish brood and assailed it. The next morning we crossed the Prut with thirty riders. . . . Singing we rode through the streets: "Rumanians, awake, awake!" We stopped in the main square. Soon 7,000 peasants assembled around us. No one knew who we were and what we wanted. But they all felt that we had come to liberate them. . . . On Monday morning I sent Potolea with fifty Legionaries to Kahul. They were to maintain order during the day. . . . At 10 o'clock we formed a marching column and marched across the Prut into Kahul. In front about a hundred Legionaries were riding in green shirts. They carried the flag. On our caps the turkey feathers waved and on our breasts the white linen crosses glowed. We looked like crusaders. And crusaders we wanted to be, knights who in the name of the cross were fighting the godless Jewish powers to liberate Rumania. . . . I only spoke briefly and said: "We shall not leave you! We shall never forget in what oppressive Jewish slavery you are languishing. You will become free! You will be the masters of the work of your hands, of your harvest and of your land! . . ."'[25] Thus Codreanu appealed to the peasants in one of the poorest and most neglected areas where trade and money-lending were largely in Jewish hands, to peasants who were neglected by the political parties and ignored by the government. There was a strong populist tendency in the Legion, glorifying the peasant's un-spoiled soul and seeking to revive the primitive values of the past. The Legionaries were sent to work with the peasants in the fields and thus to spread their propaganda among them, while the party politicians at best made speeches in the villages at election times.

The Legion itself had an élitist character and no mass membership. Out of the Legionary struggle a new Rumanian aristocracy was to emerge, not based on money or wealth, but on fortitude and strength of soul: 'as gold is purified by fire thus the true moral élite of the Rumanian nation will be cleansed in the fire of the Legionary struggle'.

[24] Codreanu, op. cit., pp. 331–4. The above is much abbreviated, as the original is rather lengthy.
[25] Ibid., pp. 338–45.

The Legionaries were to prevent the movement from moral decay, and the members from enriching themselves, from leading lives of luxury and immorality, from personal ambition and the hankering after high dignities.[26] But Codreanu realized that there must be a mass movement too if he wanted to fight elections and gain power. Thus in 1930 he founded the *Garda de Fier* ('Iron Guard') as a large national organization to fight Jewish Communism; the firm backbone of the new organization was to be formed by the Legion of Archangel Michael. While the Legion had mainly attracted students and members of the intelligentsia, the Iron Guard was to become a mass movement of the lower classes too. A special Workers' Corps was added to it in 1936, which soon had many thousands of members—in a country in which the Communist Party was suppressed as it was in Hungary. In the elections of 1931 the Iron Guard only polled 34,000 votes, 1·2 per cent of the total; but in the following year it gained 73,000 votes and five seats in parliament. The movement's main strength was in the villages, in particular those along the Prut where Codreanu had so vigorously campaigned during the previous years. In 1931 5,000 votes were cast for the Legion in Kahul alone. And these votes were gained in spite of severe persecution by the police. In 1932 the government dissolved the Iron Guard by decree; its houses were occupied and closed, the printing works at Jaşi shut.

In December 1933 the government of Ion G. Duca once more dissolved the Iron Guard and arrested thousands of the members. In reply three students killed the prime minister. Codreanu and other leaders were tried by court martial: this sentenced the three murderers to imprisonment for life, but acquitted Codreanu and the other accused and declared the dissolution illegal. The verdict caused a wave of sympathy for the Iron Guard in the country; business and industrial leaders began to support it. But Codreanu found a rival aspirant to dictatorship in the person of King Carol who with great pomp founded his own youth organization and campaigned against the political parties, at a time when totalitarianism was growing all over Europe. Each wanted his own dictatorship, and in the end bitter conflict resulted. Yet for a time the king thought that he could use the Iron Guard in his struggle against the parties: indirectly supported by the palace its strength grew quickly. In May 1935 there were 4,200 'nests'

---

[26] The above is taken from a circular of Codreanu of 12 February 1937 and from his instructions for the 'nest' leaders, point 80: quoted in *Rumänien am Rande des Abgrundes*, Bucharest, 1942, p. 157.

VARIETIES OF FASCISM IN EASTERN EUROPE

or local groups, in January 1937 12,000, and 34,000 by the end of the year. In Bucharest two large newspapers put themselves at Codreanu's disposal. In the capital food shops, restaurants, and news stands were established to defeat the Jewish traders. Later this movement spread to many other towns. In the elections of 1937 the Iron Guard gained an enormous victory and became the third strongest party in the country. It polled 478,000 votes, sixteen per cent of the total, and occupied sixty-six of the 390 parliamentary seats. After the election Codreanu publicly advocated an alliance of Rumania with Germany and Italy, 'the states of the national revolution', against the states of the Little Entente and against Bolshevism, while Rumania was traditionally allied with the other members of the Little Entente, Yugoslavia and Czechoslovakia, and with France, against any revisionist claims of Hungary and other powers.

It may have been this declaration—so contrary to the established system—or it may have been the very success of the Iron Guard in the elections which convinced the king and the government that cooperation with the Iron Guard was impossible. In any case, Carol suddenly went over to the attack and the movement suffered collapse. In February 1938 parliament and all political parties were declared dissolved; a new constitution was promulgated by decree; a single party, the 'Front of National Renaissance', was created membership in which was made obligatory for all officials; the ministers were appointed solely by the king and were responsible to him alone; the universal franchise was replaced by one based on corporations; only the king could initiate amendments to this constitution. On the day after the promulgation of the constitution, which made Rumania a semi-Fascist state, Codreanu himself disbanded the Iron Guard, to avoid, as he put it, an unnecessary loss of blood and the outbreak of civil war. But a few weeks later he was arrested with many of his followers, their houses were searched to find incriminating material, and a new trial was prepared against him. The prosecution alleged that the Legion was a terrorist organization, engaged in espionage on behalf of foreign powers, possessed hidden stores of weapons, and was preparing an armed rising. Codreanu was sentenced to ten years' hard labour for conspiracy and treason, and many of his followers suffered a similar fate, if they did not succeed in making their escape. During a night at the end of November 1938 Codreanu and thirteen others—the murderers of prime minister Duca and of an alleged traitor—were taken from their prison, tied with ropes, and strangled by the gendarmes who were escorting them. It was then announced that they had been 'shot while trying to escape'.

This deed did not bring to an end the bloody terrorism practised by both sides. In September 1939 the Legionaries in revenge murdered the 'strong man' of the Carol dictatorship, prime minister Armand Călinescu, who had carried through the campaign against the Iron Guard. Mass reprisals against the Legion followed, hundreds were shot out of hand, often innocents. To his devoted followers the murdered Captain became a martyr and a saint. Two years after his murder his remains were solemnly exhumed, together with those of the thirteen others, to lie in state in the church of Ilie Gorgani where priests prayed by their side day and night. Then 'the holy relics of the Căpitan', with those of the others, were interred in the mausoleum of the movement's 'Green House', where its other 'martyrs' were also buried. 'This week will be a week of religious devotion.'[27] In the movement itself, in so far as it survived the persecution, an even more radical and ferocious type of leader came to the fore. Many Legionaries for the time being found asylum in Germany.

After the outbreak of the second world war German influence and German control over the Rumanian economy steadily increased. King Carol more and more became a German partisan, but his régime did not gain popularity, and it suffered shattering defeats in the field of foreign policy. In June 1940 a Soviet ultimatum demanded the cession of Bessarabia and northern Bukovina—at a time when Soviet-German relations were still very close: there was no alternative but to comply, and the disputed regions were ceded to Russia. The course of the government became even more pro-German, some Legionaries were appointed to ministerial posts, anti-Semitic measures were taken, and the French and British guarantees which Rumania had accepted in 1939 were renounced. These steps, however, did not ensure German support against the revisionist claims of Hungary. In August 1940 the second Vienna Award fulfilled Hungary's claims in part and gave to her Northern Transylvania, but left the south and the Banat to Rumania, while Bulgarian claims were partially satisfied by the cession of the Southern Dobrudja. This dismemberment of the country—the loss of most that had been gained in 1919—Carol was unable to survive. After an abortive revolt of the Legionaries he was forced on 4 September to call in General Ion Antonescu who had been disgraced because

[27] The details are from the newspaper *Glasul Strămoşesc* of 1 December 1940, quoted in *Rumänien am Rande des Abgrundes*, p. 180.

of his sympathy with the Iron Guard. Two days later Carol abdicated in favour of his small son and left Rumania, accompanied by his mistress and his treasures. General Antonescu proclaimed himself *Conducator* ('Leader'), and a royal decree established the 'National Legionary State' with Antonescu as the Leader. The new government was largely composed of generals and civil servants, but Codreanu's successor, Horia Sima, became the deputy prime minister, and other Iron Guardists received important government posts. The situation seemed similar to that in Germany on 30 January 1933: the Iron Guard, although not a majority in the government, was the strongest factor within it, and it only seemed a question of time until it would push aside its rivals and exercise full power.

This, in any case, was the opinion of the Legionaries themselves, many of whom considered this a golden opportunity for settling old accounts and lining their own pockets. Many now were time-servers and opportunists, and their discipline had deteriorated. With or without authority, the Legionary Police searched houses, arrested people, tortured them, confiscated their property, or forced them to sell it at fictitious prices. Thus the Legionary Boeru took over a factory which had a value of fifty million Lei for the price of five million of which only 500,000 were ever paid. His own men then replaced the directors and managers. The government eventually listed 1,162 similar cases, and another 1,081 of outright seizures. The police did not interfere or participate. If this had been directed only against the Jews, all might have been well, but 'true Rumanians' were also among the victims. Horia Sima promised that the violence would be stopped, but was himself unable to control his unruly followers. A commission was appointed and charged with the 'adaptation of higher education to the structure of the National Legionary State'. It saw its task in purging the Legion's enemies from the teaching bodies—especially the followers of Cuza, their old rivals—and in expelling students who declined to carry out the Legion's orders. The minister of education declared: 'The teachers must be reeducated by their own students.'[28]

This state of affairs soon caused considerable friction between General Antonescu, the Leader, and the Iron Guard. In September Horia Sima had ordered the Legionaries to show 'gratitude, fidelity and complete confidence in General Antonescu because he has elevated the Legion and honoured it'. But four weeks later Sima wrote to him complaining strongly that the press was still permitted to criticize and

[28] Weber, op. cit., p. 562.

attack the régime, that the economy was not directed, and that the Legionaries were held responsible for the 'few cases of illegalities which, in most cases, have been committed in good faith'. 'Do not forget', Sima continued, 'that this is a Legionary régime, that the Legionaries are privileged, that they must be asked first, that your fatherly care must first be bestowed upon them. For two years they have been beaten, should they now suffer once more? . . . Therefore we beg you to continue on the path of the "Căpitan" and to grant us the liberty to realize our Legionary programme—a task on which we have not yet started, for until now we have been the prisoners of our own government. . . .' To this Antonescu replied that it was impossible for two conductors to direct the same orchestra: if there were within one state two police forces, two systems of justice, two political and economic leaderships, if everybody interfered, if everybody issued orders when and how he pleased, the collapse of order which had begun would continue at a fantastic pace and chaos would result. He was unwilling to allow the Legionaries and the country to become the victims of anarchy.[29] The two attitudes clearly were irreconcilable.

Worse was to follow. Antonescu decided to disband the separate Legionary Police, but the minister of the interior incorporated it with the ordinary police so that it acquired new authority. The Legionaries refused to give up their weapons. They murdered the famous historian Nicolae Iorga, the economist Virgil Madgearu, and sixty-four political detainees held in Jiliva prison, mainly chiefs of police and agents of the Carol régime, most of them without any warrant of arrest. The tortures continued unabated. There were persistent rumours of a second revolution, a 'night of the long knives' when the Legion would seize total power. One of the Legionary papers apostrophied Horia Sima: 'Horia, the man of our days, is higher than the mountains. He is like an angel and carries the archangel's sword. . . . Horia is the thought, Horia is the feeling, Horia is the light, the will, and all our strength. We stand by Horia with a fanatical faith and believe in him to our death. Horia is our commander. . . .'[30] A struggle for power between the two 'Leaders' became inevitable.

The real question at the beginning of 1941 was whether Hitler would support Antonescu or Sima. Antonescu went to Germany and succeeded in convincing Hitler that he would have to choose between the

---

[29] The correspondence is printed in full in *Rumänien am Rande des Abgrundes*, pp. 103–5.

[30] *Glasul Strămoşesc* of 15 December 1940, quoted ibid., p. 180.

two. As Hitler was preoccupied with his plans of domination and conquest in eastern Europe and for this reason needed an orderly régime
in Rumania capable of aiding him, he chose the general—exactly as in
France he supported Marshal Pétain and in Hungary the Horthy
régime, as long as they delivered the goods he required. He even
advised Antonescu to deal with the Legionaries as he, Hitler, in 1934
had dealt with the rebellious *S.A.* After his return from Germany
Antonescu replaced the minister of the interior and the chief of police
by reliable army officers; the prefects and police chiefs belonging to the
Legion were equally removed and men loyal to the general appointed
in their place. In Bucharest vast crowds protested against these changes
and soon clashed with the army and police. There was wild rioting and
looting; many Jews and others were murdered; execution squads were
formed to kill all 'traitors' and former prominent politicians under
the pretence that they were freemasons.

In the evening of 21 January Sima put forward his demands to
Antonescu: the general was to retire and his place to be taken by Sima,
with all the ministries in the hands of the Legion. On the next day the
revolt was in full swing. The public buildings and radio stations were
occupied by the Legionaries. Barricades were erected in the streets by
derailing trams and using petrol vans which were to be set alight if
the army advanced. The Legionaries from the villages were ordered
into the towns to reinforce their comrades. In Bucharest posters proclaimed: 'The freemasons of Rumania, the hirelings of England and
the Jews, have anew raised their heads. In the protection of their dark
lodges they are fomenting plans against the Axis powers and the
Legionary régime. They hate the Legionaries. . . . The enemies of
National Socialist Germany and its ideology are also the enemies of
the Legionaries! We all fight for the same ideal, the new order
of Europe. . . .' The enemies of the Legion were threatened with dire
penalties and the fate of the murdered Călinescu who had been dis-
patched to hell. The Legion's aim was: 'Life or Death at the side of
Germany and Italy'.[31] The fighting lasted for only two days. Once
more it was proved that semi-trained and ill-armed levies were no
match for a modern army. In Bucharest alone 370 people were killed.
German tanks staged a demonstration in favour of the government.
Antonescu triumphed, and the defeated Legionaries fled to Germany.
On 15 February the 'National Legionary State' was officially abolished;

[31] Posters of 22 January 1941, quoted ibid., p. 299.

it was replaced by a 'National and Social State' with Antonescu in sole control.

In Rumania—as in Hungary—the Left was insignificant and power-less; hence the Fascists could develop into a movement in favour of radical social change, advocating the distribution of the land and a directed economy which attracted many peasants, but fewer workers than in Hungary. Not only the leaders of the Iron Guard, but also many of their followers came from academic and semi-academic circles, but its propaganda and programme were populist. As in Hungary—and in Austria—the rising middle classes were above all attracted by the anti-Semitic slogans which promised to remove their successful competitors in trade and industry, in education and the professions. Codreanu combined several appeals, the religious, the social and the national, the anti-Communist and the anti-Semitic. But without his colourful personality the Legion collapsed twice in the face of a deter-mined attack by the government, in 1938 as well as in 1941. The Iron Guard did not possess the strength to seize power by itself, nor to maintain itself in the government once it had got there, factors which clearly distinguished it from the German and the Italian Fascists. The backward and underdeveloped state of Rumanian society, the dis-content among the peasants and the intelligentsia, and the absence of an effective Left, offered a chance to the extreme Right which it proved unable to seize. Its very violence and lack of discipline created ob-stacles which it could not surmount, and cost it the support of the army—a factor which proved decisive.

6 | Varieties of Fascism in Western Europe

Spain : from National Syndicalism to the Falange

Spain—like Hungary and Rumania—was an extremely backward country, with comparatively little industry, a very poor peasantry, and an unsolved land problem—a very large part of the land belonging to the Church and the nobility. But in contrast with the eastern European countries Spain had a strong—but deeply divided—working-class movement and many violent conflicts between the Left and the Right, between republicans and monarchists. The strongest force on the Left were the Syndicalists or Anarcho-Syndicalists who dominated the trade union movement, but were opposed to political action and did not participate in elections. But side by side with them there was a strong Socialist Party—divided into left- and right-wingers—and Socialist trade unions; there also was a small Communist Party and various splinter groups of the Left. Ever-present was the threat of violence emanating from the Left, especially from the Anarcho-Syndicalists who aimed at the overthrow of the established order and were extremely militant, violently opposed to the ruling classes of society and to the Church and its privileges. They had strong influence not only among the urban proletarians, but also among the landless agricultural labourers and poor peasants. Social rebellion was never far from the surface. Apart from peasant revolts, there was a tradition of revolutionary strike movements in town and country which at times had to be quelled by the machine guns of the army. The upper and middle classes reacted to left-wing violence by the employment of gunmen; they saw no reason to make concessions to the workers or the landless peasants, but clung to their traditional powers. In hardly any other country in Europe were social differences so marked and social conflicts so bitter as they were in Spain.

Yet the governments were weak and ever-changing, and political violence increased in the years after the first world war. When, in addition, the Spanish army in the early 1920s suffered disastrous defeats in Morocco popular discontent with the incompetent leaders and corrupt politicians rapidly increased. This was the situation when General Miguel Primo de Rivera, marqués de Estella and captain-general of Catalonia, in September 1923 decided to carry out a *coup d'état* to liberate Spain from 'the professional politicians, the men . . . responsible for the period of misfortune and corruption which began in 1898', when Spain had been defeated disastrously by the United States and lost Cuba. The government resigned, King Alfonso XIII requested Primo de Rivera to take office, the *Cortes* was dissolved, and the constitution abrogated. Yet it was not a Fascist régime which replaced the 'decadent' parliamentary one, but rather an old-fashioned military dictatorship with the officers firmly in control. Internal disorders were put down. Only in 1925 was an attempt made to mobilize popular support by the foundation of a new political party, the *Unión Patriótica*, to underpin the régime. Even this was not a Fascist party; beyond the veneration of nation, Church and king it had no ideology, and no momentum of its own. It was a collection of conservatives whose duty it was to support the dictatorship and to fan patriotic feelings. Although Primo de Rivera greatly admired Mussolini, he either did not have the wish or the strength of purpose to imitate his example. He even cooperated with the Socialist trade unions. Indeed, beyond patriotism, anti-parliamentarianism and the union of all Spaniards the general had no political programme. When his health began to fail and discontent spread to the armed forces the generals hesitated to prolong his authority; at the beginning of 1930 Primo de Rivera was thus forced to resign. He left Spain and died soon after. His régime left no lasting traces in the country—apart from that of military interference with politics; but that was a well-established tradition, going back to the nineteenth century.

There followed a short period of semi-dictatorship, but the king was increasingly criticized as he was held responsible for the dictatorship and the failures of the past. Republican sentiments were growing, and in the local elections of the spring of 1931 the republicans gained a majority in the major towns. They loudly demanded the abdication of the king, and even the moderate middle classes and the army officers began to desert him. Less than fifteen months after Primo de Rivera's fall the king followed him into exile, and the elections of June 1931 gave to the left-wing parties a decisive majority in the *Cortes*. A new republican constitution was adopted which for the first time made Spain a democracy; it was also strongly anti-clerical and threatened the age-old privileges of the Church. Left-wing violence, which had been suppressed by Primo de Rivera, quickly reappeared and local uprisings had to be put down by the army. They aroused widespread fears among the propertied classes while the government seemed unable to cope with the situation. The Second Republic seemed to bring a repetition of the years before Primo de Rivera's *coup d'état*. The republic was ruled by the Liberals, but they did not provide a stable government, and in the elections of November 1933 the Right gained a significant victory, while the Left was decimated.

It was in this situation of political weakness and uncertainty that some young Spaniards, mainly students or former students, began to turn towards Fascism as a solution of their country's ills. Significantly they saw these ills not only in government weakness and the loss of Imperial power, but also in social injustice and oppression. Their main inspiration did not come from Italy, but from Germany. In 1930 the two leading spirits of these groups, Ramiro Ledesma Ramos and Onésimo Redondo Ortega, both at the age of twenty-five, spent a few months at German universities where they had close contacts with National Socialist students. They returned to Spain full of enthusiasm —a Spain which they considered rotten to the core, whether it was republican or monarchist. They began to publish extracts from *Mein Kampf*, articles on Fascism and National Socialism, and fervent appeals to the young to restore the greatness of Spain which should again become 'a nation of heroic soldiers'. At the same time they favoured 'direct action' against the political Left: street fights with left-wing youth groups, the destruction of their enemies' political clubs, the acquisition of weapons, later the making of bombs. This clearly showed the influence of the Anarchists whom Ledesma Ramos eulogized, and of their practice of 'propaganda by the deed'.

In March 1931 these two young men and their disciples at the universities of Madrid and Valladolid began to publish a weekly, *La Conquista del Estado* ('The Conquest of the State') in which Ledesma Ramos proclaimed: 'We are not interested in either the monarchy or the republic. They are the concern of old men. Whatever flag may triumph—we shall oppose it . . .'; and 'Our primary goal is revolutionary efficiency. Therefore we do not seek votes, but audacious and valiant minorities. . . .'[1] Many articles attacked the decadence of Spain and contrasted it to the country's glory under the Catholic kings of the fifteen and sixteenth centuries. The nation must become heroic once more, disciplined and militarized, full of national enthusiasm. But the demands were also decidedly more radical than those of the National Socialists. The paper soon demanded the nationalization of the key industries, of transport, the banks and insurance companies, and state control of foreign trade. In June 1931 it declared: 'Long live the new world of the twentieth century! Long live Fascist Italy! Long live Soviet Russia! Long live Hitler Germany! Long live the Spain we will make! Down with the bourgeois parliamentary democracies!'[2] In Germany these might have been the slogans of the revolutionary National Socialists of Otto Strasser, although he might have hesitated to hail Hitler, to whom he liked to refer as *Adolf Légalité* or Wilhelm III.

In the autumn of 1931 the two minute groups at Madrid and Valladolid proceeded to the foundation of a party, *Juntas de Ofensiva Nacional Sindicalista* ('Groups of National Syndicalist Offensive'), or *J.O.N.S.*, the first Fascist party in Spain. Its flag, characteristically enough, was the black and red flag of the Anarcho-Syndicalists on which was superimposed the Yoke and Arrows of the Catholic kings, adopted by the *J.O.N.S.* as their emblem: the glorious past and the revolutionary present. The party manifesto demanded: respect for the Catholic tradition, Imperialist expansion, the acquisition of Gibraltar, Morocco and Algeria, the fight against any separatist tendencies, the abolition of the parliamentary system, the dissolution of all Marxist and anti-national parties, the outlawing of the class struggle, state control of the economy, partitioning of the large estates, compulsory organization of all employers and employees in national syndicates, and the countering of red violence by nationalist violence. In the National Syndicalist state of the future the youth would occupy all high offices, production would be planned, and wealth redistributed. This programme was distinctly more radical even than that of the Iron Guard or the Hungarian National Socialists.

---

[1] Quoted by Bernd Nellessen, *Die verbotene Revolution*, Hamburg, 1963, p. 51, and Stanley G. Payne, *Falange*, Stanford, 1961, p. 13. These are the two basic books on the subject discussed in this section. The quotations are from the first issue of *La Conquista del Estado*.

[2] *La Conquista del Estado*, no. 13, 6 June 1931, quoted by Payne, op. cit., p. 14.

It was bound to alienate the traditional Right; but its appeal to the Left which in Spain was strong and vigorous was likely to remain very limited. Indeed, the *J.O.N.S.* only had a following among university students, and even there it was never very large. It also attracted a few disillusioned young Anarchists.

In 1933, the year of Hitler's seizure of power—which was enthusiastically celebrated by the *J.O.N.S.*—another Fascist party was founded by General Primo de Rivera's son, José Antonio Primo de Rivera, who was then thirty years old, and well versed in the literature of Fascism and National Socialism, as well as that of Bolshevism. In August the young marqués (he had inherited his father's title) met Ledesma Ramos to explore the possibility of combining with the *J.O.N.S.* in a new party, to be called *Fascismo Español*, but Ledesma declined. Two months later, in October, Primo de Rivera founded his own party, the *Falange Española*, at a meeting in Madrid which was attended by about 2,000 people, mainly from the Right, more than the *J.O.N.S.* had ever been able to mobilize. To them Primo de Rivera explained: 'The movement now founded is not a party, but a movement *per se*, I might almost say, an anti-party. It belongs, this must be stated clearly once and for all, neither to the Right nor to the Left. On the Right there is the intention to maintain an economic order that is unjust. On the Left there is the desire to overthrow the economic order, even if this means losing much that is good. . . .' The political parties must go: 'No one was ever born a member of a political party'. To those who argued that a Fascist leader must be a man of the people, that the workers could only be won over by a man of their own kind, he exclaimed: 'Yes, we wear ties! Yes, you can say of us that we are young gentlemen (*señoritos*)! But we fight for aims which are not the concern of young gentlemen. We fight so that hard and just sacrifices may be imposed on many members of our own social group. We struggle for a totalitarian state that will distribute its fruits fairly to the small and to the big people. . . .' If it was necessary to gain their political aims they would not shrink from using violence: 'Our place is in the fresh air, under the cloudless heavens, weapons in our hands, with the stars above us. . . .'[3]

A few months later, in February 1934, the National Council of the *J.O.N.S.* met in Madrid to consider the possibility of merging with

[3] The speech is quoted by Payne, op. cit., pp. 38–41, and Bernd Nellessen, *José Antonio Primo de Rivera, Der Troubadour der spanischen Falange*, Stuttgart, 1965, no. 6, pp. 38–45.

the *Falange*. The *J.O.N.S.* too had grown in 1933; in Madrid it founded a syndicate of taxi drivers and waiters, and small groups had been formed in other Spanish towns, mainly by students. But it was still a very minor group, without any financial support. Thus they decided to amalgamate with the *Falange*, under the name of *Falange Española de las Juntas de Ofensiva Nacional Sindicalista*—not precisely a short name. The *J.O.N.S.* flag, emblem and slogans were retained, and the movement was to be led by a triumvirate consisting of Primo de Rivera, Ledesma Ramos and Ruiz de Alda. Thus Primo de Rivera had to accept radical demands and actions which many of his old friends disliked; but among the *J.O.N.S.* too distrust remained alive of the nobleman and intellectual, the *señorito*. What Ledesma Ramos and his friends opposed particularly was the tendency within the *Falange* to establish, in place of the triumvirate, a uniform leadership, the *jefatura única*, with Primo de Rivera as the *Jefe* (Leader). A motion to that effect was carried at the National Council in October 1934, but only by a majority of one; while Ledesma was appointed chairman of a new *Junta política* to work out a definitive party programme. By this curious democratic process Primo de Rivera secured his control of the movement. But three months later an open rebellion broke out against his leadership, and Ledesma and his closest friends were expelled. Their hope that many others would follow them was not fulfilled.

The *Falange*'s attempts to organize the workers and to make inroads into the Socialist movement only met with very limited success. A 'Confederation of National Syndicalist Workers' was founded in 1934. It was militant, declared its full agreement with the economic aims of the Left, denounced the 'company' unions, and wanted to infuse nationalism into the proletarian revolution. But apparently only some taxi-drivers and waiters responded to this appeal. Primo de Rivera was more successful in securing financial help from wealthy aristocrats, monarchists and financiers; but others resigned from the *Falange* whose radical slogans they disliked. Its programme, adopted in 1934, rejected the capitalist system because 'it misjudges the needs of the people, it dehumanizes private property, it pushes the workers together in unformed masses given over to misery and despair'. It advocated the nationalization of the banks and of the great public services, the redistribution of the cultivable land, the resettlement of the peasants tilling barren soil on new plots, and the expropriation of land 'acquired or used illegitimately'. 'It is insufferable that large masses live in misery, while a small group enjoys all conceivable luxury.'[4] Primo de Rivera was very conscious of the fact that his party stood for policies from which he himself and his social class were bound to suffer. During the election campaign of 1935 he explained at Seville: 'On the day when our revolution will be victorious, many on our side will lose much, perhaps everything. But in spite of this we are longing for the revolution, for we know that it is useless to enjoy privileges for a few more years while Spain is ruined meanwhile. . . .'[5] His patent sincerity assured to him the loyalty of his followers.

During 1934–35 the party developed into a proper Fascist party, with the Fascist salute, and blue shirts as the uniform, but at the end of 1935 it had only about 8,000 members. In the only elections in which it participated, in February 1936, it polled a mere 5,000 votes in Madrid, 1·2 per cent of the total, and 4,000 votes in Valladolid, four per cent of the total. Primo de Rivera himself gained 7,000 votes in Cádiz, but lost his seat, and the party did not obtain a single mandate. Only among the students—most of whom were too young to vote—it continued to enjoy strong support: its student members were more numerous than those of all other social groups taken together. The large majority of the members were under twenty-one years old. But Primo de Rivera made a virtue out of necessity and followed a strongly élitist principle, not aiming at organizing the masses, 'but to select minorities—not many, but few, though ardent and convinced; for so everything in the world has been done.'[6] Curiously enough, his contacts with Hitler and the National Socialists remained slight. When he visited Berlin in the spring of 1934 he found them depressing and divided, and he never went again. Nor does he seem to have had contacts with Mussolini and the Fascists. Indeed, it seems unlikely that either Hitler or Mussolini would have impressed this born aristocrat.

The elections of February 1936 which brought such a singular defeat to the *Falange* resulted in a decisive victory for the political Left which gained a clear majority in parliament. But this did not bring about a decline in political violence: on the contrary, the rule of the Popular Front which resulted from the election saw more and more clashes and battles between the armed gangs of the extreme Left and the extreme Right. To stem this violence the government, in March

[4] Points 10, 12, 14, 19 and 21 of the programme of the *Falange*: Nellessen, op. cit., no. 22, pp. 115–17; *Verbotene Revolution*, pp. 165–7.
[5] Speech of 22 December 1935: Nellessen, *José Antonio Primo de Rivera*, no. 20, p. 109.
[6] Speech of 17 February 1935: Payne, op. cit., p. 75.

1936, dissolved the *Falange*; most of the leaders were arrested, including Primo de Rivera, and its organization was disrupted. In revenge the party, driven underground, organized the murder of political enemies, be that local Socialist functionaries or a judge who had sentenced a young Falangist for his participation in a similar deed. From his prison cell Primo de Rivera continued to direct his movement, warning the new leaders to remain independent and not to conclude an alliance with the traditional Right or with the army; for 'the Falange is not a conservative force', and should not take part in any movement 'that is not going to lead to the establishment of the National Syndicalist state'.[7] By this time he was clearly aware that such a move was being prepared, and at the end of June he ordered his followers to support it. A few days before the outbreak of the nationalist revolt, on 12 July, he wrote in a letter: 'One of the most awful things to happen would be a national republican dictatorship. Another false attempt which I fear is . . . the establishment of a false, conservative Fascism without revolutionary courage and young blood.'[8] Primo de Rivera had lost his liberty, but neither his political independence nor his courage.

What he feared was precisely what happened. The rebellion of the generals started prematurely in Morocco on 17 July and a few days later in Spain. The military leaders talked vaguely about saving the republic, restoring order, bringing about reforms, but they had no clear goal and no programme—beyond that of destroying the Popular Front. In this hour the *Falange* found itself without leaders—they were in prison—and without any clear purpose. For the first time in its history it became a mass movement—in the parts of Spain controlled by the military *Junta*—but that only increased the confusion. The few old cadres were completely swamped, thousands hastened to don the blue shirt and volunteered for the *Falange* militia. But General Franco had no intention of adopting the revolutionary slogans and demands of the *Falange* with which he was entirely out of sympathy. He was a conservative of the old school, and his revolt a *Putsch* by the army leaders, not a social and national revolution. Primo de Rivera's warning from his prison cell had only been too justified. Ironically enough, he was tried in November 1936 by a 'people's court' for helping to prepare the revolt, was sentenced to death, and executed a few days later. As he was safely out of the way, he could become the official martyr and

[7] Editorial and circular of June 1936, quoted by Payne, op. cit., pp. 111–12.
[8] Letter of 12 July 1936, quoted by Nellessen, *José Antonio Primo de Rivera*, p. 23.

patron saint of the Franco dictatorship—a system which he undoubtedly would have opposed if he had remained alive.

With the Leader in prison—even after his death many of his followers
refused to believe in it—the leaders in the area controlled by the generals
devised the expedient of forming a *Junta* of seven members with a
chairman to lead the party until the time when the *Jefe* would reappear.
As chairman they appointed Manuel Hedilla, the former provincial
leader of Santander, a mechanic by trade, but the decisions were taken
by a majority vote, as they had been during the first year. Under
this régime the *Falange* continued to grow rapidly as many opportunists and former left-wingers joined it, partly under pressure and to
escape reprisals. But there was little direction from the centre and
organizational chaos reigned. The *Falange* militia was inefficient and
regarded with derision by the army. The party press published favourable reports on Hitler's Germany and Mussolini's Italy and even indulged in anti-Semitic propaganda—an academic issue in Spain where
there were only a few thousand Jews without any influence. But the
true Falangists preferred their own ideology, the emphasis on Catholicism and on the glorious past, to the cult of race and fatherland
which they considered pagan, as Hedilla pointed out in October
1936.⁹

By the beginning of 1937 the *Falange* leaders were divided into three
factions. There was the group around Hedilla who was supported by
the majority of provincial leaders and surrounded by pseudo-Fascist
intellectuals who were influenced vaguely by National Socialism. There
were the *Falange* traditionalists, the loyal adherents of Primo de
Rivera; and there were the newcomers, opportunists, monarchists and
conservatives who wanted to remould the party in their own sense. The
confusion among the leading group and the opposition to Hedilla who
failed to give any direction were growing apace. His critics feared that
he would try to make himself the *Jefe* under the protectorate of the
army. At a meeting of the *Junta* leaders called suddenly for 12 April
three of them announced their reasons for opposing him and declared
him deposed. He was to be replaced by a triumvirate—again a device
from the early days of the party. Of the seven members four voted
against Hedilla, who then summoned the National Council of the
Falange for 18 April, to elect a *Jefe*. But there too he only obtained a
minority of the votes, while many abstained and some voted for other
candidates. On the following day the National Council was to meet

⁹ Quoted by Payne, op. cit., p. 127.

again to elect a new *Junta política*, but this was prevented by the ruling military group.

On that day, 19 April 1937, General Franco published a decree which united the *Falange* and the *Requetés* (the militia of the Carlist monarchists) into one political formation, the *Falange Española Tradicionalista y de las Juntas de Ofensiva Nacional Sindicalista*, and combined their two separate militias into one national militia. Franco also appointed himself the leader of the new official party of the régime, while an army general was to become the commander of the militia. It was the end of any political independence or autonomy enjoyed by the *Falange* which henceforth stood under Franco's control. Its former leader, Hedilla, was arrested a few days later, tried by a military court for attempted rebellion, sentenced to death, but not executed and only placed in solitary confinement. The other leaders too were detained for shorter or longer periods. The new official party of the régime was an amorphous conglomeration of traditionalists, monarchists, militant Catholics, right-wingers and conservatives, among whom the Falangists were only a minority; all civil servants and officers belonged to it automatically. All these groups continued to have their different aims: there was no unity and no ideology, apart from that provided by Franco as the leader. But he stood much closer to the Spanish tradition of the *caudillo*, of the successful military leader and of Miguel Primo de Rivera, than to that of the original *Falange*. He steered it away from the aims and the path mapped out by José Antonio Primo de Rivera and the National Syndicalists.

Franco's new *Falange* (with the enormously long name) no longer had any political functions, nor was it allowed any political initiative. It was firmly tied to the army, with its militia commanded by army officers. The original Falangists were looked at askance by their Catholic and Conservative partners in the official state party. They distrusted the emphasis on social and economic reform which had characterized the *Falange* and considered its members radicals or crypto-Socialists. As Franco shared their views and had no intention of giving way to radical demands, the scales were heavily weighted from the outset. That the new *Falange* was not a Fascist party was clearly seen by Count Ciano, the Italian Foreign minister; when one of the early Falangists visited Italy in 1938 Ciano drew him aside and remarked that with the elderly conservatives of the new party no proper Fascist party could be built. When the civil war came to an end the influence and role of the state party became even more modest—but the same applied to the Fascist Party in Italy and to the National Socialist Party in Germany after the establishment of the one-party state. Their truly important functions had been before the seizure of power, not after it. Only that in Spain the original *Falange* was far too weak ever to attempt that goal.

It might be said that its radicalism was partly connected with this fact, that it might have shed much of this radicalism if it had ever become a mass party. Yet it recognized the ills of Spanish society far more clearly than the traditional groups and parties of the Right: whether it would ever have possessed the strength to carry out social reform unaided is impossible to say, but it does not seem likely that it could have done so. As things stood an alliance with the parties of the Left was out of the question, and any combination with those of the Right would have resulted in compromise, a compromise precisely on those issues on which the *Falange* differed most strongly from the traditional Right and from the Franco régime.

Flanders : from Nationalism to Fascism

The Belgian state founded after 1830 contained two nationalities, almost equally strong, with different languages and cultures. One, the Walloons, by virtue of their French language and their cultural links with France, were the more developed nationality and had more academically trained people: they occupied a large proportion of the leading posts in the state and the national life. The Flemings, whose language and culture were the same as those of the Dutch farther to the north, were in a less favourable position politically as well as economically, and in the twentieth century began to develop a strong sense of grievance, demanding equality of rights and of opportunity with the Walloons. As their birthrate was higher it was only a question of time until the Flemings would outnumber the Walloons. But for a long time the latter clung to their privileged and leading position and were reluctant to make concessions, either in the field of language, or in that of schools and education in general, or in the civil service and the army. The Flemings, on the other hand, could reckon on support from Holland, where some intellectuals were conscious of the common heritage and attracted by the idea of a Great Netherlands. But with the rise of a militant German nationalism its leaders too began to take an interest in Belgian affairs and to sympathize with the aspirations of their Flemish 'cousins'. In particular the Pan-German League, founded at the end of the nineteenth century,[10] considered the Flemings to be Germans and each gain of the Walloons a defeat for the German 'cause'.

These tendencies came to a head during the first world war when most of Belgium was occupied by the Germans, who strongly supported the Flemish movement. The Flemings became more radical in their political demands. A group *Jong Vlaanderen* ('Young Flanders') was founded at Ghent in October 1914; it was strongly anti-Belgian and looked to Germany as the natural protector of Flemish interests. Its programme proclaimed: 'The state and the name of Belgium must disappear. A kingdom of Flanders must be created, linked with Germany in the political as well as the military field. . . .'[11] Other nationalist Flemings, however, would go less far. Their best-known leader and speaker, Dr August Borms, advocated 'a free Flanders in a free Belgium' and wanted to be tied neither to Germany nor to France. In 1917 a Flemish National Diet met which elected a Flemish Council. Its majority desired the dissolution of the Belgian state and voted in March 1918: 'Flanders must be politically independent, with its own government, executive, legislative and judicial powers, and its own diplomatic representatives abroad. . . .'[12] These Flemish 'activists' had no mass influence, most of them were intellectuals, and only the students proved susceptible to their ideas. The movement was too obviously pro-German to arouse much enthusiasm in wider circles, at a time when it became evident that the Germans wanted to establish a protectorate over Flanders.

At the same time a movement of a very different character was growing in the Belgian army which was engaged in fighting the Germans near the Channel coast. The official language of the army was French, and its leaders were French-speaking officers. But many of the soldiers came from Western Flanders—the only part of the country not under German control. During the stalemate of trench warfare on the western front they, under the inspiration of the village clergy, tried to establish the rights of their own language within the army. Their slogan was: 'All for Flanders—Flanders for Christ', the initials forming a cross which became their emblem. The movement was not

[10] See above, pp. 28–9.
[11] A. W. Willemsen, *Het Vlaamse-nationalisme*, Groningen, 1958, p. 5. This is virtually the only monograph on the subject discussed here.
[12] Ibid., p. 34.

pro-German, nor was it anti-Belgian, and it highly respected the King of the Belgians, Albert I. But it naturally worried the army leaders who attempted to suppress it. It was thus driven underground; during the summer of 1917 an illegal organization came into being, with representatives and committees at company, battalion, regimental and divisional levels. The leader of this *Frontbeweging* was a corporal, Adiel de Beuckelaere, in peace-time a teacher in Ghent, and the subordinate leaders too were intellectuals. One of them was Joris van Severen, a law student from Ghent university, and students predominated throughout, as they did in the movement in the German-occupied parts. In July 1917 they published an open letter to the king, which in detail described the grievances of the soldiers, and demanded a Flemish army and self-government for the Flemings. The reply of the army leaders was stricter persecution than before.

Persecution, however, was unable to break up the movement which was well led and well organized, in a sector of the front which remained stable for years. But when Germany finally collapsed in the autumn of 1918 and the German army withdrew from Belgium, the Belgians' advance was so rapid and the area reoccupied so large that all coherence among the units was lost, and the Flemish leaders had no contact with each other and no control. The aims of the *Frontbeweging* could not be realized. At the beginning of 1919 the former soldiers founded the *Vlaamsche Front* ('Flemish Front') which soon developed into a political party, the *Frontpartij*, and pursued the same aims as the soldiers' movement: Flemish regiments within the army, self-government for Flanders, Flemings to decide upon all issues affecting Flanders, school teaching to be in the mother tongue, Ghent to be transformed into a Flemish university, etc. The party was strongly Catholic, and its leaders were students or former students, from Louvain and Ghent. But it had a strong influence in the countryside, mainly among the small farmers of districts close to the capital, where the upper groups spoke French or were under French cultural influence. In the elections of October 1919 the *Frontpartij* gained 6·3 per cent of the Flemish vote and five seats in parliament. One of the new deputies was a young teacher, Staf de Clercq, who was enormously popular in his country district near Brussels. Even before the election, the Flemish cause had acquired numerous martyrs in the 'activists' of the German-occupied area who were tried by courts-martial in 1919. Dr Borms was sentenced to death, and so were thirty-eight others, but the sentences were not carried out. Fifteen more were condemned to life imprisonment, and many hundreds to terms of imprisonment ranging up to twenty-five years. These harsh sentences kept the cause alive and contributed to the success of the *Frontpartij*.

In the elections of 1921, however, the party suffered some losses. A deputy elected for the first time was Joris van Severen, then twenty-seven years old, the son of a west-Flemish mayor and notary. Van Severen, like other leaders, strongly emphasized Catholicism and the Flemish national culture—as its irreconcilable enemy he denounced the Belgian state, although his own language was really French and he was deeply steeped in French culture. He was an intellectual and an artist rather than a politician, but his dynamic personality gained him great popularity in Western Flanders.[13] The setback of 1921 was overcome in 1925 when the party gained 25,000 votes and six seats. There was another considerable advance in 1929 when the party polled 132,000 votes and obtained eleven seats in the chamber. It had gained a substantial share of the Flemish vote, but Van Severen lost his seat owing to the intricacies of the Belgian voting system. By that time he had developed into a firm admirer of the doctrine of Charles Maurras and of Mussolini and a sworn enemy of the Belgian state which must be destroyed. In 1929 he founded a Flemish militia wearing green shirts and armed with clubs. He strongly influenced the students of Ghent, his old university, who were searching for a new ideology, nationalist and right-wing, looking beyond the Flemish frontiers. Among them there developed the idea of a Great Netherlands or *Dietsch* state, to embrace the Dutch, the Flemings, the Frisians and the Luxemburgers. Their journal, *Jong Dietschland*, began to propound Fascist slogans. Van Severen himself attacked liberalism and parliamentarianism, which he considered slow and sterile, lame and anti-modern. The Belgian parliament had never been popular with the Flemish nationalists: the 'modern' solution must be sought outside and beyond this system, and authoritarian ideas were gaining ground. While the majority of the Flemish students at Ghent was won over, the ex-servicemen in their majority stood aloof; their newspaper, *De Schelde*, sharply attacked Mussolini, Fascism and all Fascist ideologies.

It may have been this rejection by his former comrades, or it may have been his growing admiration for Fascism in general, which caused Van Severen to found in October 1931 his own organization, the *Verbond van Dietsche Nationaal-Solidaristen* ('League of Netherlands

[13] There is an interesting biography of Van Severen by an admirer, Arthur de Bruyne, *Joris van Severen, Droom en Daad*, Zulte, 1961.

National Solidarists'), *Verdinaso* for short, the members of which
were called *Dinasos*. (A propensity for long names was not just a
Spanish trait.) The ideological basis of the *Verdinaso* was anti-democratic and authoritarian, and it vehemently attacked the traditional
Flemish nationalists whom it assigned to the 'democratic rubbish
dump'. In the *Verdinaso* the will of the Leader, Van Severen, was law.
He issued the movement's 'marching orders'; a military discipline prevailed within it. Its uniformed militia formed the nucleus and the
backbone of the movement, the *élite* of the coming new order, which
would be a corporative state. The disorders of democracy and capitalism
must be abolished, with the political parties and the power of finance.
From Germany anti-Semitism was taken over although it was only in
Antwerp that there was a sizeable and influential Jewish community.
Van Severen was severely critical of the Dutch National Socialists led
by Anton Mussert because they were not anti-Semitic and even
accepted Jewish members, because they were allegedly liberal and
bourgeois. From Germany and Italy too came the movement's veneration of violence and the myth cultivated by it of street battles and
fights in halls with political enemies, who, in spite of their superior
numbers, were usually defeated. But the main aim was the seizure of
power, the creation of the *Dietsche Volksstaat*, the unification of all
branches of the Netherlands nation in one organic state of National
Solidarity. Power was to be seized by the *Dinasos* in Flanders as well
as in Holland by a common will, and then the two states were to be
united into one *Dietsch* state.[14] The artificial division which had come
about in the sixteenth century during the Revolt of the Netherlands
was to be eliminated for ever. With his vast self-assurance and his un-
doubted idealism Van Severen soon had a strong and enthusiastic
following among the students, but his appeal to the workers was much
less successful. Van Severen was too much an intellectual and a dandy,
and not a people's tribune. It was the same story as that of the *Falange*
in Spain, and of some of the movements in Eastern Europe. And
even the onset of the economic crisis did not bring about a basic
change. The *Verdinaso* always remained the movement of a small
minority.

A few years after the foundation of the *Verdinaso*, however, a second
Fascist movement developed in Flanders. In October 1933 the

[14] The above is a summary of Van Severen's speech to the first Diet of the *Dinaso*
students, of 31 March 1934, published in a duplicated form by the *Verdinaso* after
Van Severen's death in 1940 under the title: *Zoo sprak de Leider*, pp. 6–10.

Vlaamsch Nationaal Verbond was established, with the deputy Staf de Clercq as the Leader. It too adopted party uniforms and the Fascist salute; its flags were yellow, with the black Lion of Flanders. It wanted to terminate the domination of Flanders by the Walloons and French influences, 'the ruling liberal régime and its natural results, the suppression of classes and big capitalism'.[15] The Leader was assisted by a Central Council which consisted of those in charge of the party's central offices and the *Gauleiters* of the regions. Like the *Verdinaso*, the new party extolled the virtues of National Solidarity and aimed at the unification of all Dutch-speaking people in an organic Great Netherlands state. But Staf de Clercq lacked Van Severen's dynamism and personal magnetism. He was easily influenced and in the end always agreed with the group which brought the strongest pressure to bear upon him. Thus the *V.N.V.* never developed into an entirely uniform and strongly led party, and the local groups retained a large measure of autonomy. It was less anti-Semitic than the *Verdinaso*, but more outspokenly pro-German, and strongly influenced by the example of Hitler. In 1934 its newspaper, *Het Vlaamsche Volk*, proclaimed: 'As Germanics we Flemings belong to the spiritual Germanic front in the West. . . . If we do not want to be annihilated by the French robbers of land we must, in our centuries-old struggle, more than ever seek the support of Germany.'[16]

During the following years the *Vlaamsch Nationaal Verbond* and its press became even more pro-German. It praised the Hitler régime and the genius of its Leader and admired the national rebirth of Germany under him. Staf de Clercq was hailed as the movement's Leader. 'He is the symbol of order. The Leader thinks, the followers act.'[17] Especially the younger members were influenced by authoritarian ideas, but the ex-servicemen who formed locally the backbone of the organization less so. Propaganda was made against the department stores and in support of the middle classes, and in Antwerp there were attempts to exploit anti-Semitic feelings. In the elections of 1936 and 1939 the *V.N.V.* gained great successes, polling 168,000 and 185,000 votes, respectively, over twelve per cent of the Flemish vote, and in some rural areas as much as 20 to 35 per cent of the total. Many thousands assembled every year at the party's Diets. The figures showed to what extent the nationalist movement had grown since the early 1920s.

[15] Willemsen, op. cit., p. 315.
[16] *Het Vlaamsche Volk*, 25 February 1934, quoted ibid., p. 344.
[17] Pamphlet dedicated to the Diet of 5 May 1935, quoted ibid., p. 332.

Unfortunately they cannot be compared with those of the *Verdinaso* which did not participate in elections; its Diets were less well attended than those of the *V.N.V.*

While the *V.N.V.* became more and more a tool of German propaganda, the *Verdinaso* of Van Severen developed along its own lines. Originally, only Flanders was to join with the other Dutch-speaking regions in the *Dietsch* state, and this would mean the break-up of Belgium, which indeed was openly propagated by the *Verdinaso*. But in 1934 new 'marching orders' were issued against strong opposition of some *Verdinaso* leaders: the negative and barren attitude to the Belgian state was replaced by a more positive one; it was not to be broken up but to be conquered, not by violence and force, but by a steady development of the *Dinasos*' strength and values. The ancient Seventeen Provinces of the Netherlands were to be reunited in one *Dietsch* Empire; there was no 'Walloon' nation and no 'Walloon' culture, but the Walloons—like the Dutch and Flemings—divided into their historical provinces and units; they were not 'foreigners', but had shared the same fate with the *Dietschers* through the centuries; they were Romanized *Dietschers* and all were of common Frankish stock. An authoritarian order was to take the place of the parliamentary one; parliament was to be replaced by a High Council of the representatives of the families and hearths; the laws were to be drafted by a college of experts; liberalism, democracy and the political parties were to be liquidated. The German example was not to be copied slavishly, for every nation had to establish its 'new order' according to the laws and customs of its own existence. The Jews were not only foreigners, but dangerous and damaging foreigners, and were to be treated as such, but not in the way they had been treated in the Third Reich (this was after the pogroms of November 1938).[18] In this and in other aspects Van Severen tried to retain his independence of the powerful German neighbour—and this was only a few months before the outbreak of the second world war. The *V.N.V.*, too, was critical of the persecution of the Jews and of the Church in the Third Reich.

The changed attitude of Van Severen towards the Walloons and the Belgian state strongly affected the politics of the *Verdinaso*. Walloons were admitted as members, and special publications in French were issued to win them over. The Belgian as well as the Dutch flags were

[18] The above details are taken from two speeches by Van Severen, of 30 April 1938 and 20 May 1939, published as a *Verdinaso* pamphlet, under the title *Drie Redevoeringen van Joris van Severen*, 2nd ed., 1939.

carried in *Verdinaso* marches and demonstrations. King Leopold and Queen Wilhelmina were recognized as the rulers who were not only to be respected, but had to be supported in a political situation which became more and more threatening. Van Severen now stood for a strong Belgium and an alliance and economic union with the Netherlands. When King Leopold paid an official visit to Bruges in the summer of 1939 he was welcomed there with flowers by the children of local *Verdinaso* leaders. It was a far cry from the bitter hostility to everything Belgian which had been characteristic of his earlier propaganda. Although some ardent Flemings left the movement because they did not agree with the new course, Van Severen throughout retained the fervent loyalty of his followers: to them he remained the Leader whom they venerated beyond the grave. His mystique could not be shaken by a mere change of policy.

This mystique was reinforced by the death of Van Severen in the second world war. In May 1940, after the invasion of Belgium by the Germans, he was arrested and taken to France. There he was killed by French soldiers, together with other prisoners, during the French retreat. In the war years some of his followers collaborated with the occupying power, while others joined the Belgian resistance movement. We do not know whether Van Severen would have approved of this course, but we know that he had long been critical of the Third Reich and its policy. The leaders of the much stronger *Vlaamsch Nationaal Verbond*, on the other hand, even during the preceding years had shown a rather uncritical admiration for Hitler and his régime. It was perhaps only logical, then, that during the war they accepted large sums of German money and openly collaborated with the National Socialists, exactly as some of the earlier Flemish leaders had cooperated with the Germans during the first world war. The broad popular backing which the *Vlaamsch Nationaal Verbond* possessed did not make its leaders more independent in their actions. Above all, their organization lacked the strong leader which the *Verdinaso* had had in the person of Van Severen.

The Rexist Movement: from Militant Catholicism to Fascism

The Fascist movements in the Flemish region of Belgium for some years had no counterpart in French-speaking Wallonia, which was considerably more advanced and more industrialized. Not even the severe economic crisis of the early 1930s—which caused such a sharp rise in totalitarian movements all over Europe—had a similar effect among the Walloons. Like Flanders Wallonia was strongly Catholic, and it was from the militant Catholic youth movement that a Fascist party developed in the later 1930s. Its leader was Léon Degrelle, who was born in 1906, the son of a prosperous brewer, in the small country town of Bouillon and in his early youth saw the horrors of the first world war and of the German occupation. From 1921 to 1925 Degrelle was educated by the Jesuits of Namur; there he came into contact with the 'intellectual Fascism' of the Action française. 'Certain Jesuits . . . were the open and eager propagandists of the doctrine of Charles Maurras. Every evening the professor of rhetoric of Notre-Dame-de-la-Paix would bring into the playground . . . the number of the Action Française which had just arrived at Namur. . . . '[19]

It was Maurras who exercised a fundamental influence on the Belgian students of the 1920s. At Louvain the Action Française sold hundreds of copies every day. 'Our young men read Maurras with enthusiasm', wrote the Abbé Jacques Leclercq in 1925.[20] He presented to them a firm and well-established doctrine, a solution to the problems of the time that was in accordance with their strong Catholic and conservative convictions; the right-wing revolution preached by Maurras would solve the ills of society and invigorate it with a new spirit. In 1926 Degrelle became a student of law at Louvain university and there associated closely with the Action Catholique de la Jeunesse Belge and its organizer, Mgr Picard. Degrelle was a fervent Catholic and propagandist for Christus Rex, Christ the King. When Maurras was condemned by Rome, Degrelle and the other ardent Catholic students did not revolt but submitted. In 1931 the Catholic Action movement founded a publishing house 'Rex' and Degrelle became its director, at the age of twenty-five. In the following year he began to edit a monthly journal, also called Rex, which wanted to bring about a renewal of Christian life. Soon his publishing ventures blossomed forth into numerous journals and pamphlets directed at different groups and interests, but all supporting the idea of a Christian crusade. For his journal Degrelle went on an extended visit to Mexico to report on the persecution of the Catholics by the Mexican government.

[19] Louise Narvaez Duchesse de Valence, Degrelle m'a dit, Paris, 1961, p. 48. For Maurras and his doctrine, see above, pp. 13-14.
[20] Quoted by Jean Stengers, 'Belgium', in The European Right, ed. H. Rogger and E. Weber, Berkeley and Los Angeles, 1965, p. 142.

From fervent Catholicism it was but one step to fervent anti-Communism and anti-Marxism, and soon Degrelle's propaganda campaign became more political. He began to attack not only Communism, but also freemasonry, high finance and corruption, especially among the politicians. In the journal *Vlan* Degrelle vehemently denounced the politico-financiers, and among them he named men with a strong reputation in the Catholic associations. Prominent Catholic politicians and the Catholic Party as such were sharply criticized for their passivity and their incompetence. Financial malpractices and scandals provided Degrelle with plenty of ammunition. In November 1935 a meeting of the Federation of Catholic Associations and Circles took place at Courtrai and was addressed by the Minister Paul Segers, who was also a prominent businessman. His speech was interrupted by Degrelle and his followers. Then Degrelle took the floor, abused the party leaders in the strongest terms, and informed Segers: 'You are too old! Away with you! Do not speak of discipline and authority. You do not know what that is. . . .'[21] Soon after Degrelle published a pamphlet *J'accuse M. Segers*, which attacked the minister in violent terms as a despoiler of the economy, a trickster and a coward. This meant Degrelle's official breach with the Catholic Party.

By the beginning of 1936 Degrelle was well launched towards the foundation of his own party. He was strongly supported by many young Catholics and groups of the *Action Catholique de la Jeunesse Belge* who were attracted by his passion and his oratory. The gang of corrupt politicians must be swept away, the people whom Degrelle contemptuously called *les pourris* ('the rotters'); there must be a thorough spring-cleaning. When the *pourris* held a conference somewhere Degrelle's followers would appear with brooms to sweep the street in front of the meeting place. Degrelle travelled up and down the country and made impassionate speeches to large audiences, denouncing the politicians and the collusion between them and high finance. This propaganda fell on fertile soil as some financial crashes had made the public aware of the issue and there was a widespread *malaise* and dissatisfaction with the traditional forms of government. In Germany, too, the Sklarek and other scandals provided the National Socialists with some of their best ammunition.[22] Like the Hitler meetings those of Degrelle were superbly staged; the halls were beautifully decorated, delegations in different dress would take their places on the platform, trumpets would

[21] Quoted by Pierre Daye, *Léon Degrelle et le Rexisme*, Paris, 1937, p. 72.
[22] See above, pp. 133-4.

announce the speakers, searchlights would play on them and on the massed flags.

The programme of the new *Rex* party was published in February 1936.[23] It sharply attacked the 'politico-financial scandals' and the 'dictatorship of super-capitalism in Belgium and the Congo'. It demanded not the abolition of parliament, but a severe limitation of its functions to a control of the budget and a ratification of the laws, the shortening of its sessions to two months a year, the introduction of universal suffrage (women did not have the vote), and of the referendum to assure a 'direct contact between the people and the government'. There were numerous social demands: a rigorous control of the banks, a control of capitalism, protection for the middle and the working classes, respect for labour, the fight against unemployment by the creation of new industries, the prohibition of the employment of married women, and the return of the people to the soil. The land should belong to the peasants, but nothing was said about how this was to be achieved, whether large properties were to be expropriated or not. Wealth was to be decentralized and the masses were to be deproletarianized, but again no details were given how these goals were to be gained. There also figured, as it did in all other countries, the establishment of the corporative order, 'essentially social, based on the solidarity of the classes'. All in all it was a rather vague, socially progressive programme which promised something to everybody; but it was not particularly radical, considerably less radical than the original Fascist programmes in other countries. Belgium was not given to extremes of any kind.

Indeed, it was not in the social, but in the political field that Degrelle favoured decisive reform: the political parties were to be destroyed because they were dominated by corrupt politicians, who were themselves dominated by an anonymous oligarchy, and caused disorder in the country. Order and stability of government were to be restored by curtailing the powers of parliament and extending those of the King. He was to appoint and to dismiss the ministers—a function which parliament was unfit to exercise.[24] There was little of totalitarianism in this, but rather a return to a patriarchal system, such as Bismarck had established in Germany seventy years earlier. One of Degrelle's closest followers, the journalist Pierre Daye, expressly repudiated any

[23] The programme is printed in Louise Narvaez Duchesse de Valence, op. cit., pp. 164-5. Her book contains many other quotations from Rexist publications, and many remarks and observations of Degrelle. Apart from the books written by admirers of Degrelle there does not seem to be any study of the Rexist movement.
[24] Pierre Daye, op. cit., p. 127.

tendency towards totalitarianism, the identification of the nation with
the Fascist party, and legislation by a well-organized minority: such a
concept might be defensible, but it did not apply to Belgium.[25] Degrelle
also repudiated the use of violence and insisted that he would win by
legal methods. When someone objected that Hitler and Mussolini had
not shown any such hesitation, he replied: 'I am neither the one nor
the other, and have no intention of imitating them.'[26]

This completely new party, in the elections of May 1936, gained 11·5
per cent of the votes cast and twenty-one seats in the chamber, out of
a total of 202. The Catholics suffered most and lost sixteen seats. This
victory, moreover, was gained at a time of a rapid economic recovery
and of a sharp fall in the unemployment figures. The Flemish Nationalists also made substantial gains, while the average polled by the
Rexists in the Flemish constituencies was considerably below their
national average, only seven per cent. But in Belgian Luxemburg it was
as high as twenty-nine per cent, in Namur twenty, in Liège nineteen
per cent, and in Brussels almost the same. In the French-speaking
areas the Rexists had become a mass movement. A few days later
Degrelle was received by Leopold III, to whom he explained clearly
that what he wanted 'was power, all power, and not a ministerial
post . . . either for himself of for some of his lieutenants'.[27] His ambition was now limitless: his movement would sweep him into power.

In Flanders too Degrelle had ardent supporters, organized separately
in *Rex-Vlaanderen*, but there the competition of the *Vlaamsch Nationaal
Verbond* was almost impossible to overcome, as it stood for the same
authoritarian tendencies and appealed to the same social groups. But
in October 1936 Degrelle scored another victory. He reached an agreement with the Flemish nationalist leaders which provided for regional
autonomy for Flanders; the *V.N.V.* and *Rex-Vlaanderen* were to be
amalgamated. It seemed a great success, but it did not make Degrelle
more popular with the ardent Francophils who provided a good deal
of his support in the Walloon districts. And the agreement only lasted
eight months: it was renounced by Staf de Clercq in June 1937. The
Flemish issue proved intractable even for so versatile a politician as
Degrelle. His followers came mainly from the middle and lower middle
classes; the white-collar workers and the rural population were strongly
represented, as they were in the National Socialist and similar

[25] Ibid., p. 90.
[26] Louise Narvaez Duchesse de Valence, op. cit., p. 256.
[27] Ibid., p. 205. The election figures according to Stengers, op. cit., pp. 159–60.

movements elsewhere. But his following remained small in the industrial areas, which were strongholds of the Socialists. This was in spite of valiant efforts: young Rexist women were sent to help working-class families, and during the great miners' strike of 1936 thousands of miners' children were sent from the mining districts to live with the families of Rexists in other parts of the country. As a nucleus of the corporative order of the future, Rexist Confederations were organized for trade, industry, agriculture, artisans, the professions and even for the Congo. There were special youth groups, services for children, and protection squads to ensure order at meetings and demonstrations, commanded by a retired colonel of the gendarmerie. Those adherents who could not belong to any of these special formations were grouped in local sections dotted over the whole country.

At the beginning of 1937 Degrelle felt strong enough to organize, within one week, six monster meetings in Brussels' largest hall, the Palais des Sports. There he nightly addressed vast audiences, in a hall decorated with the black-red Rexist flags and masses of red cloth. Like Hitler, he considered red a particularly effective colour—but Degrelle did not preach social revolution. His oratory sufficed to keep up the fervour and excitement among his listeners, whose collective emotion reached its highest pitch. That too he had in common with Hitler whom he admired greatly, and apostrophied in the following words: 'The smallest place where Hitler has passed through possesses hundreds of photographs which preserve every step of the visit. The faces are ecstatic. The hands lift themselves, curved inwards, in religious gestures. The women cry, the eyes of the children are illuminated. . . . *It is above all the people who love Hitler.* To maintain the opposite would be a lie. The Hitler movement has been, and has remained, above all, a workers' movement. Hitler has lived among them under harsh conditions for years. . . . He has remained thoroughly one of the "people". He lives more frugally than any workman: never any meat; vegetables and water. He hates palaces and receptions. He constantly mingles with the crowds. . . . Simplicity and courage, that is what the people love. . . . The truth is that Hitler has the working class on his side, as no one, in any country or at any time, has ever had. . . .'[28] Hitler had achieved the 'miracle' and had won over the workers—a goal which Degrelle was unable to attain.

During the years preceding the outbreak of the second world war

[28] Article in the *Pays Réel* of 25 April 1938, quoted in *Degrelle avait raison*, Les Editions Rex, Brussels, 1941, p. 35.

Degrelle did not come closer to that goal, for his movement began to decline. His followers cried as loudly as ever '*Rex vaincra!*' But Degrelle felt that the time had come to demonstrate his great popularity. In March 1937 he ordered one of the Rexist deputies elected for Brussels to resign, and with him all those following on the Rexist list who were to replace him if this should become necessary. Thus a by-election had to be held in which Degrelle—who was not a deputy—presented himself as the candidate. But the Prime Minister, Paul van Zeeland, accepted the challenge, and the major parties (Catholics, Socialists and Liberals) did not put up any candidates of their own. Even the Church did not remain neutral; on the eve of the poll the Cardinal-Archbishop of Malines condemned *Rex* as a danger to the country and the Church, and forbade all good Catholics to vote for Degrelle. The result was a foregone conclusion. Although the Flemish Nationalists instructed their followers to vote for Degrelle, he only polled 69,000 votes, against 275,000 cast for Van Zeeland. It was a defeat. At the next general election, in April 1939, the Rexist vote dropped to four per cent of the total, and the number of their deputies to four.

After the second occupation of Belgium by the Germans, Degrelle and the Rexists cooperated with them and received large sums of German money. A Walloon Legion was formed in which Degrelle served from the bottom upwards until he became a high-ranking officer. The Legion fought with the German army in Russia, and after the withdrawal from Russia in Germany to the bitter end. Then Degrelle and some close followers succeeded in escaping, via Denmark and Norway, by air to Spain where they found asylum, and where Degrelle began to write his books.[29] In his own country his name was almost forgotten. Cooperation with the Germans—by the Rexists as well as by the Flemish Nationalists—had destroyed the basis of their movements. But Flemish 'activism' has remained a noisy and extremist group, always ready to demonstrate for Flemish 'rights' and to beat up adversaries.[30]

If it had not been for the grievances of the Flemings and their strong sense of nationalism, there might never have been a strong Fascist

[29] See, for example, *La Cohue de 1940*, Lausanne, 1949, or *La Campagne de Russie 1941–1945*, Paris, 1949 (describing the battles of the 'Walloon Legion' in Russia). Cp. also the autobiography *Degrelle* in part dictated to the Duchesse de Valence, Paris, 1961.

[30] After the war the Flemings heavily outnumbered the Walloons, and both nationalities had equal rights. In 1950 the growth rate of the population in the Flemish area was five times that in the Walloon area, 7·7 as against 1·5 per cent.

movement in Belgium, for the Rexist movement was comparatively short-lived and not supported by any profound social or national grievances. It declined as swiftly as it had arisen. It was not extremist enough to win over the masses for any length of time, and it did not develop a strong party machine led by capable leaders. Degrelle's oratory was not sufficient as a substitute for a good organization. Even in parliament his twenty-one deputies cut a poor figure. The Flemish movement had much stronger roots, going back over many years; but it was split, and its most dynamic leader, Joris van Severen, only led a small group, which mainly consisted of enthusiastic students. In general, the different Fascist groups and parties in Belgium were more right-wing conservative and less extremist than their counterparts in other countries, and in this they only mirrored the strong native conservatism. Given this, it is difficult to see how any Fascist party could ever have become strong enough to seize and to retain power by its own strength.

The British Union of Fascists

After Mussolini's victory in Italy Fascist groups were founded in Britain as they were in many other European countries. They went under different names—the British Fascists, the Fascist League, the British National Fascists, the Imperial Fascist League—but they all remained small groups on the extreme Right of the Tory Party. They were almost entirely upper and middle class in their composition, consisting of disgruntled Tories who felt called upon to save the British Empire or to preserve the predominance of the British race. The exception was the Imperial Fascist League of Arnold Spencer Leese who had joined the British Fascists in 1924 and regarded himself as a 'Racial Fascist'. Soon he was organizing his branch as an independent group; its members wore the black shirt and concentrated on anti-Semitic propaganda. Leese considered it his duty to expose 'Jewish agents' in high positions and avidly believed in the racial theories propounded from Germany, including that of ritual murder for religious purposes. Later he favoured a fighting alliance of the Nordic nations against other countries. He was a National Socialist more than a Fascist. His followers did not come from the upper and middle classes; but the Imperial Fascist League which he founded in 1929 remained very small. Its flag was the Union Jack with the swastika in the centre.

It was only during the economic crisis of the early 1930s which hit Britain severely that a larger Fascist movement came into being, and it did not originate from any of the earlier minute Fascist groups. Its founder was Sir Oswald Mosley who was born in 1896, the son of a baronet. He had a conventional upper-class education and at the age of twenty-one became a Conservative member of parliament for a middle-class constituency. But after a few years he left the Conservative Party, and in 1924 he became a Labour member of parliament, achieving minor office under Ramsay MacDonald. What Mosley found politically attractive was 'modernism', and apparently he did not find the Labour Party any more 'modern' than the Tories. In 1931 he and some of his friends thus founded the New Party, which politically stood more on the Left than on the Right, but it never flourished. Then, early in 1932, Mosley, attracted by Mussolini's Italy, went there to study the 'modern' movement at the fountainhead; to him it was largely identical with a movement of former soldiers. It was this experience that made Mosley a firm admirer of Fascism, in its Italian rather than its German variety. After his return to England he approached the British Fascists with the proposal that they should combine with the New Party in a Union of Fascists and accept Mosley as their Leader. He was to have complete control of the movement and its policy. The Fascist salute and the black shirt as the party uniform were adopted. In 1933 a Black House was established in Chelsea with a resident guard of Black Shirts. They received free accommodation and pocket money, had to do duty as guards, drivers or messengers, and led a semi-military life, with meals, parades and 'lights-out' regulated by bugle calls. The Black Shirts of the Headquarters Division regarded themselves as an *élite* and acted as an escort and protective squad for the Leader. The Black Shirts were the active members of the movement, obliged to serve it when called upon to do so; in addition there were the ordinary members who had no such obligation. By the end of 1933 there were perhaps 5,000 paying members, but it is impossible to say how many of these were Black Shirts, and how many ordinary. The party emblem was the *fasces* taken over from Italy—'the emblem which founded the power, authority and unity of Imperial Rome', a tradition 'of which the British Empire is now the chief custodian'.[31]

[31] Oswald Mosley, *Fascism : 100 Questions asked and answered*, London, 1936, p. 1. The only study available of the Mosley movement is Colin Cross, *The Fascists in Britain*, London, 1961. For the *fasces*, see above, p. 47.

In its structure, too, the British Union of Fascists was an entirely authoritarian party. Its officers were not elected but appointed, and they wielded absolute authority within their spheres. All political decisions were made by Mosley himself, who might or might not consult a small Directorate on important issues. The meetings, like the Hitler meetings, were superbly staged. In April 1934 there was a meeting in the Albert Hall which was opened by a fanfare of trumpets; a double file of Black Shirts carried the Union Jacks and Fascist banners into the hall and took up their position near the platform; then, after a short pause, Mosley appeared, alone; at the end, the Black Shirts time and again chanted: 'Mosley! We want Mosley!' Six weeks later there was a monster meeting at Olympia, which became notorious because of the violence used by the Black Shirts to silence and remove all hecklers and interrupters, in the best *S.A.* style. National Socialist influence also became evident a few weeks later when Mosley came out in support of Hitler after the purge of the *S.A.* on 30 June 1934. It became even more evident when Mosley, at the second Albert Hall meeting in October, identified himself with Hitler's anti-Semitism: 'Not on grounds of race or religion, but on the fundamental principle of Fascism, we declare that we will not tolerate an organized community within the state which owes allegiance not to Britain, but to another race in foreign countries. . . . We shall not fight Germany again in a Jewish quarrel.'[32] The Jews, as Mosley put it, 'must put the interests of Britain before those of Jewry, or be deported from Britain. . . . The Jews as a whole, have chosen to organize themselves as a nation within the Nation and to set their interests before those of Great Britain. . . .' Jews must be treated as foreigners and not be permitted to become officials or members of parliament. 'Anyone in the service of the State under Fascism must be entirely British.'[33]

In the political field Mosley demanded that the political parties and the party system must be abolished, but not parliament. But 'a Parliament elected under Fascism will be a technical and not a political Parliament. The franchise will be occupational and not geographical. Men and women will vote according to their industry or profession. . . .'[34] The functions of this parliament should be curtailed, it should only deal with general problems, while the details should be decided by a National Council of Corporations. This and twenty-four

[32] Cross, op. cit., pp. 126–7.
[33] Mosley, op. cit., points 95 and 98.
[34] Ibid., point 14.

individual corporations should control the economic life. A Fascist Grand Council—as in Italy—should assist the king in the choice of the prime minister. There should be a strong government which would be given power to act by the people. 'By giving Government power to act, Fascism brings not the end of freedom but the beginning of freedom. Real freedom is economic freedom. . . .'[35] For obvious reasons nothing was said about political freedom. But all these aims were to be achieved 'by legal and constitutional means. We seek power by the winning of a Parliamentary majority.'[36] Mosley also promised social reform, an attack on poverty and unemployment, public works and a health service; 'the rule of the financial gangster' must be terminated.

During the years of the depression Mosley, in contrast with the other Fascist groups, was able to attract many of the young or fairly young, from the lower middle as well as the working classes. The latter often came from the militant Independent Labour Party which was declining in influence. They were not attracted by the cautious policy of the official Labour Party, nor by the small Communist Party which never gained a large working-class following. In the East End of London, with its large Jewish population, the Fascist leaders were of proletarian origin. There great Fascist marches were organized in the mid-1930s which met with organized left-wing resistance. To protect the marchers and the open-air rallies violence was systematically and ruthlessly applied by the Black Shirts. But this weapon misfired, for many of the less extremist adherents of the movement disapproved of it. While the movement's open anti-Semitism attracted many in the East End, it looked to most others, especially those with strong national feelings, like an import from Germany. Mosley's association with Hitler was not popular in Britain. Nor was anti-Communism a live issue in a country in which Communist influence was so limited. Yet in the elections to the London County Council of March 1937 the Fascists scored considerable successes in the East End, obtaining twenty-three per cent of the votes in Bethnal Green North-East, and nineteen per cent in Stepney.

With regard to Hitler's policy Mosley laboured under a complete illusion. In his opinion, there was a fundamental difference between the Germany of the Kaiser and that of Hitler. The former 'rested on a system of export capitalism conducted by Judaic finance which

[35] Ibid., point 9.
[36] Ibid., point 16.

challenged us on the markets of the world, and emphasized that challenge with naval rivalry that threatened our Empire'. Hitler's conception, however, was 'exactly opposite to that of the Kaiser. The new German does not desire a world wide Empire, for he believes that racial deterioration will result from such racial intercourse, and that the new German has another mission in the world than to elevate savages. . . .'[37] To Mosley, therefore, the interests of the two countries were not opposed to each other but complementary. But this was a complete misreading of Hitler's mind and aims, and even of German racialist doctrine. It is true that Hitler would have liked a British alliance, but only to further his dreams of world conquest, and his policy was bound to clash with British interests. Early in 1936 the name of the movement was changed to 'British Union of Fascists and National Socialists'—another sign of growing German influence. There was some opposition to the change in the Policy Committee, but Mosley without any difficulty carried the majority with him.

Mosley as a Leader undoubtedly possessed personal magnetism and had an inventive mind. But—like José Antonio Primo de Rivera—he suffered from two handicaps: he came from the upper classes and never shed their mentality, and he was an intellectual, devising a blue-print for a Fascist Britain, rather than applying himself to practical issues of politics and organization. The British Union for some years attracted large numbers, but most of them did not stay for long. An internal estimate for 1938 gives only 3,000 active members and another 15,000 inactive ones. By then perhaps 100,000 people has passed through the ranks of the movement. In the provinces it was still extremely weak. In 1937 its candidates polled 29 votes in Southampton, 41 and 51 votes in Edinburgh, 97 and 98 in Sheffield, 74 and 106 in Leeds: minute figures which show that the Fascists had failed to gain a mass following.

After the outbreak of the second world war their leaders and many members were arrested for the duration, and the movement simply collapsed. Although attempts were made after the end of the war to revive it, it never again acquired a large following. Its association with Hitler marked it as unpatriotic in the eyes of the majority, and the violence it employed lost it many sympathizers. The post-war political climate did not favour any tendency towards a revival of totalitarianism or intolerance, and even the gradual liquidation of the British Empire

---

[37] *Oswald Mosley's Tomorrow We Live—British Union Policy*, London, n.d., pp. 65–6.

did not arouse any widespread opposition on the Right. Mosley's methods no doubt were less violent and less extremist than those of Hitler or Codreanu, but they were too extreme for the large majority of his countrymen. As there was no Communist danger, and no nationalist grievances on account of a lost war or unfair treatment by a dominant group, other important factors which Fascism might have exploited were absent. The national climate and the political structure did not favour its growth, and Sir Oswald Mosley was neither a Hitler nor a Mussolini.

The Austrian Heimwehr

Austria, after the first world war, lost her Empire and became a small republic with far too large a capital, Vienna, which no longer served the needs of an Empire. Furthermore, Vienna was Red, dominated by left-wing workers' and soldiers' councils, while there was little industry in the other parts of the country and the prevailing political mood— in Carinthia, Styria, the Tyrol—was conservative and anti-Marxist. Styria and Carinthia were threatened by claims of the new Yugoslav state to border areas with a mixed population, and as on the German eastern frontiers, guerilla warfare soon developed between irregular forces fighting over disputed areas. On the Austrian side these were defended by free corps similar to those which were founded in Germany—and they could equally well be used to fight Marxism or Bolshevism at home.

On a local basis these para-military associations continued to flourish long after the immediate danger of Yugoslav attacks had passed. The units were well supplied with funds by the industrialists as a counter-weight to the Marxist trade unions, but they also received help from abroad. Money and weapons for the Styrian units were sent by similar organizations from Bavaria, especially the ill-famed *Orgesch* (Organization Escherich) which was arming for civil war in Bavaria. The local authorities, too, rendered every conceivable help, above all the governor of Styria, Dr Rintelen, so that the Styrian *Heimatschutz* (Home Defence) possessed even guns and aeroplanes. Its leader was a local lawyer, Dr Walter Pfrimer, who as a student had been a member of a *Burschenschaft* and an ardent follower of Schönerer; his ideas were pan-German and *völkisch* as those of Schönerer had been. His units wore the swastika and carried the German black, white and red flag in addition to the white-green of Styria. In the Tyrol another lawyer, Dr Richard Steidle, held a similar position; he was a native of the South Tyrol (Alto Adige) which had to be ceded to Italy. His forces too were supplied with weapons by the *Orgesch* from Bavaria. After the failure of the Kapp *Putsch* in Berlin in March 1920 he acquired an energetic chief of staff in the person of Major Waldemar Pabst, who had escaped from Germany and took up residence in Innsbruck, another link with the German counter-revolution.

The collapse of the Habsburg monarchy, the lost war, and the inflation which resulted from it provided these units with many recruits: officials, ex-servicemen, small farmers, rentiers, members of the professions—groups which had been hit by the economic and social changes resulting from the first world war. They all hated Red Vienna, its strong working-class movement, its cosmopolitan culture, its parasites and profiteers. But for several years these para-military units had only local importance, and no clear programme. In 1927, however, strong fear and hatred of the Marxists were aroused anew through the burning down of the Palace of Justice in Vienna by embittered crowds and the general strike proclaimed by the Socialists after the police had fired on the demonstrators. The *Heimwehren* (Home Defence Units) succeeded in defeating the strike everywhere and could welcome many new recruits eager to stem the Red tide. Their many local units for the first time acquired a centralized leadership and direction. Hitherto their programme had been merely anti-Marxist, but now it became anti-parliamentarian, aiming at the establishment of an authoritarian state based on corporations or estates, for which Italy provided the example. The government of Dr Ignaz Seipel saw in the *Heimwehren* welcome allies in its struggle against the Socialists. The *Heimwehr* organization was strengthened, and valuable connexions were established to officers of the police and of the army. But the units continued to wear local insignia, colours and costumes. Their politics, too, often were of a local colour, clerical or national, and national either in an Austrian or a pan-German sense. The local clergy often supported the movement and gave it their blessing.

These efforts were strongly supported by the right-wing government of Hungary, headed by Count István Bethlen, which was established after the suppression of the Hungarian Soviet Republic in 1919.[38] On the initiative of Count Bethlen Mussolini began to take an interest in the *Heimwehr* movement, which in the past had been inspired by

[38] See above, pp. 170-2.

German examples and German support. When Bethlen met Mussolini in Milan in April 1928 he suggested to the *Duce* that he should
help the *Heimwehren* with money and weapons, so that their organization could be brought to full strength and a right-wing government
could be formed in Austria. Mussolini agreed to the proposal and promised that he would transfer one million lire and the required weapons
to the *Heimwehren* if they undertook to seize power within the foreseeable future. Two months later Dr Steidle handed to Bethlen a
memorandum which pointed out that the *Heimwehr* was in a state of
transition from a purely military formation to a 'state-political' organization; through its impetus the *Heimwehr* would force the bourgeois
parties to revise the 'semi-Bolshevist' constitution which had been
adopted under the pressure of the Viennese mob. This memorandum,
with its naïve phraseology, was immediately sent from Budapest to
Rome, where the Fascist foreign minister, Dino Grandi, declared that
his government agreed with the aims of the *Heimwehren* and would
pay them the sums requested. But he insisted that the *Heimwehr*
leaders must sign a declaration that, after their seizure of power, they
would consider the question of the South Tyrol (with its largely
German-speaking population) as non-existent. This declaration
Steidle duly sent to Budapest, and two weeks later the Italian government put 1,620,000 lire at the disposal of the Hungarians for transfer
to Austria.[39] There, however, the willingness of the *Heimwehr* leaders
to renounce any claim to the South Tyrol aroused strong opposition,
even in their own ranks.

In consequence of these events the ideology of the *Heimwehr* movement became increasingly pro-Fascist. When it submitted its programme to the Austrian chancellor in 1929 this included the erection
of 'the authoritarian state based on estates and on Fascist foundations'.
Its leaders began to dream of a march on Red Vienna. In May 1930
several hundred *Heimwehr* leaders at Korneuburg took an oath which
betrayed strong Fascist influence. It sharply rejected 'western democratic parliamentarianism and the party state. In its place we want to
put the self-government of estates and a strong leadership of the state.'
It also proclaimed: 'We are determined to take over the state and to
remould it and its economy in the interests of the entire *Volk*. . . . We
are determined to bring about an independent development of the
economy on a corporative basis. . . .' On the same day Dr Pfrimer

[39] These documents have been published from the Hungarian archives by Lajos
Kerekes, in *Österreich in Geschichte und Literatur*, vol. ix, January 1965, pp. 1–13.

declared: 'On all sides the conviction was evident that here in Austria only Fascism can save us. We must make an attempt to seize power. . .'[40] During the following weeks the Korneuburg oath was taken by the *Heimwehr* units all over Austria.

There was, however, very little unity among the *Heimwehr* leaders. In September 1930 Dr Steidle was removed from the leadership, and his place was taken by Prince Ernst Rüdiger Starhemberg, the scion of an illustrious Austrian noble family, who was aided by Dr Pfrimer. Starhemberg had pan-German and anti-Semitic leanings. He accepted the post of the minister of the interior and, in the elections to be held in November 1930, headed the list of the so-called *Heimatblock*. But Pfrimer demanded from him that the elections must not take place and prepared for the march on Vienna to be undertaken in October. The elections did take place, but Starhemberg's list only gained 228,000 votes and eight seats in parliament—a defeat that the more radical elements had foreseen. The result was a severe crisis and, on the side of the extremists, an increased determination to organize a *Putsch*. The Fascist tendencies within the *Heimwehr* became more pronounced and were fostered from Italy. Weapons were supplied in quantity. In the spring of 1931 Pfrimer proclaimed that not the people were ruling, as alleged in the constitution, but the party bosses who merely feathered their own nests: it was high time that this unconstitutional state was overthrown by a 'liberating *coup d'état*'. A programme drafted in May stipulated the elimination of 'the liberal and demagogic party system and the liberal and capitalist economic order', in favour of the 'idea of estates based on ancient German democracy'.[41]

The long-awaited *Putsch* and deposition of the government were finally attempted by Pfrimer in September 1931. In Styria the attempt was at first entirely successful. The heavily armed *Heimwehr* units occupied many smaller places and surrounded the capital of Styria, Graz. But the other leaders did not support him, and the march on Vienna never started. The authorities reacted with unusual mildness, and the units with their weapons were permitted to disperse peacefully. Pfrimer and other local leaders were put on trial, but they were acquitted, the jurymen joining the accused in giving the Fascist salute. The failure of the *Putsch*, however, led to further acrimonious disputes

[40] Quoted by Josef Hofmann, *Der Pfrimer-Putsch*, Vienna and Graz, 1965, pp. 20, 24, and by Ludwig Jedlicka, in the *Journal of Contemporary History*, vol. i, January 1966, pp. 138–9.
[41] Hofmann, op. cit., pp. 37, 55.

among the leaders and, in Styria, to a split. There the units following Pfrimer concluded a pact with the National Socialists and were soon absorbed by them, while Starhemberg formed his own units. He began to realize that it was easier to gain power in alliance with the state and its apparatus, hence he moved closer to the governing Christian-Social Party, which was now headed by Chancellor Dollfuss. This did not mean that the *Heimwehr* gave up its aim of setting up a totalitarian state, for this could also be done in cooperation with the Christian-Social Party. Mussolini continued to send to Starhemberg ample supplies of arms and money.

This support, indeed, was now more essential than it had ever been, because in January 1933 Hitler became the German chancellor, and the Austrian National Socialists were rapidly gaining ground. Already in January 1931 Major Pabst pointed out to a Hungarian visitor that their quick growth could partly be explained by the fact that they collected contributions from their members and thus were financially independent, while the *Heimwehr* relied too much on subsidies from industry and foreign countries. But it was the internal rivalry between its leaders, the ambiguity of its political programme, and its basic conservatism which militated against the *Heimwehr*. It was now faced by a much more extreme movement which was strongly supported from Germany and promised to fulfil the old dreams of the Pan-Germans, while a specifically 'Austrian' ideology had not struck root.

In August 1933 Chancellor Dollfuss met Mussolini at Riccione. There Mussolini demanded an openly pro-Fascist course in Austrian internal policy, for which end he intended to use the *Heimwehr* as a pressure group. To prevent Austria from falling under German sway, all Austrian forces were to be united under the slogan of national independence. A few weeks after the meeting Dollfuss outlined to the so-called 'Fatherland Front' his own programme for a political reconstruction on the basis of corporations or estates. But this did not satisfy the *Heimwehr* leaders who—in accordance with Mussolini—wanted a Fascist Austria. Dollfuss, however, depended on *Heimwehr* support, for the Fatherland Front was too weak and too disunited to defend the government against the Socialists on the Left and the National Socialists on the Right. It was hardly more than the Christian-Social Party under a new name, and it never developed into a dynamic Fascist party. Austria did not become a Fascist and totalitarian state, in spite of all Mussolini's efforts.

At the beginning of 1934 the undersecretary of state in the Italian Foreign Office, Fulvio Suvich, visited Vienna; for Mussolini was determined that the programme of Riccione must be carried out, that the political parties, especially the Socialists, must be eliminated, and that Austria must be transformed into a corporative state on the Italian model. Dollfuss was still hesitating, but the *Heimwehr* leaders loudly demanded a change of the political structure in the Fascist sense. In the Tyrol they mobilized their units, engaged in deeds of violence, and issued their demands in the form of an ultimatum; the provincial government was to be assisted by a committee drawn from the para-military formations. Similar demands were raised in Styria and in Upper Austria. Above all, the Socialists were to be deprived of their remaining influence and positions. Thus the scene was set for the government's measures against the Socialists which provoked their revolt in February 1934. It was soon drowned in blood, and their party was dissolved.

On 1 May 1934 Starhemberg was appointed vice-chancellor and Dollfuss' deputy as the leader of the Fatherland Front, which the *Heimwehren* hitherto had declined to join. On the same day a new constitution was promulgated which abolished parliamentary in favour of authoritarian government. Parliament was no longer to be elected. The deputies could no longer debate government proposals, but only accept or reject them. Membership was to be based on corporations, seven of which were envisaged: for industry, trade, agriculture, the professions, the civil service, etc. Each was to include employers and employees; but most of the corporations never came into being, and the whole constitution remained an artificial edifice.

In July 1934 Chancellor Dollfuss was murdered by National Socialists, and again it was Mussolini's support that saved Austria and the semi-authoritarian régime established there. Yet this régime was increasingly menaced by Germany and the Austrian National Socialists who received German support and could shelter there in case of need. After the destruction of the Socialist Party and the trade unions it was no longer possible to play off one opponent of the régime against the other, and this had earned for itself the undying hatred of its victims. Meanwhile the *Heimwehren* disintegrated further, and many of their members joined the National Socialists who appealed to the same sentiments and were growing in strength. With this the Fatherland Front was unable to compete: it had no revolutionary fervour, it was too bourgeois and too conservative. In these circumstances the experiment to transplant Italian Fascism to Austria was bound to end in failure.

Not Mussolini, but Hitler triumphed in Austria, where he had grown up and where he had received his decisive political impulses. His policy of *Anschluss* was carried to success by a genuine Fascist party, the Austrian National Socialists, who continued to grow in spite of government persecution. Their mass appeal was based on Pan-Germanism which had been a strong current for decades, the ideal of generations of students—and Germany was now a strong power from which a magnetic influence emanated. In Austria, Pan-Germanism had been strongly reinforced by the peace settlement of 1919 which deprived Austria of her old provinces, but forbade her to join the new German Republic. Twenty years later the victorious western powers were willing to concede to the Austrian-born dictator what they had prohibited in 1919. Thus Fascism triumphed in Austria, but it was of the German, not the Italian variety, and it meant the subordination of everything Austrian to the new masters in Berlin. Berlin, not Vienna, was the capital of the 'Greater Germany' ruled by the Austrian lance-corporal.

| # The Fascist Movements

The Fascist movements which arose in Europe during the 1920s and 1930s were very different in character, and they mirrored the entirely different national backgrounds of the countries in which they developed. Some were more conservative, and others more radical in their demands and their actions. Some were violently anti-Semitic, and others were not. Some took revolutionary action and staged armed revolts against the government, while others insisted on the legal way as the only possibility of attaining power. Some acquired a strong following among the lower classes, while others remained almost entirely middle and lower middle class. With so much variety, it might be asked what they had in common, and with what justification we can speak of Fascism in the singular. The following pages are an attempt to discuss these common traits—the factors which distinguish Fascism from other contemporary movements, whether right-wing or left-wing.

The Fascist movements, as has been emphasized by other writers,[1] had much in common in their ideology—so much that they were able to borrow from each other. They were not only strongly nationalist and violently anti-Communist and anti-Marxist: that they had in common with other parties and groups of the extreme Right, such as the Nationalist parties of Italy and Germany. The Fascists not only hated Liberalism and democracy and the political parties, but they wanted to eliminate them and to replace them by a new authoritarian and corporative state. In this state, there would only be one party; its hierarchy would overlap with that of the state, and its machinery would take over functions of the state. Its members would be the only ones entitled to hold high state offices. Ideally, there would be an

---

[1] Especially by Ernst Nolte, *Three Faces of Fascism*, London, 1965.

identity of party and state, although in practice much friction between them arose in Germany as well as in Italy. Again in theory—though not always in practice—the Fascist party was strongly élitist in character. Its early members considered themselves called upon to save and to lead their nation, and many Fascist parties did not aim at attracting a mass membership, or stipulated periods when no new members would be accepted. The Fascist parties were conceived as tightly organized semi-military machines with which state and society were to be conquered; in all of them, para-military associations or militias—clad in black, brown, green or blue shirts and uniforms—played a very important part. They contained the 'activists' who had to bear the brunt of the struggle for power. The seizure of total power was their aim.

Part of the movements'·ideology was a powerful myth, a myth of the nation and the race. It usually took the form of territorial expansion as the goal, a Greater Germany, a Greater Finland, Imperial conquest in Africa, a Great Netherlands state, an Empire. The movements also glorified and venerated the past: the Roman Empire of antiquity, the Spain of the Catholic Kings, the Seventeen Provinces of the Netherlands, the Germanic or the Turanian glories of earlier centuries. This myth was the religion of the twentieth century, fervently believed in however slim its connexion with reality. To the historical myth belonged the movements' flags and emblems: the swastika as a symbol of Aryanism, the *fasces* of the Roman Republic, the yoke and arrows, the Flemish lion, the crossed scythes or arrows. Above all, there was the myth of the 'Leader' who was venerated like a Saint by the faithful, who could do no wrong and must not be criticized, who was God-given, and to whom superhuman qualities were attributed. He possessed a personal dynamism and magnetism which could arouse vast crowds to frenzy and ecstasy. Whoever has attended a Hitler meeting in Germany will remember the passions which he was able to arouse, the atmosphere of religious frenzy and devotion. His magnetism later made battle-hardened generals tremble in his presence. The magnetism exercised by some of the other Fascist leaders—Codreanu, Primo de Rivera, Van Severen, Degrelle—seems to have been equally powerful,[2] and less artificial than in the case of Hitler, who carefully cultivated

[2] That the same applied at the local level has recently been shown by an interesting study of the Dutch National Socialist movement in the small town of Winterswijk: G. A. Kooy, *Het échec van een 'volkse' beweging—Nazificatie en Denazificatie in Nederland 1931–1945*, Assen, 1964. There the local N.S.B. leader was a very popular vet.

his mystique. There were other cults which characterized the Fascist movements, notably a cult of violence and 'action'. In Germany and elsewhere the myth of the street battles and battles won in meeting halls remained very much alive, as did the memory of the movement's 'martyrs' who 'march in spirit with us in our ranks'.[3] In Rumania and Germany this cult reached religious proportions. In no other party did the myth play such a vital part. To it also belonged—in the cases of Hitler and Codreanu—the myth of the devilish propensities of the Jewish race and its dreams of world power. Both love *and* hatred were cultivated by the Fascist movements.

Unlike many middle-class or working-class parties, the Fascists appealed to all social groups, from the top to the bottom of the social scale. Excluded were only those who were their favourite objects of attack: the profiteers, the parasites, the financial gangsters, the ruling cliques, the rapacious capitalists, the reactionary landowners. But even there exceptions were made if it suited the Leader's book. There is no doubt, however, that certain social groups responded much more strongly to the Fascist appeal than others. This is particularly true of those who were uprooted and threatened by social and economic change, whose position in society was being undermined, who had lost their traditional place, and were frightened of the future. These were, above all, the lower middle classes—or rather certain groups within them: the artisans and independent tradesmen, the small farmers, the lower grade government employees and white-collar workers. Perhaps even more important in the early stages were the former officers and non-commissioned officers of the first world war for whom no jobs were waiting, who had got accustomed to the use of violence, and felt themselves deprived of their 'legitimate' rewards. In Italy, in Germany, and elsewhere the 'front' generation played a leading part in the rise of Fascism. For its members fighting was a way of life which they transferred to the domestic scene. They loved battles for their own sake.[4] It is no accident that the most important Fascist movements had their origin in the year 1919, the year of the Hungarian and Munich Soviet republics, of civil war which aroused fear and hatred in many hearts. Those who had been badly frightened did not

---

[3] In the words of the 'Horst Wessel Song' which became the German national anthem. Horst Wessel was one of the early 'martyrs' who was shot by Communists in Berlin.

[4] Thus Codreanu in a revealing passage of his autobiography: *Eiserne Garde*, Berlin, 1939, p.11.

easily forget. The occupation of the factories in northern Italy in the following year had the same effect.

This does not mean, however, that the lower middle classes acted on their own—in a revulsion from liberalism and parliamentarianism—or in their own interests to bring about Fascism. In a recent work on a Marxist topic it was stated that the lower middle classes adopted a policy to 'use that power [of the state], even increase it, for their own ends till they reached the superstates of Nazi Germany and Fascist Italy'.[5] This is a gross oversimplification of a very complex process by which members of the lower middle classes were recruited by Fascist parties in many different countries; but they did not take any initiative as a social group; nor did they intend to use the power of the state 'for their own ends'. An earlier sociological analysis, based on the Italian example, suggested that a development towards Fascism was possible in Italy because there the bourgeoisie was weak and the proletariat strong and particularly well organized, having achieved a dominating position in certain parts of the country.[6] While this was true of Italy, it was much less true of Germany—where the proletarian revolution had been decisively defeated in 1919—and not at all true of certain underdeveloped countries, such as Hungary and Rumania. From what has been said in the preceding pages it emerges that Fascist movements could develop in countries with a very strong left-wing movement—such as Italy or Spain—but equally in countries where the opposite was the case. It does not seem that the relative strength of the bourgeoisie and the working class had much to do with the rise of Fascism. There is more truth in the assertion that this rise was due to a malaise, a maladjustment of capitalist society, the victims of which were the lower middle classes more than any other social group.

Apart from the groups already mentioned, there were the youngsters at school and university who became ardent believers in Fascism at an early stage. They were fed up with the existing society, bored with their daily duties, and strongly attracted by a movement which promised a radical change, which they could invest with a romantic halo. These youths came from middle-class or lower middle-class families. They could not easily find the way into the Communist camp. But they found the weak and changing governments of the post-war period

[5] J. P. Nettl, *Rosa Luxemburg*, London and New York, 1966, vol. ii, p. 554.
[6] Franz Borkenau, 'Zur Soziologie des Faschismus', *Archiv für Sozialwissenschaft und Sozialpolitik*, vol. lxviii, 1933, p. 521. It is somewhat ironical that this was published a few weeks *after* Hitler had come into power.

utterly unattractive. In the Weimar Republic, in the post-war Italian kingdom, in the corrupt governments of Rumania, in the powerless governments of Spain, there was nothing to fire the enthusiasm of youth: they were dreary and pedestrian, the offices filled with mediocrities and time-servers. It was this, rather than any economic threat, that led so many idealist students into the Fascist camp. Similarly, many young officers and soldiers of the post-war generation were attracted by visions of national greatness and the promise of a revision of the peace treaties. A perusal of the autobiographical notes[7] compiled by men who joined the National Socialist Party in its early years shows that pride of place belongs to a strong nationalism, the desire to see Germany strong and united again, freed from the 'chains of Versailles', and also from the faction fights and the 'horse-trading' of the political parties. This often went together with hatred of the Communists and Socialists, and with anti-Semitism. Those who joined the Party were usually very young; they loved the frequent fights and battles in which they got involved together with their comrades, as well as the uniforms and the propaganda marches.

For the success of Fascism other factors, too, were essential. In the first place, there was the devastating economic crisis which made millions unemployed and threatened the economic existence of many more millions. If it had not been for the vast inflation of the German currency which undermined the very foundations of society, followed by the slump of the early 1930s, Hitler would not have been successful in Germany. Nor would Mussolini have been in Italy if it had not been for the post-war economic crisis and the fears which it aroused in the middle classes. Many other Fascist movements owed their growth to the slump of the early 1930s, a slump that found all governments helpless and passive. Essential, too, was the help rendered by sections of the ruling groups and governments, or the support of the army and high-ranking officers. Without this, there would have been no march on Rome and no Mussolini government. Without the support rendered by the Bavarian government and army the National Socialists would not have become a mass party in Munich in the early 1920s. Later, the ambigious role of the *Reichswehr* leaders and their deep contempt of the Republic proved of inestimable value to Hitler, as did the financial contributions which he received from certain industrialists. The Iron Guard would not have become a mass movement if it had

[7] There are many hundreds of these autobiographical notes in the *Hauptarchiv der NSDAP*, now in the Bundesarchiv at Koblenz.

not been supported for a time by King Carol and industrialist circles. In Spain the revolt of the generals thrust the *Falange* into prominence. In Finland and in Hungary the army provided invaluable help for the Fascists. This factor must not be overestimated in its importance, but neither must it be overlooked.

It has recently been stated that 'the German crisis was *sui generis*'. 'Though Fascism had spread throughout Europe, the German variety came to be unique. It was unique not only in the way it managed to displace the revolutionary impetus, but also in the primacy of the ideology of the Volk, nature and race. . . .'[8] As far as the *völkisch* ideology was concerned it was not unique, but it had its close counterparts in the racial theories propounded in Finland and in Hungary—two countries inhabited by non-Indo-European peoples. The 'Roman' ideology of the Italian Fascists and the theory of the common 'Dietsch' origin of the people of the Netherlands belong into the same category. Moreover, the Italian Fascists were considerably more successful in destroying 'the revolutionary impetus' than were the National Socialists. The former's punitive expeditions killed the revolutionary movement in Italy; but in Germany this was accomplished by the Free Corps before the National Socialist Party came into being. This is not to deny that its growth was very much facilitated by the existence of *völkisch* and anti-Semitic beliefs in certain circles, but this was only one of the factors which aided its rise. The others were the lost war, the sense of humiliation and the fierce nationalism resulting from the Treaty of Versailles, the occupation of the Ruhr and the reparations' issue, the weakness and unpopularity of the Weimar Republic, the inflation and the economic crisis, the fears and the insecurity of the middle and lower middle classes. All these combined to make the rise of Hitler possible, and all were paralleled by similar developments in other European countries. Even Hitler's ferocious anti-Semitism was matched by the same tendency in Hungary and in Rumania.

Were the Fascist movements revolutionary? No doubt many of them demanded radical social changes and reforms, especially in Eastern Europe and in Spain where these were bitterly necessary. But in the more stable and conservative atmosphere of north-western Europe these movements were much less radical. The Italian Fascists and the German National Socialists were radical in their original demands, but both shed most of this radicalism fairly soon. If many

[8] George L. Mosse, *The Crisis of the German Ideology*, New York, 1964, p. 315.

Fascist leaders insisted that they must come into power in a legal way, this does not prove that their movements were not revolutionary. Even if this insistence was not just useful propaganda, the Fascist movements did aim at a fundamental change of the political structure— the abolition of parliamentary government and democracy—and the replacement of the ruling groups by a new *élite*. Once in power, they naturally had to use many of the old experts, civil servants and generals, but these were no longer in command. They received their 'marching orders' from the new leaders who often came from entirely different social groups, far below the level of the old ruling classes. The Fascist 'revolution' was not fought out in the streets and on the barricades, but in the ministries and government buildings. In this sense there was a 'seizure of power'. Power was handed over by the old ruling groups to the new leaders, and they used this power for their own ends.

Between the aims of the new and those of the old rulers there was a superficial similarity—the expansion of Germany or colonial conquest in Africa—but in reality there was a vast difference. What Hitler aimed at was not German expansion, and not even a Greater Germany, but world conquest. He did not care for the fate of the Sudeten Germans, the South Tyrolese or of any other German minority, but was willing to sacrifice them on the altar of his ambition. Mussolini's methods of conquest were often quite irrational, subject to his vision of a 'Roman Empire'. No one could seriously maintain that the two dictators acted in the interests of their countries. There is much truth in the assertion of Hermann Rauschning that the Fascists carried through a 'revolution of nihilism'. The Hitler Youth used to sing a song which prophesied that Europe would be aflame when the *Germanen* went down; Europe was in flames, but she has recovered. Fascism was the product of a deep social and economic crisis, a crisis of European society.

8   Neofascism

The Second World War ended with the downfall of the Fascist regimes, first in Italy, and then in Germany; they were discredited by the collapse of their policies of conquest and expansion, by the ruthless suppression of all opposition, and by the inhuman treatment meted out to their enemies. In both countries, democratic parties and trade unions slowly resumed their political activities, under the watchful eyes of the Allied forces of occupation. Yet all over Europe many thousands of convinced Fascists and National Socialists survived the war, often embittered by arrest, trial and exclusion from public office. It was only a question of time before they would try to organize themselves, to take up the struggle once more against liberalism and democracy, against undesirable aliens and alleged Communist subversion. Indeed, as the war brought with it the advance of Soviet power into the heart of central Europe and the forced conversion of most of eastern and central Europe to Communism, the fears which had been such a powerful promoter of the Fascist movements received a strong confirmation in fact. And there were millions who were uprooted and driven from their homes, who fled from the advancing Red Army or were expelled from Poland and Czechoslovakia, many resentful and eager for revenge. When things became more settled in postwar Europe new dangers threatened alleged racial purity, foreign workers migrating to the more affluent countries, or immigrants from the former colonial empires of the victor states. Although prosperity returned to Europe much more quickly than after the First World War, there were once more severe economic crises, high unemployment and rapid inflation which fifty years earlier had driven masses of the discontented into the arms of the Fascists. Thus a Fascist revival in one country or the other could almost be expected.

Yet thirty-five years after the end of the war there is no Fascist mass movement anywhere in Europe, but only a plethora of small groups and parties some of which are openly Fascist or National Socialist, while others disclaim this epithet and proclaim their loyalty to the democratic order. One or the other party may gain adherents for a time and poll a large following in an election; but this has usually been followed by decline and disintegration, often accompanied by internal conflicts and rivalries between different 'Leaders'. Awareness of the threat of Fascism has grown considerably, and with it a readiness to combat the danger in its early stages. In several countries, legislation has hampered the spread of Fascist or racist propaganda, and has even led to the dissolution of Neonazi organizations. Anti-Fascist propaganda has been more vigorous than that of the Fascists whose financial subsidies from big industry and agriculture seem to have dried up. In the Communist states of eastern Europe, once hotbeds of Fascism, many former Fascists have found shelter under the new masters, but no legal Fascist groups could survive. In western Europe, Fascist organisations have on the whole remained particularly small in the countries occupied by the *Wehrmacht* during the war where revulsion against National Socialism was especially strong, and where Fascist leaders such as Degrelle, Doriot, Mussert or Quisling collaborated with the occupiers.

In France, Fascism has remained negligible; organizations such as *Ordre Nouveau*, founded in 1969, have been dissolved; in the last election two groups of the extreme right between them won less than one per cent of the vote. In Belgium, the Flemish *Volksunie* has a paramilitary protection unit which is strongly racist and anti-Communist, but it has only a few hundred members. In Holland, there is a Netherlands *Volksunie* which was founded in the early 'seventies and has a Leader; it participated in the election of 1977 under the slogan 'Keep the Netherlands white!', aimed at foreigners and immigrants from the former Dutch colonial empire; but it polled only 33,000 votes, 0.4 per cent of the total. Detachments of Flemish and Walloon nationalists have taken part in right-wing rallies in Germany, and the meetings of former members of the Armed *S.S.* have provided similar opportunities for 'international' gatherings, but all these activities have been on a small scale. The overthrow of right-wing military dictatorships in Greece, Portugal and Spain has deprived the extreme right of international backing and prestige. There seems to be little chance of a come-back of the military in any of these countries, much as the Spanish army may feel provoked by the terrorism of the extreme Left and the Basque separatists. At the end of 1978 a leading British weekly published an article with the heading 'Where have all the Fascists gone?'[1]. The answer, if we look at Europe since the Second World War, would be that only in three countries important Fascist revivals have occurred: as one might expect, in Italy and Germany, and, somewhat surprisingly, in Britain.

Italy

Italy differs from other European countries in so far as one Neo-fascist party, founded soon after the war, has held the stage without interruption for well over thirty years, while elsewhere such parties have grown and disappeared again in profusion. This party is the *Movimento Sociale Italiano* which was founded as early as 1946 by former prominent Fascists. It was inspired above all by the revolution-ary beginnings of Italian Fascism in 1919[2] and by the attempt of Mussolini, after his arrest and his liberation by the Germans, to found a radical Fascist Republic, the Republic of Salo on Lake Garda: a republic that was powerless and depended on German support. The recognized Leader of the M.S.I., Giorgio Almirante, was an under-secretary of state in the Republic of Salò. Its programme was based on a return to the Fascism of the Origin, uhtainted by any compromise with the monarchy or the established powers, and demanded the elimination of the 'parasitical plutocracies', the establishment of a hierarchical public order, a state based on corporations instead of trade unions, state intervention in labour conflicts, an end to 'the parties' political terror', a return to the colonies across the Mediter-ranean. Soon thousands of Fascists released from imprisonment or returned from the colonies joined the M.S.I. But its mass basis was centred not in the north, but in the Italian south which had not known the struggle of the Italian partisans and the Republic of Salo and continued to be extremely poor and backward, in spite of all the post-war efforts to found industries there. In the referendum of June 1946 the vast majority in the Italian south voted in favour of the retention of the monarchy, while the majority of the Italians voted against. In the first postwar election of 1948 the M.S.I. polled only two per cent of the vote but won six seats in the chamber, all in the south[3]. During the following years it worked in alliance with the monarchists

[1] *The Economist*, 16 December 1978, p. 23.
[2] See above, pp. 49-52.
[3] See Petra Rosenbaum, 'Neofaschismus in Italien', *Aus Politik und Zeitgeschichte*, Bonn, 7 December 1974, pp. 14-19, and *Neofaschismus in Italien*, Frankfurt, 1975, pp. 36-40.

and became a typical party of notables of the south-Italian type. The unsolved problems of the south were to provide the M.S.I. with endless opportunities for propaganda, with possibilities for compromises and temporary alliances with the ruling Christian Democratic Party, and on occasion with the chance of exploiting mass discontent and revolt. While the north saw rapid industrialization and became prosperous, the south stagnated and the gap between them widened. Millions of southerners migrated north or across the Alps in search of a living.

In 1951 the M.S.I. won eleven seats in the regional parliament of Sicily with slogans such as 'The Mediterranean as Italy's Living Space' and 'Return to Work in Africa' and thus consolidated its position in the south. When it made further advances in local elections there the Minister of the Interior, Mario Scelba, proposed a bill to dissolve the movement and the para-military associations of the right in accordance with the Italian constitution. But obstruction tactics delayed the acceptance of the bill, and in the general election of 1953 the M.S.I. gained a further success, emerging with 5.9 per cent of the vote and 24 deputies in the chamber. In several regions of the south it cooperated with the ruling Christian Democrats and participated in the sharing out of the lucrative public posts. Contributions to the party began to flow, and it became difficult to proceed against it by legal methods; the Scelba law was forgotten. But while the party leaders worked within the existing system, adapted themselves to parliamentary procedures and cooperated with other parties of the Right, these tactics were opposed by the radical Fascists. Conflicts developed within the party, and more radical groups, such as *Ordine Nuovo* and *Avanguardia Nazionale*, broke away from it. The latter was anti-Semitic and racist and demanded the destruction of the democratic system and its replacement by a regime of 'true order'. *Ordine Nuovo* openly sympathized with National Socialism, published translations of *Mein Kampf* as well as works by Gentile and Mosley, aimed at a 'national and social revolution', and adopted as its motto that of the *S.S.*: 'Our Honour is Loyalty'. Both groups, however, remained small. There were other, even more extremist organizations, such as the *Squadre d'azione Mussolini*, harking back to the days of the Fascist *squadre* and equally committed to violence. In Rome and elsewhere they demolished offices of left-wing parties and attacked people in the streets, while the police remained passive. Much more important were the Fascist unions, the *Sindicati Nazionale dei Lavora-*

tori, founded in the early 'fifties by a leader of the M.S.I. to oppose the genuine unions. They soon had a mass membership, especially in the south, where they supplied the employers with 'reliable' workers.

The elections of the late 'fifties and the 'sixties did not bring the M.S.I. further successes: it polled 4.8, 5.3 and 4.5 per cent of the vote in three general elections between 1958 and 1968. Parliamentarian Fascism did not seem to lead the party anywhere, and the young radicals reproached the leaders with arranging themselves within the system and reaching agreements with the Christian Democrats. Open conflicts broke out at the party congresses. When the party leader, Arturo Michelini, protested against the term of Neofascist to be applied to the M.S.I. and recommended abandoning all Fascist slogans and methods, Almirante protested in the name of all those who desired a Fascist revolution. He was then appointed a member of the party presidium but lost many followers who considered him an opportunist. *OrdineNuovo* called for a boycott of the elections and its leader, Pino Rauti, established links to Neofascist groups in other countries. The youth and student organization of the M.S.I. sharply criticized the traditionalist attitude of the leaders which in their eyes was passive and non-Fascist. They and other groups of the extreme Right preached political violence and the spirit of revolutionary Fascism. They organized camps with para-military exercises and weapon training. Violent clashes occurred with left-wing students and workers. When Michelini died in 1969 Giorgio Almirante became the party's leader; he had always been a radical Fascist, opposed to the party notables from the south and loyal to the Fascism of the Salo Republic.

The year 1969 saw a sharpening of political and social conflict, colossal strikes, student riots, permanent government crisis, a growth of violence and political terror, committed by groups of the extreme Left as well as the Right. The government seemed unable or unwilling to solve the problems facing the country, to restore law and order and to maintain stability. Fear of left-wing subversion grew, while the 'opening to the left' (a coalition of the Christian Democrats with left-wing parties) became a real possibility. Groups of *Squadre d'azione Mussolini*, *Ordine Nuovo* and *Avanguardia Nazionale* practised terror against the left and resorted to bombing. At the end of the year a bomb exploded in the agricultural bank of Milan; it killed sixteen people, and eighty-eight were seriously wounded. The police sought the perpetrators among the local anarchists and only years later arrested some Fascists. But the principal accused succeeded in escaping abroad in spite of close confinement. The trial was postponed several times; it came to an end early in 1979 but without the three chief criminals. The elections of 1970 brought the M.S.I. only a small success, an increase of its vote from 4.5 to 5.2 per cent, and that after an extended crisis of the coalition government of the Christian Democrats with the Socialists. Many members of the lower middle classes began to look to the M.S.I. as a bulwark against the growing threat from the Left, the power of the unions, and the disintegration of authority and society. The slogan of 'the cursed rule of the parties' served to mobilize those who were alienated by the practices of the bureaucracy, corruption, mismanagement in the state industries, the ruling cliques and interest groups.

These tendencies erupted in the summer of 1970 in the revolt of Reggio Calabria, situated in one of the most neglected areas of the south. The issue was whether Reggio, Catanzaro or Cosenza should become the capital of the new region and reap the benefits expected from the transfer of authority. Since Reggio's rivals had far better connections in Rome, the Italian government announced that Catanzaro was to be the regional capital, and Cosenza the seat of a new university. There were strikes, mass demonstrations and riots in Reggio; public transport was brought to a halt by enraged labourers and peasants; a local M.S.I. functionary violently attacked the rule of the parties. New rioting occurred when it was announced that Reggio was also considered unsuitable for the establishment of a new centre of heavy industry. An action committee organized by the Fascist union planned deeds of violence against the party offices of the Christian Democrats and the left-wing parties which were burned. The hordes mobilized by the committee were joined by Neofascist students and pupils from the towns of Sicily, such as Catania and Messina, and by the Black Shirts of a nearby para-military camp. By the end of July the press of the M.S.I. which had at first adopted a cautious attitude openly supported the revolt and the slogan of a 'free and independent Reggio'. From there punitive expeditions were sent out to Catanzaro and Cosenza. The battles with the forces of the executive during which public buildings, post offices and stations were burned down lasted until September. M.S.I. propaganda pictured the organized violence as the justified wrath of the people who had risen against the corrupt rule of the parties. In 1971 the compromise was adopted that the regional council was to sit alternatively in Catanzaro and in Reggio.

The revolt of Reggio demonstrated how the initiative passed to the Fascist radicals whom the party leaders used as their executive arm and on whom the M.S.I. depended.

In his press conferences Almirante constantly emphasized the threat of a Communist takeover: Italy must use force to eliminate the threat. For the elections of 1972 his slogan was simply Law and Order, an 'order of a just hierarchy of rights and duties'; the corporative system was the guarantee of social peace; the colonies were to be returned to Italy, and strikes to be prohibited; the young must learn the ideals of élitism. In the elections the M.S.I. had its greatest success so far and gained nearly nine per cent of the vote in the country as a whole: much less in the north and as much as 15 per cent in Palermo, 20 in Naples, 21 in Reggio, 23 in Catania. It was a rebellion of the south against mismanagement, neglect and central government. But the M.S.I. had also cleverly exploited the dilemma of the ruling Christian Democrats who posed as the barrier against the Communist threat but were no longer able to govern without Communist support. Almost three million votes were cast for the combined list of the M.S.I. and the National Right. The voters came above all from the middle and lower middle classes, officials, white-collar workers, soldiers, academics, and included the impoverished urban masses of the south. With fifty-six seats in the chamber and twenty-six in the Senate the M.S.I. became the fourth strongest party in the country.

During the following years, however, local and regional elections did not bring the M.S.I. the expected successes, in spite of the continuing weakness of the government and the growing disillusionment with the coalition of the Christian Democrats and the Left. In the general election of 1976 the M.S.I. dropped to just over six per cent of the poll, while the Communists obtained nearly thirty-five per cent, rivalling the strength of the Christian Democrats. Although none of the fundamental problems facing Italy had been solved and the threat of Communism had clearly not receded, although there was severe unemployment and an ever-growing academic proletariat, the large majority of conservative Italians continued to see in the *Democrazia Christiana*, and not in the M.S.I.,´ their protector against the left-wing danger. Indeed, more recently the Christian Democrats have recovered some strength; they remain by far the strongest party without which no government can be formed. In the general election of June 1979 they suffered only very slight losses, while the Communists were reduced to 30.4 per cent of the total. The M.S.I. which once more campaigned for 'order' lost equally and polled only 5.3 per cent. This defeat was at least partly due to the squabbles and infighting within the movement. In 1976 half the parliamentary deputies left and founded the National Democratic Party. They accused Almirante of having ruined their cause through his radicalism and of driving the party into isolation. In southern Italian towns youth groups of the M.S.I. publicly threatened and severely wounded left-wing pupils. The M.S.I. organized veritable pilgrimages to the grave of Mussolini in his native village of Predappio. The Neofascist trade union called strikes on the railways so as to convince the workers that the left-wing unions were bankrupt and called on the workers to take their fate into their own hands. But these tactics only frightened the adherents of the traditional Right.

Thus the dichotomy between the more traditional Italian Right led by noblemen, academics, officers and industrialists and the terrorist revolutionary Fascists has continued. The leadership of Almirante who tried to integrate them in one party did not succeed. Perhaps this is the most important cause of the rather moderate success of Italian Neofascism, of its failure to exploit the conditions of almost permanent unrest, corruption, instability and political terrorism. As these conditions are likely to continue, the M.S.I. will remain part of the Italian political scene, but is likely to occupy a position on its fringes rather than in the centre. Though Rome has been conquered many a time, a conquest based on the backward south is not a practical possibility, and another March on Rome is out of the question. Only in alliance with the *Democrazia Christiana* could the M.S.I. hope to gain influence and power, and this too seems to be a vain hope.

Germany

Germany was shattered even more than Italy by the war and the total collapse of the dictatorship. It was also more tightly controlled by the forces of the occupying powers which divided Germany between them. Thus it took several years before any extreme right-wing party emerged from the ruins, and none of them could proclaim itself openly National Socialist. This was also due to a general revulsion against the dictatorship, for example in the postwar German press and literature, when the vast atrocities committed were revealed. In East Germany, no pro-Nazi party was permitted, and in West Germany the federal courts several times prohibited pro-Nazi parties and organizations, which were then dissolved by the authorities. In contrast with Italy, there has thus been a bewildering kaleidoscope of parties and groups which all disclaimed

National Socialism, but in reality perpetuated its ideology to a larger
or smaller extent. A common denominator in their ideology was the
opposition to the democratization that occurred in the Federal Republic, especially to the powerful influence gained by the trade unions, and
to any rapprochement with Communism in the East. As the number of
Jews left in Germany is pitifully small, anti-Semitism has been replaced by Xenophobia, directed at the hundreds of thousands of
foreign workers who have made their home in Germany without being
integrated into German society, and who—contrary to the statistical
evidence—are held responsible for the growth of crime.

In contrast with Italy, however, there is no neglected and impoverished south; millions of expellees and refugees have been absorbed into
the economy. Economic recovery and stability have been remarkable,
in spite of the oil crisis, and so has been the continuity of government,
led by either of the two large parties, the Christian Democrats or the
Social Democrats. These factors largely account for the relative lack of
political extremism, whether of the right or of the left, in complete
contrast with the years of the Weimar Republic. The middle-of-the-
road parties dominate the political scene. The political terrorism
practised by the Red Army and other factions has caused strict defen-
sive measures of the authorities, but the democratic system has survived. Above all, the strident German nationalism of the Wilhelminian
and post-Wilhelminian periods has subsided in favour of pragmatism
and the satisfaction created by economic prosperity. No one seriously
contemplates marching eastwards to new conquests, not even to
reunify the two Germanics. Appeals to 'blood and soil', to the Germanic virtues, to racial superiority, to military glory no longer evoke
an echo. France is no longer the 'hereditary enemy'. The political
atmosphere has changed completely. It is these factors which account
for the very limited success of Neonazism in Germany.

In the late 1940s, when Allied restrictions on German political life
were lifted, two extreme right-wing parties were founded. Both significantly incorporated the word *Reich* (evoking echoes of Bismarck as
well as Hitler) in their names, and one also the word Socialist which
had been so misused by the National Socialists. This was the *Sozialis-
tische Reichspartei*, founded in 1949 by Dr Fritz Dorls who had early
on joined the N.S.D.A.P. but later broken with it out of sympathy with
Otto Strasser's revolutionary National Socialism.[4] Dorls was an out-
standing organizer and a ruthless demagogue, and the party was organized in accordance with the Leadership Principle. It also had

4 See above, pp. 124, 137, 141.

Protection Squads, the members of which wore white shirts, black riding breeches and jackboots. The Party Council consisted of the founders, the regional party leaders and members coopted on the proposal of the party chairman who was entitled to add further members; it was the most important organ of the S.R.P. With propaganda methods copied from the past it tried to win over the masses of the disappointed and uprooted. Its propaganda was anti-Semitic and anti-democratic; the leading German politicians were accused of treason; the attempt on Hitler's life on 20 July 1944 served as the material for a new stab-in-the-back legend. The party's leader in Schleswig-Holstein (where Nazi influence had been particularly strong) was Otto Ernst Remer, an officer who was promoted by Hitler for his part in squashing the military coup of 20 July in Berlin. In the S.R.P. meetings due homage was paid to those fallen in the war as well as to the comrades still in prison or captivity, and occasionally to 'the victims of the gallows of Nuremberg' (where the principal war criminals had been hanged). The party soon had tens of thousands of members. In the elections to the Diet of Lower Saxony in 1951 it gained eleven per cent of the vote and fifteen seats—27 per cent in Aurich and Rotenburg, 28 in Lüneburg and 33 in Diepholz. At least in some parts of Lower Saxony, the S.R.P. clearly had become a major party and posed a threat to the new order. Thus late in 1951 the German government appealed to the constitutional court in Karlsruhe to declare the S.R.P. anti-constitutional because it was a successor to the N.S.D.A.P. according to its leaders, programme, propaganda and form of organization. Twelve months later the constitutional court accepted the evidence submitted and declared the party dissolved because its programme and ideology were very close to National Socialism and it rejected plural democracy and the democratic parties. Remer escaped to Egypt; after an amnesty he returned to Germany, was later tried on criminal charges and once more fled abroad. The party disappeared from the political scene.

The other, rather similar party, founded at the same time, was the *Deutsche Reichspartei*. It glorified the ideas of war and the *Reich*, demanded greater living space for the Germans, and tried to win over the former National Socialists. The party claimed to be conservative and not socialist, but its hierarchy and structure followed the National Socialist pattern; orders emanated from the top. The D.R.P. proclaimed its loyalty to the 'whole and undivided history of the German nation' and to 'the people's community' (as the National Socialists had done). Most of its membership was concentrated in Lower Saxony, where it polled 8.1 per cent of the vote in 1949; but in 1953 it fell to 3.5 per cent. In the federal elections the party obtained only 1.8 per cent in 1949, and by 1961 was reduced to 0.8, so that it was unable to gain any seats in the Bonn parliament. The decline was obviously due to Germany's growing prosperity and the absorption of the refugees and war victims by the West German economy. After the foundation of the N.P.D. in 1964 the D.R.P. dissolved itself. Many of its functionaries and members joined the new rising party of the Right.

There were also many organizations of the refugees and expellees who formed their own *Landsmannschaften;* among them that of the Sudeten Germans achieved some international notoriety for its revisionist demands. Active within it was the *Witikobund*, an élitist league which was joined by many leading Sudeten National Socialists. It agitated violently against 'the colossal sell-out of our fatherland', which it claimed outdid even the Treaty of Versailles; but it never had a large following. Most of the leaders of the Sudeten German *Landsmannschaft* preferred to join one of the major German parties and to work within them for their aims, but without any notable success. More dangerous was *Nation Europa*, based on the survivors of the German and non-German units of the *S.S.* in the Second World War. Like similar organizations of exservicemen it hailed the 'European spirit' in Hitler's war against Russia and considered the war an anti-Bolshevik crusade. It also propagated a new stab-in-the-back legend, held that all opposition to National Socialism was treason, adhered to a new racialism and glorified the Arabs' struggle against Israel. *Nation Europa* was finally dissolved by the German authorities. The principal organisation of *S.S.* ex-servicemen is the H.I.A.G. which has about 20,000 members and aims at achieving equality in the treatment of the *S.S.* men with former German soldiers. But as about 500,000 men served in the Armed *S.S.*, 20,000 is not a very impressive figure. Organizations such as these try to perpetuate the legend of the 'defence of the Occident against the flood of Bolshevik nihilism' by the German army, from general to private soldier, as one ex-servicemen's journal put it in 1964.[5] Journals such as these naturally disclaim any responsibility of Germany for the outbreak of the Second World War and hail the publication of any book that holds 'that Germany in 1939 did not desire any war and put forward the most moderate demands imaginable': thus the *Sudetendeutsche Turnerbrief* (which continues the *völkisch* traditions of the Sudeten German sports clubs) in August

[5] *Kyffhäuser*, no. 6, 1964, quoted by A. Hübner, 'Rechtsradikale Jugendgruppen in der Bundesrepublik', in I. Fetscher (ed.), *Rechtsradikalismus*, Frankfurt, 1967, p. 139.

1962.[6] They deny that six million Jews were killed by the National Socialists and at best concede a much smaller number of victims who allegedly died because of the exigencies of the military situation. Yet the very middle-aged warriors of the Second World War have not been able to arouse great enthusiasm for the military cause. The younger German generation has followed very different ideals and ideologies, often the very opposite of those of their fathers.

The most important of the many extreme right-wing organisations of postwar Germany was founded in 1964, with a name that did not emphasize the idea of the *Reich* or of socialism: the National Democratic Party (N.P.D.). For a time it was more successful than any other in exploiting anti-liberal and authoritarian tendencies in West German Society, the resentment against the unions and the foreign workers. Although its some-time leader, Adolf von Thadden, had not been a National Socialist, nearly half its local functionaries and three quarters of its leading officials were connected with National Socialism, and many had occupied prominent positions before 1945. Many of them, including von Thadden, had had posts in the *Deutsche Reichspartei*. The N.P.D. soon had a large membership, rising by June 1965 to about 15,000 and two years later to over 25,000. Among its voters, men and Protestants were more strongly represented than women and Catholics, and middle-aged men more strongly than any other age group. It is more difficult to establish the social composition of the party's following. It seems that peasants and workers were under-represented but that other social groups were fairly evenly represented; apparently there was no specially strong support from refugees and expellees from the eastern territories.

The N.P.D. programme emphasized above all German nationalism: 'The robbery of ancient German soil and the partition of Germany are elements of a deed of violence. . . . The claim to the Sudetenland must not be abandoned by any one, be that government or party. . . ' The allegation that Germany alone was responsible for the two world wars was a 'lie', and the fight against it the task of the whole nation.[7] The entry of the United States into the war was attributed to 'the activity of certain anti-Fascist and anti-German Jews'.[8] The number of Jews

[6] Comment of the *Sudetendeutscher Turnerbrief*, August 1962, on the book of the American historian Hoggan: quoted by E. Weick, 'Gibt es einen "Rechtsradikalismus" in der Vertriebenenpresse ?', ibid., p. 108.

[7] N.P.D. programme quoted by H. Maier and H. Bott, *Die NPD*, Munich, 1968, pp. 67, 87.

[8] *Deutsche Nachrichten*, quoted ibid., p. 35.

killed during the war was estimated 'reliably' as between 350,000 and one million. As to the concentration camps, 'the N.P.D. regrets that in these camps political enemies of the Third *Reich* were imprisoned together with criminals.'[9] The Munich leader of the N.P.D. even declared in 1965: 'There never were any crimes in National Socialist Germany. These slanders are only the propaganda of international Judaism and the Jewish press.'[10] In the same year the N.P.D. journal, while not denying 'the crimes of the Hitler era', claimed that 'the right radicalism of the Zionists carries perhaps more conscious guilt for these crimes than the whole German people'.[11] The same journal earlier wrote that Heine, because he was a Jew, could not possibly have been the greatest German poet after Goethe.[12] There were also repeated attacks on radio and television as the destroyers of German culture, on the worshippers of internationalism who allowed the national characteristics shown in artistic values to whither away, on all who undermined and denigrated the national culture. The same slogans and appeals were used by the Nationalists and the National Socialists in the days of the Weimar Republic, yet the constitution of the N.P.D. proclaimed that it was without any reservation loyal to liberal principles.

In the general election of 1965, only ten months after its foundation, the N.P.D. polled only two per cent of the vote and did not gain a single seat. But then its successes multiplied. In November 1966 it obtained 7.9 per cent in Hesse and 7.4 in Bavaria and gained eight and fifteen seats respectively in the two Diets; in Ansbach, Bayreuth and Nuremberg it even polled between thirteen and fifteen per cent. In Land elections in the following year it won seven per cent of the vote in Lower Saxony, 8.8 in Bremen, and in 1968 as much as 9.8 in Baden-Wurttemberg, the traditionally liberal south-west of Germany. Usually the success was particularly marked in towns and districts with a strong National Socialist tradition. But serious conflicts broke out between different N.P.D. leaders, principally between old Nationalists and more radical younger functionaries, and von Thadden was unable to integrate these conflicting tendencies. In the federal election of 1969 the party polled only 4.3 per cent and—on account of the five per cent

[9] N.P.D. Politisches Lexikon, quoted by R. Kuhnl, G. Ahrweiler, M. Maessen, R. Rilling and R. Tellers, *Die NPD*, Berlin, 1967, p. 94.

[10] Josef Truxa on 18 June 1965, quoted by J. D. Nagle, *The National Democratic Party*, Berkeley-Los Angeles, 1970, p. 77.

[11] *Deutsche Nachrichten*, no. 52, 1965, quoted ibid., p. 74.

[12] *Deutsche Nachrichten*, no. 7, 1965, quoted by R. Kühnl and others, *Die NPD*, Berlin, 1967, p. 144.

hurdle—did not win a seat in the Bonn parliament. This failure marked
the beginning of its decline. Since then its vote has dwindled: to 0.8
per cent in the general election of 1972, and to 0.3 per cent in 1976,
when only 123,000 votes were cast for the N.P.D. in the whole of West
Germany—and that in spite of large unemployment and economic
difficulties. According to an estimate of the German authorities, in 1978
the party had about 9,000 members left only a fraction of whom were
actively working for it.

In June 1977 the party organized an all-German rally at Frankfurt,
which was also attended by activists from Austria, Belgium, France and
Italy, but it was unable to mobilize more than 4,000 adherents. Its
youth organisation, the Young National Democrats, at the end of 1977
had perhaps another 1,500 members. There Neonazi tendencies were
clearly evident and their federal conference in 1977 took place under
the old Nazi slogan: 'Smash the Red Front and the Reactionaries!'.[13]
Meanwhile von Thadden was replaced as the party leader by Martin
Mussgnug, but this did not provide the N.P.D. with a more charismatic leader. In recent years, reports on the N.P.D. have almost disappeared from the columns of the German press, with the exception
of occasional references to one of its 'actions'. Thus the Munich N.P.D.
organized an 'Anti-Holocaust Action', to undo the effect of the showing
of the American Holocaust film—an action promptly prohibited by the
mayor of Munich. Apart from the lack of a charismatic leader and the
intervention of the authorities, the opposition organized by the students
and some trade unions has contributed to the party's decline. Usually
the party's Protection Squads overreacted badly to any organized
opposition, so that the party which espoused 'law and order' became
associated in public opinion with violence and disorder. The voters
who wanted to oppose the ruling Social Democratic-Liberal coalition
government had in the Christian Democratic Party and its Bavarian
associate a more effective counterweight available than the small
N.P.D. The Christian Democratic parties succeeded in integrating the
conservative and right-wing vote.

Apart from the 'respectable' parties of the extreme Right, there exist
in West Germany—exactly as in Italy—more extremist Neonazi
groups, mainly of young people. The authorities have listed twenty
or more of these, but they are very small, counting between them
about 1,300 'activists'. Their members tend to look with contempt at
the cautious tactics of their elders, at the meetings of 'old comrades'

[13] These data are taken from a report by the Minister of the Interior of North
Rhine-Westphalia on 'Rechts- und Linksradikalismus', Düsseldorf, 1978, pp. 7-9.

at which much beer is consumed and the battles of the last war are fought anew. Such Neonazi groups collect, or steal, weapons and symbols of the Third *Reich*, celebrate Hitler's birthday, sing old Nazi songs, and smear swastikas and anti-Semitic slogans on shops, banks and public buildings. Sometimes they use posters and other propaganda material produced in the U.S.A. by the 'N.S.D.A.P.-Foreign Section', such as 'Don't buy from Jews!'. As such activities are legally prohibited, they are only reported when the police arrest the culprits or when anti-Semitic slogans appear prominently. These groups apparently do not possess a significant number of sympathizers and differ from each other on points of tactics and ideology. Yet the number of 'right extremist incidents' registered by the police has risen from 616 in 1977 to 992 in 1978 and 890 during the first six months of 1979, so that the Minister of Justice in November 1979 asked for new and more energetic legislative measures against the perpetrators. The German authorities also noticed that some of the small Neonazi groups have adopted tactics of political violence, such as arson, bombing, raids on army barracks and bank robberies, which they have borrowed from the extreme Left. But it has to be borne in mind that the German economy, German society and the whole political system are far more stable than those of Italy—and incomparably more stable than those of the Weimar Republic fifty years ago. While this remains so Neonazism does not represent a serious danger, and the small Neonazi groups are unlikely to gain any mass influence.

Britain

In the period before the Second World War, the political traditions of Britain and the comparative stability of her institutions did not favour the growth of a Fascist mass movement, and the British Union of Fascists remained a fringe movement.[14] After the war, Sir Oswald Mosley's efforts to revive it and to stage a come-back did not meet with any greater success. Two changes, however, helped to create conditions more favourable to the growth of an extreme right-wing movement: the rapid loss of the Empire and the concomitant foundation of independent states in Africa and Asia, all more or less hostile to the remaining white minorities, and the mass of immigrants from the Commonwealth, without whom the British economy could not function, but who nevertheless aroused intense antagonism wherever they settled en masse. Although British political institutions remained on the whole stable, the precarious state of the economy, the power of the unions,

[14] See above, pp. 219-23.

large strikes, inflation and the rapid fall in the value of the pound have added strong elements of insecurity to the domestic situation. These factors, and especially the race issue, have provided Fascist or semi-Fascist organizations with their opportunity. Several of them, often in conflict with each other, came into being in the 'fifties and 'sixties, but none became a mass movement.

In 1954 a former leading member of the British Union of Fascists, A. K. Chesterton, a scholar and intellectual, founded the League of Empire Loyalists. He had broken with Mosley after the German occupation of the Sudetenland in 1938 and had fought in the war; he was a patriot and at the same time strongly anti-Semitic, anti-Communist and anti-American. Like so many Fascists, he believed that Jewish banks were responsible for the Russian revolution, that Jewish finance capital was identical with Bolshevism, and that the Moscow-Wall Street alliance aimed at the ruin of the British Empire and the establishment of world power. The League wanted to be an élite and sought influence rather than power, but it suffered from internal conflicts and schisms. While it had about 3,000 members in 1958, by 1961 there were only a few hundred left. In 1957 Colin Jordan resigned because the League would in principle accept Jewish and non-white members. In the next year John Bean left and founded the National Labour Party, and Jordan established his own White Defence League. But in 1960 Bean and Jordan joined hands in the British National Party, to free Britain from 'the domination of the international Jewish-controlled money-lending system' and to safeguard 'our Northern European folk'. The new party organized demonstrations at railway stations when trains arrived carrying immigrants from the ports. Its members sang: 'Red Front and Jewry will finally fall, Our race and nation will smash them all'.[15] In 1962 the party split because Bean strongly disapproved of Jordan's close ideological links with German National Socialism, 'to the neglect of Britain, Europe and the White World struggle'. In 1964 Bean stood as a candidate in the general election at Southall and gained nine per cent of the vote on a programme of stopping all non-white immigration.

Jordan in his turn, on Hitler's birthday in 1962, founded the National Socialist Movement with a birthday cake covered by a swastika and spoke of Britain's 'shame' in causing Hitler's defeat. The national organizer of the new movement was John Tyndall, but in 1964 he was expelled by Jordan on account of his British Fascist orientation, as opposed to the pro-Nazi brand favoured by Jordan. A police search

[15] Quoted by M. Walker, *The National Front*, London, 1977, pp. 34, 36.

at Jordan's home and headquarters produced weapons as well as Nazi flags, jackboots, uniforms and swastika armbands. At a summer camp in the Cotswolds, organized to form a National Socialist 'World Union', Jordan was appointed World Leader, with the American Lincoln Rockwell as the second-in-command, 'to protect and promote the Aryan race and its Western civilization'.[16] In 1966 the police discovered that the total membership of the movement was 187 of whom only 35 were still active; there were another 271 active supporters without voting rights 77 of whom still subscribed. After his expulsion Tyndall founded the Greater Britain Movement which regarded 'a pure, strong and healthy British race as the principal guarantee of Britain's future' and wanted 'marriages between Britons and non-Aryans' to be forbidden to protect the race.[17] Tyndall also advocated the adoption of apartheid on the South African model and British support for the white regimes in South Africa, for the white settlers were fighting 'for our cause and our future, the future of British civilization the world over'.[18] But his movement too remained very small and lacked the resources to fight an election.

Early in 1967 the British National Party, the League of Empire Loyalists and the Racial Preservation Society combined to form the National Front. The new party, at the outset thus had about 1,500 members, most of them from the British National Party. Its aims were: to fight Communism, to oppose the gangs of old politicians, to stop all immigration and to achieve the repatriation of non-white immigrants. 'The N.F. regards International Communism as the number one enemy of civilisation, and it repudiates the idea of "detente" with the Communist world while the latter seeks only the destruction of the West. We believe that only strength and the will to use it will keep the Communists at bay.' But the party considers 'International Monopoly Capitalism' as dangerous an enemy as Communism, and 'in fact the two represent different means to the same end: a world tyranny'.[19] Indeed, the hoary tale of the identity of Communism and capitalism has figured repeatedly in N.F. propaganda. 'Communism is not, as is supposed, a revolutionary uprising of the people against capitalism but a capitalist creation, sustained and nurtured by Capitalism through all its trials . . .'; 'Communism in Russia was created with the financial

[16] Ibid., pp. 40-41.
[17] Quoted ibid., p. 71.
[18] Quoted ibid., pp. 80-81.
[19] *National Front Statement of Policy*, s.d., p. 5.

backing of Wall Street international bankers such as Kuhn Loeb and Co. and the Warburgs . . .'; 'the "Russian" Revolution was financed mainly by Jewish bankers in the United States, Germany and Sweden. "German" Communism was of no different origins—apart from Marx himself, Lassalle, Liebknecht and Rosa Luxembourg (all Jews) being the most prominent promotors. . . .'[20] Even Liebknecht was made a Jew, and Rosa Luxemburg's name was misspelled.

Officially, the National Front distinguishes between anti-Semitism and anti-Zionism and claims that it is only anti-Zionist, for Zionism is 'imbued with a sense of racial destiny that knows no bounds, and brooks no opposition in its drive for mastery and world power. . . . Its extent is so great as to make it a threat to the survival of the West. . . .'[21] N.F. members declare that they are not anti-Jewish and that Jews are welcome to join the party. But its organ, *Spearhead*, has also carried anti-Semitic statements: 'Jewry wishes all races to mongrelise themselves—except itself; all nations to lose their sense of special identity—except its own. . . .'[22] The early editions of *Spearhead* —before its editor Tyndall joined the N.F.—had a regular column 'Gleanings from the Ghetto', signed Julius, which specialized in violent anti-Semitism and proclaimed: 'it is the Jews who are our misfortune: T-h-e J-e-w-s . . .'. Its first issue included an article 'Some Social Achievements of the Third Reich' which praised Germany's compulsory Labour Service 'of a year or so' and some other institutions of Hitler's Germany. In September 1967 *Spearhead* announced that Tyndall's Greater Britain Movement was joining the National Front to establish unity on the extreme Right. The N.F. also advocates Britain's withdrawal from the Common Market and 'repudiates the Treaty of Rome, since that Treaty was signed as a betrayal of election promises'. But characteristically, the main reason for this opposition is a racist one: Britain's entry was 'only the first step . . . ultimately culminating in the tyranny of One World Government carried on by an international élite'; its aim is to 'mongrelise' the different nations, 'and we could all unite into one final multi-racial antheap'.[24] It is the

[20] Quotations from *Spearhead*, no. 92, 1976, p. 6; no. 94, 1976, p. 10; no. 103, 1977, p. 11.
[21] *Spearhead*, no. 75, May 1974, p. 7.
[22] *Spearhead*, no. 53, June 1972, p. 13.
[23] *Spearhead*, no. 1, 1964, pp. 5-6; M. Billig, *Fascists—A Social Psychological View of the National Front*, London-New York, 1978, pp. 127-28.
[24] *National Front Statement of Policy*, s.d., p. 2; *Spearhead*, no. 58, November 1972, p. 8.

old fear of 'mongrelisation', of 'degenerate mestizos' of mixed blood, which had inspired Houston Stewart Chamberlain at the dawn of the twentieth century.[25] The same 'deadly peril' was stressed by Chesterton at the first annual conference of the N.F. in October 1967; but he also warned against another danger, that of racist extremism.

Leaflets of the National Front have attacked the chain stores, monopolies, the political parties, the Common Market, inflation and called for a moral cleansing of Britain. Tyndall proclaimed: 'We have to raise that [political] temperature several degrees if people are to awake and something is to be done. Enthusiasm has to be created, and that can only be achieved by an appeal of dynamic force which arouses feelings of the masses . . .'.[26] Yet there can be little doubt that only one issue was likely to do so—that of race. The expulsion of all Asians with British passports by General Idi Amin and their reception in Britain caused widespread popular protests. When the refugees moved into new homes and jobs the N.F. could exploit the issue to the full. A plane carrying West Indians and black American tourists was met on landing in May 1976 by N.F. members shouting: 'Don't unpack, you must go back!' and 'This is England, not Pakistan'. In the general election of February 1974 the N.F. fielded fifty-four candidates and polled only 76,000 votes. But eight months later its candidates gained over 113,000 votes, and as much as 9.4 per cent of the vote in Hackney and Shoreditch and over eight per cent in Tottenham and in Wood Green, all in Greater London. In local elections in 1976 forty-eight N.F. candidates in Leicester between them won 43,733 votes, an average of eighteen per cent.[27] Two months later, in a council election at Deptford, the N.F. together with the National Party polled a higher percentage than the Labour Party. Although these clearly were exceptional cases they show what support the party was able to win in areas with a large non-white population at a time of economic recession and large unemployment. At the beginning of 1974 the N.F. had thirty branches and fifty-four local groups, most of them in south-east England; it was very weak in the West country, Scotland and Northern Ireland. Late in 1978 *The Economist* estimated that the party had about 10,000 members,[28] but other estimates are higher. Among its members, young militants are prominent, some of them no doubt attracted by the violence so often

[25] See above, pp. 30-31.
[26] *Spearhead*, no. 87, September 1975, p. 15.
[27] Figures taken from Walker, op. cit., pp. 126, 173-75, 198.
[28] *The Economist*, 16 December 1978, p. 23.

aroused by N.F. rallies. Like similar parties elsewhere, the N.F. has organised its own Defence Squads against attackers from the Left.

The progress of the National Front has been clogged—as that of the German and Italian Neofascists—by internal conflicts and splits. At the annual conference of 1970 Chesterton was unanimously reelected as the Leader, but he was considered too old and he always spent the winter months in South Africa. Only a few months after his reelection the majority of the N.F. Action Committee asked him by letter to resign as chairman. From Cape Town Chesterton replied by resigning from the party. When Tyndall declined to succeed him John O'Brien, a former Conservative, was chosen as chairman in the absence of a more suitable candidate. He later described the atmosphere at N.F. head-quarters as 'a frightful atmosphere of mutual distrust and intrigue. Clique against clique. There was the Brown clique, there was the Tyndall clique . . .'.[29] In July 1972 O'Brien left his office, ostensibly for a holiday, but then secretly returned and sent a circular to the members that eight members of the N.F. Directorate had resigned and formed a new organization. Now John Tyndall took over the chairman-ship of the National Front in addition to the editorship of *Spearhead*. But his leadership too was soon challenged, this time by a more mod-erate group. When he proclaimed in *Spearhead* in 1974 'although we admit to a marked preference to [*sic*] democratic methods so long as such methods can be found which will work',[30] the opposition to him grew. In his place the party Directorate elected Kingsley Read as the new chairman, and Tyndall as his deputy. On both occasions there was a tie which was resolved by the chairman's casting vote—and Tyndall was determined to regain the chairmanship. He bitterly attacked the editor of *Britain First* because he had rejected Mussolini and the cult of the Leader. At the annual general meeting of October 1975 Tyndall moved that in future the N.F. chairman was to be elected by the party, and no longer by the Directorate. The meeting ended in chaos. Tyndall sent his supporters to party headquarters to occupy it, but they discovered that the vital files had already been removed by Kingsley Read who denounced the illegal occupation by the Tyndall faction. In November the party's Disciplinary Tribunal expelled Tyndall from the party and suspended nine other members. But five weeks later they were reinstated by the High Court, whereupon Kingsley Read and his followers seceded and founded the National

[29] Walker, op. cit., p. 103.
[30] *Spearhead*, no. 79, September–October 1974, p. 2.

Party. Its leaders retained the party headquaters and membership files, but early in 1976 the N.F. obtained another court order which forbade the National Party to use the files. The large majority of the branches and perhaps two-thirds of the members remained loyal to Tyndall and the N.F., while the National Party was joined by only twenty-nine branches and local groups.

In the general election of 1979 the National Front fielded more than three times as many candidates as in October 1974 and tried to exploit the resentment of the voters on two issues: that of race and that of the Common Market, with its concomitant high food prices and the common agricultural policy. The N.F. called for the compulsory repatriation of all immigrants and for a British withdrawal from the Common Market. 191,000 voters—many more than in 1974—expressed their rejection of the existing party system by voting for National Front candidates. But none of these was able to muster more than a few thousand votes and all lost their deposits, landing the N.F. with a debt of £45,300. If one compares the election results in the eighty-six constituencies where the N.F. ran a candidate in 1974 as well as in 1979, it turns out that in these cases its vote actually fell from 113,613 to 64,541 votes, a decline of over forty-three per cent. This striking decline was probably due to the fact that racial tension had somewhat abated, and perhaps even more important, that the intensified clash between Labour and Conservatives—after the bitter winter of 1978-9—made many disgruntled ex-Conservatives return to the fold. This severe defeat has brought about new internal strife and infighting within the National Front, and it seems very unlikely that it will play a major part in British politics in the foreseeable future.

In the 1920s and 1930s Fascist movements mushroomed all over Europe. They were the product of the deep social and political crisis caused by the First World War and of the extreme reaction to the threat of Bolshevism', which was another fruit of the war and its aftermath. These movements were inspired by the example of Benito Mussolini, and later by that of Adolf Hitler, who ruthlessly coped with the dangers which threatened to engulf bourgeois society. Millions saw in Fascism the solution to all their problems and anxieties. Yet the advance of 'Bolshevism' into the heart of Central Europe has not brought about the rise of similar movements on any such scale. Partly this is no doubt due to the defeat of the Fascist dictatorships in the Second World War and the revelation of the countless atrocities committed by them. Furthermore, in spite of the oil crises and severe unemployment European society in the 1970s is much more stable and prosperous than it was in the 1930s. National hatreds and feelings of national and 'racial' superiority can hardly flourish in the Europe of the Common Market and many other 'European' institutions. The countries of Western Europe have drawn much closer together and have got to know each other far better than in the inter-war period. The Neofascist parties have been able to exploit exceptional circumstances, such as the extreme poverty of the Italian south or the racial issue in Britain; but even then their leaders proved unable to arouse the masses as their predecessors did so successfully. Even the fear of 'Bolshevism' has receded although almost half of Europe has passed under Russian domination. In Germany as well as in Italy, traditional Christian Democratic parties have succeeded in integrating the conservative Right and the propertied classes which have become reconciled to the democratic order. The working classes too have been integrated into the existing social order and no longer pose a threat to the middle and lower middle classes. The whole political and social climate has changed to such an extent that a Fascist revival, in any way similar to that of the 1930s, seems extremely unlikely.

Bibliography

This selective bibliography contains mainly books written in English and, where none exist, written in French or German, and only exceptionally those in other languages.

The only book which deals with Fascism as a whole—in France, Italy and Germany—is Ernst Nolte's interesting *Three Faces of Fascism*, London, 1965. In contrast with the present study, his book focuses almost exclusively on Fascist ideology. Another book which has been of great value to the writer is *The European Right*, edited by Hans Rogger and Eugen Weber, Berkeley and Los Angeles, 1965. The first issue of the *Journal of Contemporary History*, London, January 1966, was devoted to 'International Fascism, 1920–1945'.

Austria

The antecedents of National Socialism are investigated by Andrew Gladding Whiteside, *Austrian National Socialism before 1918*, The Hague, 1962; and in his chapter on 'Austria', in *The European Right*, pp. 308–63. There is a useful short biography on *Dr Karl Lueger* by Kurt Skalnik, Vienna, 1954; and a much more interesting one on 'The Political Career and Influence of Georg Ritter von Schönerer' by John Christopher Peter Warren, a London Ph.D. thesis of 1963 which is unfortunately unpublished.

The most important study of the 'Heimwehr' movement is Josef Hofmann, *Der Pfrimer-Putsch*, Publikationen des Österreichischen Instituts für Zeitgeschichte, vol. iv, Vienna and Graz, 1965. A number of interesting documents on the 'Heimwehr' have been published by Lajos Kerekes, 'Italien, Ungarn und die österreichische Heimwehrbewegung 1928–1931', *Österreich in Geschichte und Literatur*, vol. ix, 1, January 1965. They are discussed by Ludwig Jedlicka in the *Journal of Contemporary History*, January 1966, pp. 127–44. Reports on the Austrian National Socialists in 1923 are to be found in the *Nachlass* of Colonel Max Bauer in the Bundesarchiv at Koblenz, no. 81.

Belgium

The most interesting accounts of the Rexist movement are written by protagonists of Degrelle: Pierre Daye, *Léon Degrelle et le Rexisme*, Paris, 1937;

260

and Louise Narvaez Duchesse de Valence, *Degrelle m'a dit*, Paris, 1961. A selection of Degrelle's articles can be found in: *Degrelle avait raison— Recueil des textes écrits par Léon Degrelle entre 1936 et 1940 dans le 'Pays Reel'*, Brussels, 1941. For the background see: Jean Stengers, 'Belgium', in *The European Right*, pp. 128–67.

Britain
The only book on the British Union of Fascists is: Colin Cross, *The Fascists in Britain*, London, 1961. Sir Oswald Mosley's programme can be found in: *Fascism—100 Questions asked and answered*, London, 1936. See also: J. R. Jones, 'England', in *The European Right*, pp. 29–70.

Finland
The only available studies of Finnish Fascism are by Marvin Rintala: *Three Generations—The Extreme Right in Finnish Politics*, Bloomington, Indiana, 1962; and his chapter on 'Finland', in *The European Right*, pp. 408–42. Useful too are the books by John H. Wuorinen, *Nationalism in Modern Finland*, New York, 1931, and *A History of Finland*, New York, 1965.

Flanders
There does not seem to exist a satisfactory study of Flemish nationalism in any major language, but A. W. Willemsen's *Het Vlaams-nationalisme 1914–1940*, Groningen, 1958, is a very interesting book. Interesting too is a biography of *Joris van Severen* by Arthur de Bruyne, Zulte, 1961, written by one of his admirers. The Hoover Library at Stanford possesses several collections of Van Severen's speeches, published by the *Verbond van Dietsche Nationaal-Solidaristen*, some printed and others stencilled.

France
There are two important works in English on the *Action française*: by Eugen Weber, Stanford, 1962, and by Edward R. Tannenbaum, New York, 1962. Cp. also Eugen Weber's chapter on 'France' in *The European Right*, pp. 71–127. The writings of Jacques Doriot—such as *La France avec nous!*, Paris, 1937, and *Le Mouvement et les Hommes*, Paris, 1942—are of small interest. Two studies on Charles Maurras are contained in D. W. Brogan, *French Personalities and Problems*, London, 1946.

Germany
The antecedents of National Socialism have been investigated by: George L. Mosse, *The Crisis of German Ideology—Intellectual Origins of the Third Reich*, New York, 1964; Peter G. J. Pulzer, *The Rise of Political Anti-Semitism in Germany and Austria*, New York and London, 1964; and Fritz

Stern, *The Politics of Cultural Despair—A Study in the Rise of the German Ideology*, Berkeley and Los Angeles, 1961. A National Socialist historian, Walter Frank, has written a biography of *Hofprediger Adolf Stoecker und die christlichsoziale Bewegung*, Hamburg, 1935. Important sources on this topic are: Paul de Lagarde's *Deutsche Schriften*, Göttingen, 1886, and Houston Stewart Chamberlain's *The Foundations of the Nineteenth Century*, English transl. by John Lees, London, 1911.

Several of Adolf Hitler's works have been translated into English: *Mein Kampf*, New York, 1939; *Hitler's Secret Book*, New York, 1961; *The Speeches of Adolf Hitler*, ed. by Norman H. Baynes, London, 1942; and *Hitler's Table Talk 1941–1944*, London, 1953. The best biography is by Alan Bullock, *Hitler—A Study in Tyranny*, London, 1962. Useful too is Konrad Heiden's *Der Fuehrer*, London, 1944.

Important are further some recent German studies, such as: Georg Franz-Willing, *Die Hitlerbewegung—Der Ursprung 1919–1922*, Hamburg, 1962; Hanns Hubert Hofmann, *Der Hitlerputsch*, Munich, 1961; Albert Krebs, *Tendenzen und Gestalten der NSDAP*, Stuttgart, 1959; Werner Jochmann, *Im Kampf um die Macht*, Frankfurt, 1960; and the documents edited by Ernst Deuerlein, 'Hitlers Eintritt in die Politik und die Reichswehr', *Vierteljahrshefte für Zeitgeschichte*, vii, 1959, pp. 177–227, and *Der Hitler-Putsch*, Stuttgart, 1962. Equally valuable are some books written by leading National Socialists: Ernst Röhm, *Die Geschichte eines Hochverräters*, Munich, 1928; 7th ed., Munich 1934; Joseph Goebbels, *Vom Kaiserhof zur Reichskanzlei*, Munich, 1934; *Das Tagebuch von Joseph Goebbels 1925/26*, ed. by Helmut Heiber, Stuttgart, 1961. An interesting study of the National Socialist rise in a small German town is: William Sheridan Allen, *The Nazi Seizure of Power—The Experience of a Single German Town 1930–1935*, Chicago, 1965; London, 1966.

A vast quantity of hardly used material on the National Socialist Party is contained in the 'Hauptarchiv der NSDAP', now at the Bundesarchiv at Koblenz; for the present study the vols. 76, 78, 82, 88, 97, 100, 104, 107, 109, 111, 116–17, 120, 125, 513–14, 528–33 have been used, which contain material on the early years of the party; so does the *Nachlass* of Julius Streicher, ibid., from which the vols 9, 13 and 72 have been used. For the early 1930s the *Nachlass* Krebs, ibid., has some new material. The Hoover Library at Stanford possesses one file of the 'Gau Gross-Berlin' which contains material on the Stennes group and lists of those who were expelled from the National Socialist Party in 1931.

Hungary
A mass of material can be found in C. A. Macartney, *October Fifteenth—A History of Hungary, 1929–1945*, 2 vols, Edinburgh, 1956. A more specialized study is István Deák's chapter on 'Hungary', in *The European Right*, pp. 364–407, which is based on his unpublished M.A. thesis, at Columbia University.

Italy

The most useful biography of Mussolini in English is: Laura Fermi, *Mussolini*, Chicago, 1961. Of the far more detailed Italian biography by Renzo De Felice only two volumes have so far appeared: *Mussolini il rivoluzionario* and *Mussolini il fascista, 1921-1925*, Turin, 1965-66. Mussolini's *Autobiography*, London, 1937, is of small interest.

On Italian Fascism there are in English the following useful books, most of them written by Italians: Federico Chabod, *A History of Italian Fascism*, London, 1961; Hermann Finer, *Mussolini's Italy*, London, 1964; A. Rossi, *The Rise of Italian Fascism*, London, 1938; Salvatore Saladino, 'Italy', in *The European Right*, pp. 208-60; Gaetano Salvemini, *Under The Axe of Fascism*, London, 1936. There is an interesting article by Adrian Lyttleton, 'Fascism in Italy—The Second Wave', in the *Journal of Contemporary History*, January 1966, pp. 75-100. Of great interest for the atmosphere in Italy in the early 1920s is Italo Balbo, *Diario 1922*, Milan, 1932.

Important for the general background are: Margot Hentze, *Pre-Fascist Italy*, London, 1939; Dennis Mack Smith, *Italy—A Modern History*, London, 1959; Robert Michels, *Sozialismus und Fascismus in Italien*, 2 vols, Munich, 1925; Wilhelm Alff, 'Die Associazione Nazionalista Italiana von 1910', *Vierteljahrshefte für Zeitgeschichte*, xiii, 1965, pp. 32-63; Luigi Salvatorelli and Giovanni Mira, *Storia d'Italia nel periodo fascista*, Turin, 1956.

Rumania

The only available studies of the Iron Guard are the important ones by Eugen Weber: 'The Men of the Archangel', *Journal of Contemporary History*, January 1966, pp. 101-26, and 'Romania', in *The European Right*, pp. 501-74. For the background see: C. Kormos, *Rumania*, Cambridge, 1944; Henry L. Roberts, *Rumania—Political Problems of an Agrarian State*, New Haven, 1951; Joseph S. Roucek, *Contemporary Rumania and her Problems*, Stanford, 1932; Pavel Pavel, *Why Rumania Failed*, London, n.d. Invaluable as source material is : Corneliu Zelea Codreanu, *Eiserne Garde*, Berlin, 1939; and equally a government publication, *Rumänien am Rande des Abgrundes, 21.-23. Januar 1941*, Bukarest, 1942.

Russia

The only articles in English discussing the question of a 'Russian Fascism' are those by Hans Rogger: 'Was there a Russian Fascism? The Union of the Russian People', *Journal of Modern History*, xxxvi, 1964, pp. 398-415; 'The Formation of the Russian Right', *California Slavic Studies*, iii, 1964, pp. 66-94; and 'Russia', in *The European Right*, pp. 443-500.

Spain

By far the most valuable book in English is: Stanley G. Payne, *Falange— A History of Spanish Fascism*, Stanford, 1961. There is a selection of the

speeches and writings of José Antonio Primo de Rivera, edited by Bernd
Nellessen, Stuttgart, 1965, under the title: *José Antonio Primo de Rivera, Der
Troubadour der spanischen Falange*, Stuttgart, 1965. This was preceded by a
short book of the same author: *Die verbotene Revolution—Aufstieg und
Niedergang der Falange*, Hamburg, 1963. For the background see: Raymond
Carr, *Spain, 1808-1939*, Oxford, 1966; Gerald Brennan, *The Spanish
Labyrinth*, Cambridge, 1943; and Hugh Thomas, *The Spanish Civil War*,
London, 1961.
Important books in English on Fascism, published after 1967 (date
of the first edition of *The Rise of Fascism*)
Robert Benewick, *The Fascist Movement in Britain*, 2nd edition,
London, 1972
Karl Dietrich Bracher, *The German Dictatorship—Origins, Structure
and Effects of National Socialism*, London, 1971 (German edition,
Cologne, 1969)
William Carr, *Hitler—A Study in Personality and Politics*, London, 1978
F.L. Carsten, *Fascist Movements in Austria—From Schönerer to Hitler*,
London, 1977
Alan Cassels, *Fascism*, New York, 1975
Paul Corner, *Fascism in Ferrara 1915-1925*, Oxford, 1975
Joachim C. Fest, *Hitler*, London, 1974 (Pelican—German edition,
Frankfurt, 1973)
Alastair Hamilton, *The Appeal of Fascism—A Study of Intellectuals and
Fascism 1919-1945*, London, 1971
M. Lackó, *Arrow-Cross Men—National Socialists 1935-1944*, Budapest,
1969
Walter Laqueur (ed.), *Fascism—A Reader's Guide*, London, 1976
(Pelican 1979) Contributions by 12 historians and political scientists
Adrian Lyttelton, *The Seizure of Power—Fascism in Italy 1919-1929*,
London, 1973
Jeremy Noakes, *The Nazi Party in Lower Saxony 1921-1933*, Oxford,
1971
Joseph Nyomarkay, *Charisma and Factionalism in the Nazi Party*, Min-
neapolis, 1967
Geoffrey Pridham, *Hitler's Rise to Power—The Nazi Movement in
Bavaria 1923-1933*, London, 1973
Otto-Ernst Schüddekopf, *Revolutions of Our Time—Fascism*, London,
1973
Albert Speer, *Inside the Third Reich*, London, 1970 (German edition,
Berlin, 1969)
Hugh Thomas (ed.), *Jose Antonio Primo de Rivera—Selected Writings*,
London, 1972
Henry A. Turner (ed.), *Reappraisals of Fascism*, New York, 1975
Andrew G. Whiteside, *The Socialism of Fools—Georg Ritter von
Schönerer and Austrian Pan-Germanism*, Berkeley-Los Angeles-
London, 1975

Index